LIFE AND WORK IN INDIA

LIFE AND WORK IN INDIA:

EMBODYING A SHORT SKETCH OF THE HISTORY AND PROGRESS OF KATHIAWAR FROM 1865 TO 1899

ROBERT B. BOOTH

GYAN

Published by

Gyan Publishing House
5, Ansari Road
Daryaganj, New Delhi-110002
Phone: 011-47034999, 9811692060
E-mail: books@gyanbooks.com

Distribution Network
gyanbooks.com
India, USA, Canada, UK, Australia

ISBN: 978-93-7169-304-2 (PB)

First Published, 1912

2nd Impression 2025

Printed at: Gyan Press, Delhi.

LIFE AND WORK IN INDIA
Author: ROBERT B. BOOTH

Life and Work in India.

Life and Work in India:

EMBODYING

A SHORT SKETCH OF THE HISTORY AND PROGRESS OF KATHIAWAR FROM 1865 to 1899.

(Being in some part a reprint from a report by the Author in 1880.)

BY

ROBERT B. BOOTH. M.Inst.C.E.

(Late Engineer to the Kathiawar Political Agency).

1912.

Contents.

List of Illustrations.

Introduction.

I have often been asked by friends to put my notes on Indian work and life connected with my long service in Kathiawar into readable book form, but I did not think they would prove of interest to other people, especially now that twelve years have elapsed since my retirement. However, the putting the notes together has been a great pleasure to me; it has been like living the good old days over again, now that I am getting on in years and can only enjoy an active life in memory.

In the following pages, to make certain subjects more immediately intelligible (instance Chapters VI. and VII), I have considered it best to sketch their history and development at once over a number of years, instead of taking them piecemeal from time to time, mixed with other matter, and subsequently to refer to a few of the most interesting items more particularly.

I have tried to avoid unnecessary detail, technical or otherwise, but in the matter of speeches made on special occasions by persons holding high positions, being intimately connected with the welfare of the province in various directions, I felt bound to put them in without much or any curtailment.

Introduction

CHAPTER I.

ARRIVAL IN BOMBAY.

VARIOUS EXPERIENCES—FIRST VISIT TO KATHIAWAR.

It was one early morning in July, 1864, that I arrived in Bombay from New Zealand. The steamer lay out in the harbour, which is one of the finest, best protected, and most extensive, I believe, in the world. The passengers were landed in small native boats at Mazagon Bunder, where, on stepping ashore, I was assailed by a host of half-naked coolies, determined to take possession of myself and my belongings, while they maintained a deafening jabber at the top of their very unmelodious voices, in a language unknown to me. I was presently relieved from my difficulties by the appearance of a Parsee dressed in a long white cotton gown or coat, with red leather slippers on his bare feet, and a tall shining brimless hat on his head. He addressed me in good English, procured me a buggy, and directed the driver to take me to some hotel he named, and informed me my " kit " would speedily follow me on a coolie's head.

After a lengthy drive through the native town and some shady roads, we arrived at the hotel called Pallonjee's, at Byculla, the only hotel then, I believe, patronised by Europeans in the island. It was a great rambling place with large rooms surrounded by verandahs.

The heat was, to me, terrific, and in my New Zealand clothing, I was already melting from every pore.

I was escorted to my room by a native domestic, who endeavoured in very broken English to give me a deal of information which I could make nothing of. One end of the room was occupied by a bedstead enclosed on every side by mosquito curtains of thin muslin. Large doors with venetian shutters opened on to a trellised verandah, and a punkah was suspended over a black table and two chairs.

Presently Mr. Pallonjee, the landlord, appeared, a genial, smiling, stout and middle-aged Parsee, who at once took possession of me in a fatherly way, explained in good English that he knew my brother, Booth Sahib, very well; Sahib often lived in his hotel; very good man and good friend, Mr. Booth Sahib. "Would I want breakfast? Then go Bombay, see brother? Very good, buggy ready soon," and so on.

It was a drive of three miles through the native city to reach the fort of Bombay, where all the great mercantile offices were situated. The heat, mugginess, and peculiar spicy (?) smell of the locality were oppressive to my unacclimatised senses, and the noise in some parts was deafening. The artisans appeared to follow their calling in the open streets, or partly so at any rate. In one locality all the inhabitants were coppersmiths, and they energetically worked away in the front of their shops, hammering their copper vessels, chattering and shouting with their neighbours and passers-by, and keeping up a continuous pandemonium of sound. Further on were various and numerous shops filled with every description of European and native merchandise, and many fine tall buildings, and residences of rich Hindoos and Parsees, with their strangely coloured walls, verandahs and projecting balconies. There were no footpaths, and the population occupied every part of the roadway, while the "jehus" continued to shout "bar jao" (get out of the way) incessantly. Having reached the end of this part of the native town, we emerged on to a wide flat esplanade, which was then being laid out in straight roads, while the sea, which extended along the south-west face, brought with it a cool, invigorating air, very welcome after the stifling atmosphere of the close city roads. Another mile brought me into the old Fort and landed me in a close narrow street, with immensely high buildings on either side, comprising warehouses and godowns below, and offices above.

I was directed to one of the large open doorways and from thence up a dozen or so flights of steep stairs, till I at length arrived at an opening with a red screen across the entrance. Within was a spacious room sprinkled with numerous tables, at which sat native clerks, Hindoo and Parsee, each with his own special punkah swinging over his head, pulled by a nearly naked coolie, lying on his back on the floor, apparently asleep, while one black leg moved, pendulum-like, up and down, with the end of the punkah rope held between his toes. Nobody paid any attention to the intruder until I enquired for whom I sought, when a dignified-looking old Parsee came courteously forward, shook me by the hand, and hoped I had had a pleasant voyage. I was ushered then behind another screen, where I beheld my brother himself, seated before an excellent lunch, a mug of iced beer at his elbow, and another coolie swaying a punkah overhead.

The "tiffin" was very welcome indeed, and when we had discussed that, and had a chat and a cheroot, he left me for half-an-hour to finish up urgent work in the office. This completed, he dived into a recess behind another red screen, and presently emerged, ready for the outer world.

We proceeded to the street and entered his office shigram, a covered-in, hearse-like conveyance on four wheels, and drove to some establishments to order a fit out, in the form of wearing apparel, more suited to the climate than what I possessed. At 5 p.m. we drove to a railway station and left for Bandora, a suburb ten miles away, where my brother's bungalow was situated, and *en route* I was introduced to several men who were, like him, going out to their homes after the business of the day.

On arrival at Mahim station, a smart dog cart, in charge of a black syce (groom) in livery, awaited us, and my brother taking the reins, the three miles to Bandora were quickly covered, and we found ourselves under the porch of a picturesque one-storeyed bungalow with gardens all round, wide verandahs, large shady rooms filled with every luxury, and long easy chairs, in one of which reclined my brother's chum, Sedgewick, who had preceded us.

Bandora is a narrow peninsula running into the sea. On one side the land rises abruptly, while on the other it takes the form of a long slope, open to the prevailing and favourite south-west winds. My brother's bungalow, among many others, stood about half-way up this slope, commanding a fine view of the ocean and the waves breaking on the rocky coast-line below. The soft, cool evening air felt delightful following the intense and stifling heat of the city, and all our surroundings conduced to a feeling of comfort and restfulness.

The European homes of Bombay, especially in those rosy days of mercantile prosperity, were usually luxurious, and they were needed after the long days spent in the busy marts and offices of the city.

Dinner dress was, of course, a *sine qua non*, and the fashion then during the hot season was white, or, at any rate, a white cotton jacket in lieu of the black swallow tail, and silk cummerbund, or sash around the waist, in lieu of a vest.

The well-appointed dinner table was a blaze of flowers, and we dined " à la Russe " on the best of everything in the form of food and liquor, a revelation indeed to the New Zealand bushman.

After dinner two or three men from neighbouring bungalows turned in, and all adjourned to easy lounge chairs in the cool verandah, where we smoked and chatted till drowsiness sent us to our respective couches for the night. So ended my first day in Bombay.

My brother was representative at Bombay of the large firm of Stephen Burstall and Co., cotton merchants, of Liverpool, Hull, and Bombay. He had been some three years in India, where his previous extensive experiences in Liverpool had given him a position of considerable importance in the cotton trade.

Bombay was then in its zenith of commercial prosperity, owing to the American war, during which it enjoyed a monopoly in the cotton trade, and my brother's services would, in the following year, be crowned by a partnership in the firm he represented.

The following morning we were all up early for chota hazri (the little breakfast) of tea, toast and fruit, to sustain us for a walk before the heat of the day commenced. At 8 a.m. we bathed, and immediately after breakfast drove to Mahim for the train to Bombay. At 1 p.m. we lunched at the Bombay Club, not at that time housed in the palatial building it now occupies. In the evening an hour was spent in the Apollo Bunder rooms, then a favourite resort, which, to some extent, took the place of the present fashionable Yacht Club.

Bombay was then commencing its transition stage; most of the old fort walls had been dismantled, but none of the fine Government buildings which now adorn the Esplanade had been erected. During the hot season a part of the Esplanade was used for the pitching of tents, in which the Europeans lived for coolness, and the laying out of the present fine roads and planting of roadside trees had not yet commenced. At Colaba were the extensive cotton yards and factories, barracks, and most of the oldest established residences, and the present existing fine church had been erected. On

Malabar Hill, across the Backbay, was the residence of H.E., the Governor, Sir Bartle Frere, and those of the largest number of the rich city merchants and Government officials, etc.

The growing wealth of Bombay at this period produced a state of feverish excitement which eventually proved disastrous to many. It was a daily event to notice the formation of new companies for all manner of projects, few of which ever reached maturity. One of the most extensive schemes was the reclamation of Backbay, by cutting down a portion of Malabar Hill, and throwing it therein. The shares were readily applied for and ran up to enormous premiums. The concession from Government was obtained, a company formed, and work put into hand. All this is so much a matter of history that it is not necessary to refer to it here. The only reclamation carried out before the company failed was that upon which the present railway to Colaba and the fine Queen's road along the sea face were constructed, and so far an excellent work was accomplished, but any further extension ot the original scheme would have proved anything but an unmixed blessing.

My first occupation in Bombay was a seat in the office of Messrs. Ritchie, Stewart and Co., one of the largest mercantile firms, which had in co-operation with it the important firm of architects and engineers—Messrs. Scott, McClelland and Co.

After a short period I was appointed under the joint firms as manager of the Victoria Bunder Works, which comprised the building of extensive cotton presses, and the reclamation of a portion of the foreshore towards Colaba for the formation of jetties and docks for the same company.

There was also a shipbuilding yard, in which were constructed the large iron barges which we employed for the carriage of reclamation material from islands or the mainland, across the harbour.

It was a very interesting charge, although for the six months during which I remained there I felt myself more in the position of a pupil than otherwise. I now settled down to my new work, commenced to pick up Hindoostani, became the possessor of a smart dogcart, and a Persian Arab horse, good in saddle and harness, read my paper in the train each morning as I went to business, repaired to the Apollo Bunder after office hours for a cheroot and cocktail, and home to dinner and billiards. I omitted to mention that my brother and his chum possessed a billiard-room in their bungalow, in all of which I was now full partner.

On one of these homecomings an accident happened to my brother which narrowly escaped costing him his life. A party of us were riding from Mahim to Bandora, He was mounted on a favourite grey Arab called "Backbay," leading, when, on rounding a sharp corner up the hill near Bandora the horse slipped sideways and came down a crasher. My brother fell violently on his head and lay apparently dead. We quickly procured a cot from a bungalow near by and carried him home, fortunately no great distance, and sent for a doctor. He was unconscious for some hours, and had a bad cut over the eye. On examination, however, he was found to be otherwise uninjured. The eye wound was stitched up and a day's rest set him on his legs again.

Strangely, a very sad and fatal accident occurred not long after at the very same spot, resulting in two deaths. There was at the outer corner of the road bend, on the steepest part of the hill, an old disused well, with no other protection than a low parapet wall about two feet high. A party of gentlemen and ladies had gone from Bombay in a wagonette and pair for a day's picnic at Bandora.

On returning late in the evening the horses, in going down the curved hill, became restive, with the result that the wagonette capsized on to the old well, pitching three of the party, two ladies and a gentleman, therein. The ladies immediately disappeared into the slimy, stagnant water; for the moment the others were too astounded and helpless to render aid or know what to do. Then one of the party, Captain Briscoe, of the P. and O., jumped in, dived, and brought up the two ladies in succession. In both cases life was extinct. It was supposed they were killed instantaneously by striking the wall as they fell. The condition of the poor husband and father, who were present, can be imagined. Captain Briscoe received the Humane Society's medal for his plucky act.

Six months after my appointment to the Victoria Land Reclamation Company the property was sold at a large profit, and I, in common with the entire staff, was presented with a douceur of six months' pay, which in my case amounted to a little over £240.

My brother, during his occasional holidays, visited Poona, then, as now, the official station hill and society centre, civil and military, of the Presidency. On one occasion I accompanied him. He was a member of the Eastern Rifle Association, who held their annual shooting meets at Poona and Bombay, and was one of the most successful competitors for prizes. Breech-loaders were not invented in those days, but the rifles used in the competitions were very splendid weapons with their telescopic and frying pan sights, wind gauges, etc., and the shooting was from 500 to 1,000 yards. I also paid a visit to Matheran, a wooded plateau some thirty miles inland, rising 3,000 feet abruptly above the plain, and in company with a few youngsters from Bombay enjoyed a fortnight's sojourn there immensely, riding hill ponies, sketching, etc.

A member of our party was an inimitable caricaturist, and one of our escapades, I recollect, was the burglarious entering of a vacant bungalow, and decorating the walls within with numerous illustrations of life on the hill, executed with a burnt stick, which some of the party produced from a fire provided for the purpose. Some of the sketches were really clever, but I am afraid the owners of the residence did not eventually appreciate them as we did.

Snipe shooting also, in those early days, was excellent, and I made frequent visits with my brother to Dyser and the Thana river, Bassein, etc., for this purpose. The railway between Surat and Bombay was not yet completed, and we used to go up to Thana on lorries. The snipe were found in numbers on the paddy (rice) fields.

I did not remain in the Victoria Land Reclamation Company after the sale of the property, but immediately before my leaving a serious accident occurred, fortunately unattended with loss of life. This was the collapse of an immense press building under construction. I forget the company to which it belonged, but the architects were the firm I was employed under. The building covered a great area of land immediately inside the gateway of the Bunder. The outer walls were masonry, and the great iron girders to carry the floors were supported over the interior on iron columns, while their ends rested on the outer walls.

The workmen and coolies, of whom some two hundred were engaged in the building, had all left for their dinner hour, and I had just passed from below the building on my way from the Bunder and was mounting the stairs to my office, when, without any warning, the entire structure fell with an astounding crash, filling up in an instant the entire roadway

I had just walked upon with a mass of masonry, girders, columns, and scaffolding. Of course, it was put down to scamped work on the part of the contractor.

About this time I was invited by a friend, a Mr. Thomas, to take a trip with him to the Province of Kathiawar, where he had some business in connection with cotton to attend to, and we would be likely to get some shooting. Having nothing to do, I gladly assented. Taking only a small swag with a gun and rifle each, we proceeded by train to Surat and from thence crossed the Gulf of Cambay in a small sailing boat, a native craft of perhaps five tons' capacity. The voyage should not exceed, on an average, twelve hours, but with us it occupied much more, for at first we had no breeze, and had to trust to oars. Towards midnight a land breeze sprang up, which sent us out of our course, and the choppy, jerky motion, added to the smell of fish oil and garlic, laid me low. I never experienced a more unpleasant night. At noon the following day, under a broiling sun, we landed at Gogo on a shingle beach, twelve miles from Bhavnagar; but it was evening before we were recovered sufficiently to move on or to procure a bullock cart to take us to our destination.

We eventually arrived in a very hungry and dilapidated condition at Bhavnagar at midnight, where we discovered Thomas's friend, Mr. Drennan, located in a small room on the top of a bastion on the old city fortification. This was the only accommodation possible for a European visitor in those days. Here we were regaled with chowpatties and tea, but even that was luxury after the day and night we had experienced.

Bhavnagar was then, as now, one of the greatest cotton marts in Western India, and enjoyed an important trade with Bombay by means of small sailing craft, called pattimas. Mr. Drennan was the only European there, and he was but an occasional visitor. He was the pioneer among Europeans to open up cotton trade and industries in Kathiawar, and had already started small steam gins and presses at Dholera, Dhundooka and Wudhwan.

We spent two days at Bhavnagar. The "business" portion of the trip did not, I recollect, occupy much time, and so we slaughtered a considerable amount of game in the way of black buck, Neilghai (blue bull), partridge, etc. The skins of the big game we left with Drennan to have dried and forwarded by boat to Bombay.

Resuming our journey, I was provided with a camel (a mode of conveyance which, like olives, one needs to acquire a taste for), while Thomas rode a horse of Drennan's. The first day we proceeded half-way to Dhollera, camping with an engineer who was employed on the road which the Government was then projecting in the locality.

The following day Thomas made an early start and rode ahead for Dhollera, while I, mounted on my camel with gun and rifle, decided to shoot my way quietly and take the full day for it. That morning I made a wonderfully lucky shot at a black buck, at a distance, measured immediately, of 400 yards. The animals were unusually wild, and there was no cover on the dead flat land. The buck was alone and steadily kept out of ordinary range, and moving. At last, in desperation, I fired over and ahead of him as he walked along proudly with his head erect. He dropped on his haunches and apparently could not get his hind legs under him again. I discovered that the bullet had broken both his legs above the hocks! As Thomas asked me to fetch meat as well as skins, we hung the beast under the camel and proceeded. I added a number of partridge and hares, and presently sighting in a swamp several huge birds I had not seen before, I secured one of the largest without difficulty, as they were very tame. This enormous bird, about four times as large as a goose, was tied by the feet to the back of the saddle and hung down over the camel's tail. Decorated as we were, it may be imagined what a spectacle we presented as we rode into the town of Dhollera late in the evening. It was speedily evident that the inhabitants were very considerably struck with it. They gathered round in constantly increasing numbers, gesticulating and talking loud and angrily, and some went so far as to try to stop the camel. The driver spoke to them, seemingly in an endeavour to pacify, but I could not understand what was wrong. Fortunately at this moment Thomas, with Mr. Kleinknecht, an assistant of Drennan's, appeared on the scene, and the latter after some difficulty contrived to appease the crowd by explaining the circumstance to the village elders, and we were permitted to proceed to his house. Kleinknecht now informed me that I had unwittingly committed an act of sacrilege, and deeply insulted and offended the villagers by carrying slaughtered animals into their Mahajin town, and had he not arrived when he did, the villagers would in all probability have maltreated or killed me. The Mahajins are a bigoted sect of Hindoos whose religion teaches them to destroy no life, not even the most dangerous or vilest, and they consider themselves and their surroundings to be polluted by the presence or touch of dead flesh. They believe that their souls, after death, pass into the bodies of the lower animals.

Dhollera was at one time an important port, but the creek which connected it with the Gulf of Cambay was now silted up so considerably as to render the navigation of it, even for small vessels, increasingly difficult.

After two days passed in this, to me, very uninteresting and desolate district, we proceeded on our way to Wudhwan. I obtained the loan of a big Persian horse from an engineer called Robb, which I was glad to exchange for the camel. Our first journey was a short one—fifteen miles—to Ranpur (this district, although within the Province of Kathiawar, was regulation, or British territory), where was a large bungalow occasionally occupied by the Collector of Ahmedabad. We rode through at night, and found on arrival only a perfectly empty house—not even a chair or cot, and, of course, no food. We tied our animals to trees in the compound until the syces would arrive, lit pipes, and sat on the stone steps till sleep overcame us, and we lay down on the bare choonam floor, with saddles for pillows, until daylight. The horses managed to pick up a little food from the stunted grass in the enclosure, and they carried us gaily into Limri, a distance of, I think, twenty miles, by mid-day. Here we put up in a mallee's (gardener's) hut in a large overgrown garden on the south bank of the Bhogava, opposite the town, and the mallee procured us milk and chowpatties, and subsequently some food was sent us from the Durbar, together with native cots and mattresses, and grass and grain for our tired animals. Here we spent a restful day under the shade of the banian trees and soothed by the creaking of a koss drawing water from a well hard by. In the afternoon we went out after buck and shot two fine ones.

Limri was fifteen miles from Wudhwan, and as it was our last stage we decided to do it comfortably. The syces were sent on overnight, and we started with our rifles in the early morning. Five miles on, as we passed the first village, we came on a herd of antelope, and one fine buck, which I determined to possess, if possible. Dismounting, I gave the horse to a village lad to hold, and went to stalk the buck, but failed to hit him, and when I returned I found the horse in an excited state trying to break away from the boy. Seizing the bridle-rein it came away in my hand—the beast had gnawed it through! With a bound, and darting his heels in my face, the vicious brute bolted, first for an old man who was riding a small tattoo. This animal he seized by the neck and bowled him over, man and all, and then galloped to the next village, two miles distant, where I followed on foot, running most of the way. I found him standing knee deep in the tank, feeding on the sedge grass. He was quiet enough now, and allowed me to lead him out with the rein round his neck, but he was so dead lame that after mending the bridle and mounting, I found he was unable to carry me. I took him to a house on the outskirts of the village, handed him over to the first man I met, and started on foot for my eight-mile walk. It was a hot and dusty tramp over a flat, uninteresting level with scarcely a tree or bush and intersected here and there with dry sandy river beds. On reaching Wudhwan city I found I was still three miles from the camp or political headquarters. Near here I came across a small herd of deer and shot one of them; but as I was unable to carry it, I left it and went to the station, where I found Thomas and Kleinknecht. After I had some food, we all returned for the deer but found only the skin and bones, while a score of vultures sat around, gorged and stupid.

At Wudhwan Civil Station Drennan had erected a cotton press and ginning factory, and built a comfortable bungalow. The station was only recently formed by the political agent, Colonel Keatinge. I little thought, on this my first visit to Kathiawar, that ere long I would visit it again and that it was destined to be the scene of my life's work.

From Wudhwan we travelled to Ahmedabad, about eighty miles; a bullock cart carried our kit and servants, while we walked and shikarred each day. We camped out at night on the bare ground,; there were no roads or rest houses in those days—all that was left for me to do in the future. We obtained a great number of deer-skins and small game. From Ahmedabad we proceeded to Bombay by railway, after a most enjoyable trip of over a month.

Among the many valued friends of my brother whom I met during my stay at Bombay, were Mr. and Mrs. Robert Warren. He was Resident Engineer on the B.B. and C.I. Railway. And on my return from Kathiawar they very kindly invited me to visit them at their bungalow near the

Bassein Bridge. Here I spent a delightful time boating on the fine river, and shooting, varied with trips on the open line, visiting works and practising a little with the theodolite, taking trigonometrical observations, etc.

Mrs. Warren was an accomplished musician, vocal and otherwise, and I have pleasant recollections of musical evenings at the Bandora bungalow, where she and my brother took leading parts.

CHAPTER II.

THE RAILWAY SURVEY.

It was late in 1865 that orders were received by the Bombay, Baroda and Central Indian Railway Company to carry out a trial survey for a line of railway it was proposed to construct between Neemuch and Wasad, to connect with the existing line at the latter place. The length would be about two hundred miles, and it was to pass down the ghāts south of Neemuch, through the Bheel country, and along the Mahi Valley.

Through my brother's interest I was appointed one of the assistant engineers for this survey. The engineer-in-chief was Mr. Thomas Foy, M.I.C.E., an old and experienced officer on the staff, and his four assistants were Messrs. Hargrave, Clerke, Kirkman, and myself.

We journeyed by G.I.P. Railway to Bhurhampore, and from thence by shigram to Neemuch *via* Mhow, then, as now, one of the great military centres in India, our camp equipage accompanying us on bullock carts. The journey was about 150 miles, broken only by a few days' stay at Mhow, for the procuring of fresh conveyances.

The road from Mhow to Neemuch was a common cart track, along which at every twelve to fifteen miles were placed rest houses or travellers' bungalows, where we were usually able to procure cots to sleep on and a "sudden death" meal. The puggie (watchman) in charge of these isolated buildings is a jack of all trades, cook included; but as travellers do not frequently call at the habitations unexpectedly, it was rare that any supplies were available, beyond possibly the tin of preserved soup, of doubtful freshness, or such like. The puggies, however, invariably kept a number of domestic fowls to meet such hasty calls on their resources, and within a few minutes of a traveller's arrival, he would notice a stampede of the birds around the enclosure with the owner in chase. Fifteen minutes subsequently, one or more of these animals, as might be required, would be served up spatchcocked, stewed, or grilled, with a plate of chowpatties (thin cakes of dough, fried in butter). It is marvellous how quickly the Indian cook will produce such a meal, and how well he will do it under apparently the most adverse circumstances.

Of course, we had our servants and an abundance of food with us on this occasion, and were not always dependent on the bungalow factotum.

The journey occupied fifteen to twenty days, and on our arrival at the military cantonment of Neemuch, we occupied a couple of very comfortable houses while arranging for the commencement of the survey.

Here Mr. Foy, under the orders of the Government, was supplied with a company of the Bheel Corp, with a native officer in command, for protection and escort of camp equipage, and a large number of mules for the carriage of tents, office kit, and general impedimenta. To each of us was appointed a fixed number, as we might at any moment be sent on separate duty. The arrangements were conducted under military rule and exactness. At five a.m. the bugle sounded for turning out, and five minutes later the tent kanauts (walls) fell down. At half-past five breakfast was served in the open, and at six o'clock the survey was under weigh.

On our departure, the entire camp was packed up, placed on the mules, and removed to the next position indicated by the Chief. At 1 o'clock we stopped for an hour's rest and refreshment, prepared and sent on to us in tiffen baskets by coolies. Then we surveyed till nightfall, and found our new camp prepared for us as before, bath, dinner, bed all ready and very welcome.

The Chief was under orders to conduct the survey in two separate lines, the object being to determine the best available gradients down the ghats, and he was directed to seek for and carry one survey, if possible, by the valley of the Jakim river, supposed to have its source not far from Neemuch.

At this period no trigonometrical survey had been made of the country we were traversing, and such maps as were extant were crude and frequently incorrect.

For ten miles, until we struck the ghats, it was a flat plateau, with scarcely any vegetation beyond short yellow grass, and bounded by the sky line. On approaching the edge of the steppe, an immense panorama sloped away below us, hills and spurs, range upon range, for the most part densely clothed in forest growth. It looked as it was, an almost unpopulated wilderness of forest, without track or roadway of any description, and it was through some 100 miles of this we were to penetrate with two lines of survey.

Hargrave and I worked one ; he ran the line with theodolite, while I followed, taking the section. We had with us fifty or sixty Bheel axemen, whose duty was to clear the way indicated by flags, through the jungle, and this needed to be very accurately done to enable the surveyor with theodolite to lay down a perfectly correct line and for the leveller to take an accurate section of the same.

The Bheel axemen were remarkably expert, and the rapidity with which trees, shrubs, tangled grass and undergrowth fell before them was marvellous.

Soon after entering the ghats the Chief was at fault as to the position of the Jakim river, and had proceeded with the other survey party on a trip of inspection to a village called Dowlapani, said to be some 12 miles down the steppe. At this juncture Hargrave got ill and was obliged to lie up for a day, and it gave me an opportunity of doing a bit of exploring on my own account. Taking a gun, I started alone through fairly open jungle, eastwards along the ghats. Knocking over now and again a grey partridge or peafowl, of which there were numbers about, I must have wandered some three or four miles, when I came on a solitary native carrying a load of wood. An endeavour to converse with him proved a failure, but he pointed ahead, and repeatedly mentioned the word Jakim. Soon we emerged on an open stretch of ground and a shallow pool, behind which, on a rising knob, stood a cluster of huts, mostly in ruins. I followed my companion to the place and found about half-a-dozen miserable-looking natives in it. It was evidently a deserted village, or very nearly so, but so far as I was able to understand the few inhabitants, the name of the village and river was Jakim.

Mr. Foy desired that we should make sketches of any of the country about, which might strike us as being of use, and I always carried with me a sketch block and pocket compass.

I now proceeded to make a rough map of my day's walk, and laid down thereupon, as near as I was able, the position of the river and deserted village.

In the evening I returned to camp, laden with a supply of partridge and a couple of fat peafowl, a welcome addition to our larder, and Hargrave, to whom I showed my sketch map, thought it might be valuable to the Chief.

In the morning we started on our survey, and in the course of a week carried it to Dowlapani, where Mr. Foy and the others were camped.

The Chief, on scrutinising my map, immediately directed me to return to Neemuch with Clerke and run a fresh survey from thence to the deserted village, and pursue the valley of the river from that point until further orders.

We covered the twenty-two miles back to Neemuch the following day on foot, took one day's needed rest, on the evening of which we laid off the fresh line and ran it out a couple of miles, ready for the next morning's start. In the open, only long observations were needed, and we arrived on the bank of the Jakim at nightfall, our angle of deviation from the original survey line proving very accurate and taking us almost direct to the point we desired to strike. Following the course of the river the gradients were more uniform, and easier for survey, as the jungle was much more open, and in three days our course led us as we anticipated to Dowlapani, where, after plotting up, the Chief was well pleased at the result.

It was now early in February; although the days were oppressively hot, the nights in these high altitudes were often very cold, and occasionally slight frosts occurred. The survey proceeded steadily and made good progress till the ghats were passed, and we found ourselves on the plains and approaching the valley of the Mahi. After every third or fourth day we stopped survey, to plot up the work, and decide whether alternative lines would have to be tried.

I must now make a slight diversion and recount a somewhat unusual occurrence to take place on a railway survey. This was neither more nor less than my own marriage. I had, strange as it may appear, and as it was in my then circumstances, engaged myself some months previously to a young lady in Bombay, with no intention, of course, of any immediate marriage—that was to await better times. Now, however, the young lady, who was an orphan, living with her adopted mother, was suddenly placed in an embarrassing position, as the latter was obliged to return to England at once.

At the time that this news reached me, the Chief was on the point of despatching one of his assistants to Bombay with important papers, and to bring back money for survey expenses, and I obtained leave to execute the commission.

There was but one horse on the survey, belonging to Kirkman. I borrowed him, and with three mules and two extra servants, I started at midnight with a Bheel guide, which we renewed from village to village. In four days with forced marches we arrived at Wàsad, where, leaving the escort with directions to await me at Baroda, I proceeded to Bombay by the night train, executed my business the day I arrived, got married the following day, and took my wife back with me to the survey. Returning, we left the railway at Baroda, where my men had a small tent and dinner ready for us. Here the same evening I purchased an excellent saddle horse for myself, and after a few lessons my wife was able to ride the other animal, which was steady (One of her wedding presents was a side saddle and bridle.) We travelled during the night, being cool, and there was a brilliant moonlight. All our belongings were packed on mules, which the men rode turn about. On the night of the fourth day we reached the camp, which had moved only a few miles during my absence.

So far from the young wife being any obstacle, she proved a considerable acquisition to the survey party, assumed the management of the camp, and rode off each morning at the head of the mule train; indeed, under her guidance, we became a very social party for the rest of the time.

More than half the survey was now accomplished, and by far the most difficult part—namely, the trial for gradients down the ghats and the passage through the heavy forest land in the Bheel country. Now we were running along the Mahi valley, and one bit of difficult work was at Lunawada, where some very rough country and forest-clothed hills had to be negotiated. Once, while checking a line of levels, over a steep cliff, I had occasion to be let down a precipice by a rope. On reaching nearly to the bottom I tumbled into the branches of some salary trees, which happened to be covered with red ants, half an inch long, a kind of wasp. They attacked me in myriads, got inside my shirt, up my trousers, into my hair, and stung me terribly all over my body. It was days before I entirely recovered, but I had to work all the same.

The country here was also infested with wild bees, and an amusing adventure with them occurred one day. Mr. Foy carried with him throughout the survey a number of fowls, and engaged a boy specially to look after them. His tent was pitched near a cluster of dead trees around which the servants had fixed the cooking arrangements and hen-coops. There happened to be a swarm of bees in a hole in one of the dead stumps, and when we were having late breakfast the next morning (it being a plotting day, when we stayed for work in camp) there was a sudden shouting and stampede of all hands ; the bees, resenting the presence of their visitors discovered themselves, and attacked everyone within reach indiscriminately. All the fowls were stung to death, and the entire camp cleared out for safety, more or less suffering from the attack. Nobody could be induced to go near the trees till sundown, when the bees had retired to rest.

All the Bheel country was infested with monkeys—they were in thousands of all sizes, many as large as men. On passing through the forest on my way to Wasad, I committed an act I have since regretted. I shot a monkey ; I cannot tell why I did it. Hundreds were accompanying us, jabbering and jumping from tree to tree, scampering before and behind, in their usual curious and friendly way. Probably never before had they seen such visitors to their forest home. A huge fellow was jumping some hundred yards ahead, and almost unconsciously I took a snap shot at him with my rifle, and unfortunately hit him. He took to moaning and crying in a most plaintive way, more like a child than anything else. A couple of men rushed over and secured the beast with a rope, when in an instant, fully a thousand monkeys came bounding in from the adjacent trees, making a terrific jabbering and apparently in the most intense excitement. A mule walla called out—" Maro ! Sahib, Maro ! (kill him, Sahib, kill him) which I did at once, with a bullet through the head. The monkeys seemed a bit appeased at this, probably thinking their comrade was unhurt, and we, keeping close together, got away as speedily as we could. The Bheels subsequently declared that we were on the point of being attacked, and had I not silenced the animal and left him, we would probably have been torn to pieces.

There was abundance of game, panthers, sambhur, and tigers in these jungles, but we had little time for amusement, and beyond obtaining a deer or small game now and then for food, did nothing in the sporting way.

By the first week in May we finished the survey up to Wasad, and left for Baroda, ten miles distant, to work up plans and sections. This occupied some two months. Then orders were received to disband the extra staff, and I found myself free and without employment.

CHAPTER III.

APPOINTMENT AS LOCAL FUNDS ENGINEER TO POLITICAL AGENCY OF KATHIAWAR—JOURNEY THITHER.

We stayed, my wife and I, at Baroda during the rains, where we occupied a comfortable little bungalow and joined in all the gaiety of the station. For a little time Clarke stayed with us. One evening I lent him my horse for a ride while we were out driving, and on our return we learnt that the horse had thrown him just outside the compound and bolted for the city, his old home. Notwithstanding the utmost endeavours made by the station staff officers I never saw that horse, saddle or bridle again.

At the end of this time I received the sad news of my father's death. My brother, hearing of his illness, had already gone home. It was now the end of August. We moved to Bombay, and I was getting anxious about finding further work, when I received a call from the Engineer-in-Chief of the B.B. and C.I. Railway to come to his office. Mr. Richmond received me cordially, informed me that Mr. Foy had reported in high terms of my services in the survey, especially in relation to the Jakim Valley route, and he was now happy to tell me that he had recommended me for an appointment as District Engineer in Kathiawar, that Colonel Keatinge, the Political Agent, had been to consult him on the subject the previous day, and I was to proceed with him (Mr. Richmond) to Poona the following day for a personal interview with the Political Agent. This was excellent news to take to the wife, and indeed we had cause to feel relieved and elated, for my finances were at a very low ebb.

I took my wife to stay with friends at Colaba until my return, and met Mr. Richmond at the railway station in the morning.

At Poona I put up at the Royal Hotel and dined at the Western India Club with Mr. Richmond and Mr. Curry, the agent of the railway, and on the following day I went, by appointment, to call upon Colonel Keatinge. He was a tall, fine-looking man, who had won his V.C. in the Mutiny, and was now one of the ablest administrators in India. His manner was kind but bluff and short, and he seemed to learn all about me with a few questions and looking very intently at me all the while. The examination was apparently satisfactory, for in less than ten minutes he informed me that I was appointed Local Fund Engineer to the Kathiawar Political Agency, that I would receive my official appointment in Bombay the following day; then he laid out some maps of the Province and proceeded to show me what he wanted done on my arrival, and expected me to take up my appointment within a week.

It was too late to catch the train for Bombay that day, so I dined again at the Club, where I received congratulations from my two powerful friends, and arrived the following evening at Bombay.

My brother was still at home, and the time of his return was doubtful. He had experienced a heavy reverse to his prospects owing to the late mercantile crisis which involved many houses, including his, in partial ruin. He was now concluding arrangements with his home constituents for starting business on his own account.

Our preparations for Kathiawar were soon made, but I had to provide the needed outfit and instruments.

We journeyed by train to Ahmedabad, 315 miles, then the terminus of the B.B. and C.I. Here we procured two bullock carts for our kit, and a covered bullock shigram for ourselves to convey us to Wudhwan, 75 miles distant, where my work was to commence. We had brought from Bombay two servants, a cook and butler.

Our start from Ahmedabad was an unfortunate one. We left late in the evening, intending to travel during the night, but in crossing the wide sandy bed of the Sabermati river, although our light shigram got over safely, the kit carts both stuck, and no exertions on the part of the drivers could induce the bullocks to pull them out.

Assistance was impossible until morning, and there was nothing for it but to take out the bullocks and leave the carts until then. We slept in our shigram on the bank. During the night heavy rain came on, causing the river to rise some feet, and at daybreak we were able to discern only the tops of the kit carts, the rest being under water; a little more rain would have carried them off entirely.

It was some hours before the men were able to cross and procure the necessary assistance, and nightfall was again upon us before we were ready for the journey, with one half of our property ruined with wet.

From this point to Veerumgam, 30 miles, there existed a sort of Government road, and properly we should have kept to it, and at this season journey *via* Veerumgam, but the ghariwallas stupidly advised our taking the direct route adopted during the fair season, which led along low ground adjoining the great "ran" which extends northwards from the Gulf of Cambay. Of course we were in the ghariwallas' hands and were led by them.

Our first halt the following morning for breakfast was by a prickly pear hedge and a clump of trees, surrounding a cultivator's well. A number of monkeys were disporting themselves near by, and being of a friendly disposition, and no doubt accustomed to being fed by travellers, they proceeded, to the evidently increasing alarm of our Bombay cook, to make prying excursions amongst his boxes and parcels. The poor cook, fearing to offend his visitors, imbued them with greater courage, and presently one of the largest bounded on to the cook's back as he stooped over his fire. This was the last straw; with a shriek of terror he threw up his arms, and ran for his life. We saw that cook no more.

We resumed our journey all day and throughout the following night, and discovered the mistake we had made in taking the direct track. The entire country was more or less under water; the cart track we were obliged to keep to was worn a foot or more in depth into a kind of ditch or drain filled with water, and in this we journeyed on from village to village, four or five miles apart, at the rate of a mile an hour.

In the morning we would draw up at a village and creep on to the bank of a tank, where it was dry, take out some pillows and rugs for a seat under a tree, procure some firewood, milk and butter from the village, and improvise a meal as best we could. Then on again, with fresh animals if we could get them; if not we would give the old ones a few hours rest and food.

The country was uninteresting to a degree, an everlasting green and yellow flat, with villages in their clumps of trees dotting the plain a few miles apart.

Six weary days and nights of this travelling brought us, or rather a part of us, to Wudhwan Civil Station. The two kit carts were again stuck in a dry ditch some miles behind, where they remained till the next day.

Wudhwan Civil Station was one of the headquarters of the Political Agency, where resided the First Assistant to the

Political Agent, Mr. Herbert Birdwood, I.C.S., who, with his wife, received us most hospitably, and very pleased we were to find ourselves in a comfortable bungalow once more.

The Station had only recently been formed by Colonel Keatinge, and possessed as yet but a few shops and a Thanna, in addition to the assistant's residence. A small cotton-pressing factory had also been erected by private merchants.

The place was 66 miles distant from Rajkote, and I found orders from the Political Agent awaiting me in Mr. Birdwood's hands, directing me to carry a road survey with me from Wudhwan to Choteela, 36 miles. A native surveyor, by name Khanji Mackangee, was sent to assist me.

No trigonometrical survey had yet been undertaken for this province, and the existing map provided but a very crude and often incorrect idea of the country, but I resolved, in the first place, to survey the existing cart-track, with adjacent land, as a guide for further observations.

I had my small hill tent and camp furniture with me, and Mr. Birdwood supplied me with what further I required.

On the second day I started, leaving my wife with the Birdwoods, who had kindly proposed her remaining with them until I had completed a portion of the work.

I speedily discovered that my assistant, Mr. Khanji, had never used either theodolite or level, and as there was no time to educate him, I was obliged to use both instruments myself, and fill in both field-books, leaving the chaining only to him.

Being merely a flying survey of the present cart-track and adjacent country, I ran it up to Choteela in eight days, plotting up the day's work each night.

From Choteela to Rajkote, 30 miles, a road line had already been laid down by Colonel Keatinge himself with the assistance of his native surveyors, and a rough, unbridged road had been constructed, so it was not needed that I should have any survey to do on this section.

I rode back to Wudhwan on a camel during the night to fetch my wife. I purchased from Mr. Birdwood a pair of Decanny bullocks and a country cart, over which I fastened a cover of bamboo matting, filled the interior with grass, and laid a mattress thereupon; this was the conveyance in which my wife drove from Wudhwan, and in which we both drew up at the residence of the Political Agent of Kathiawar on a forenoon in the month of November, 1866.

I may remark, in passing, that in these days the Province of Kathiawar did not possess even one horse-carriage, nor scarcely a road upon which one could be driven. The means of locomotion were on horse or camel back, shigrams or country carts, and with the Chiefs, elephants.

We stayed as guests at the Kothie for a few weeks until we procured a bungalow in the Military Cantonment, and Colonel Keatinge had initiated me into his scheme for the public improvements he had in view, and for the carrying out of which he had obtained the sanction of the Bombay Government to my appointment.

Previous to this time, the charge of the few imperial buildings and other Government property in Rajkote were ostensibly under the charge of the Executive Engineer at Ahmedabad, but now that the Political Agent had in projection a heavy annual expenditure on the part of the Chiefs, for the furtherance of road communications and other necessary works of public improvement throughout the province, most of which would be carried out independent of Government direction or supervision, he represented that it was necessary to have professional assistance unconnected with any control or advice beyond that of the Political Agent, himself acting for and with the States.

Before proceeding further with this sketch, it will be well to give a short description of the Province of Kathiawar in its political relation to the Bombay Government, and what was the general nature of the scheme for reform and improvement inaugurated by Colonel Keatinge, in which I was more or less intimately connected in my professional capacity for thirty-three years.

CHAPTER IV.

DESCRIPTIVE OF THE GOVERNMENT OF THE PROVINCE, FEATURES OF KATHIAWAR, ETC.

The Province of Kathiawar, forming the southern portion of Guzerat, is a peninsula situated between Sind and the port of Bombay. It is bounded on the north by Guzerat, south by the Indian Ocean, west by the Gulf of Kutch, and east by the Gulf of Cambay.

Its area is about 20,000 square miles and the population, at the time to which I refer, was about 2,300,000.

The province is divided into 186 states, classified according to their rank; thus there were four (now seven) first-class states owning territories of between 3,000 and 4,000 square miles, and drawing revenues of between £200,000 and £300,000 per annum. Of second-class there were nine (now eight) with revenues of £50,000 to £100,000 per annum. In the third-class, seven, and so on, some of the smallest possessing incomes of not over £1,000 per annum.

Up to the beginning of the nineteenth century the chieftains' principal occupation was warfare amongst themselves.

The northern portion of the Province had been conquered by the Mahrattas, who established the payment of a yearly tribute from the Chiefs, and the Gaekwar of Baroda obtained a similar supremacy over the south.

In 1817 the Peshwa ceded to the British Government his share of the Kathiawar tribute, and in 1820 the Gaekwar agreed to his share being collected by the British Government and paid through them, also that Baroda should send no troops into the Province or make any exactions except through the agency of the British Government. In 1820 a Political Agent, subject to the Government of Bombay, was appointed to reside in the Province with a military force at his command. The Chiefs were required to disband such troops as they entertained, to cease the repairs and erection of forts, and betake themselves to the improvement of their states, and to bettering the condition of their people.

A system of government was established, taking Rajkote as the headquarters, military and political. This had worked pretty satisfactorily for the general peace, and therefore to a certain extent prosperity of the Province, up to the date 1865, at which this sketch properly commences.

Colonel Richard Hart Keatinge, V.C., at this time appointed Political Agent in Kathiawar, was a man of original, powerful, and practical mind. He was not content with merely the obligation placed upon the Chiefs for peace and proper conduct; he saw that for the ultimate prosperity of the country something more was needed than merely to keep the Chiefs in subjection from fear of the paramount power. He saw the ignorance of the people and the worse than ignorance of their natural rulers, who since their usual avocations of war and rapine had been put a stop to had, for want of other and better employment, sunk to a lower state of existence physically and morally than before, while the so-called educated officers ot their courts, for the most part foreigners called in to carry out the official routine of reform and government, were often the real masters, and used their temporary period of power and office to amass wealth, and further demoralise the States, rather than advance the public good.

Colonel Keatinge divided the Province into four districts or prants, in each of which he created a civil station as a headquarters for an assistant Political Agent, with the necessary courts and offices for carrying out the judicial and executive jurisdiction of his district. It would be the duty of these officers also to travel about the prants in their charge, hearing complaints, advising the Chiefs, punishing crime, and generally entering into all the wants of the people and the country.

Rajkote, the Civil and Military headquarters, occupied a pretty central position in the Province. The Military Cantonment and the Civil Station lay side by side, connected through their entire length of about a mile by a single roadway, on either side of which, in the Military camp, were situated the compounds with residences of the officers, their mess, bungalows, orderly rooms, etc., while separated therefrom and in different localities were the lines for the native infantry, cavalry, artillery and parade grounds. The residences were not Government property and were of the crudest design and construction, many of them almost unsafe to live in. The roads and compounds were roughly fenced with prickly pear or cactus, and in but few instances was any attempt made at ornamentation or gardening. The sepoys' lines were constructed by themselves as a part of their duty, as well as for Government economy, and were mud-walled, with roofs of Dutch tiles laid over split bamboo framing. Each single sepoy was allowed one room 10 ft. by 10 ft. in a corner of which he cooked his food. The married quarters were a trifle larger.

The civil residences at that time comprised the Kothie, or principal bungalow, where resided Colonel Keatinge and his family, a large squat building with gardens of some small pretensions around it, and near by were the public offices, courts and waiting hall, for transaction of agency business. Further along were the residences of Captain Hebbert and Captain La Touche, assistant Political Agents, and the civil surgeon, Dr. Joynt, also another residence in which resided Captain Lloyd, the administrator of Rajkote and Limri, two states, the Chiefs of which were minors and wards of Government. There was also a Mission House, where resided the Revd. Mr. Wells, of the Irish Presbyterian Mission. An English Church of diminutive dimensions was situated in the Military lines, where a Church of England Chaplain officiated, and a Roman Catholic Chapel, chiefly for the use of the Portuguese and Eurasian inhabitants, occupied a site in the civil station. There was one schoolhouse, a civil hospital and a jail in civil limits. The native Bazaar, in which were the shops and stores for supply, was situated within Military limits.

Adjacent to the civil station, and separated by an unsavoury nallah, lay the Rajkote city, bounded on its opposite side by the Adji river, which, during the monsoon season, was often a considerable torrent, but in the fair season, a wide sandy and rocky river bed with a shallow stream in which the inhabitants of the city (some 20,000) and their cattle, washed, drank, and bathed in common. The city, which was enclosed by fortified walls, was about a mile in length, and a quarter of a mile wide, with narrow tortuous streets along which only a single cart could pass, and even that in some parts with difficulty.

It was the custom of the country to build their town streets crooked and irregular, under the supposition that in time of war the many angles and turns would afford shelter and protection. There were four principal gates constructed on the usual plan for purposes of defence in case of attack. The outer gate, which was placed at right angles to the city wall, opened into a court from which a second gate at right angles to it led into the city. The court as well as the city was protected by walls and bastions of great strength, loopholed above, and subtended by platforms in the masonry

THE KHOTIE RAJKOTE, AS IMPROVED IN 1886.
(*See page* 26.)

GAECWARI SOWARS, 1866.
(*See page* 27.)

from which the defenders could shoot. The gates themselves were remarkable structures, placed between walls of solid masonry 6 to 10 ft. thick, these huge teak doors, 10 to 12 ft. wide by 20 to 30 feet high, were made of powerful framing sheeted with teak planking from 2 in. to 3 in. in thickness, closely studded with large iron spikes projecting six inches from the face. The armouring was designed as a protection against elephants, these animals being usually employed during war for forcing the gates by pushing their full weight against them.

There was no recognised system of drainage or sanitation, or even cleanliness of any description; offal and filth were thrown into the streets, to be partially devoured by the domestic cows and pariah dogs, and partly swept away by the city scavengers periodically, but indeed the pariah dogs, vultures, crows, and cows formed the main scavenging community of all the native towns at this period, and but for them epidemics, which were rampant enough at most times, must have decimated many localities.

The above description of Rajkote would refer generally to most Hindoo or Mussulman towns at that period.

There were quartered at Rajkote a regiment of native infantry a squadron of cavalry and a mountain battery of artillery with European officers in command; these numbered ten or twelve, some of whom were married. The civil element comprised the Political Agent and his family, two assistant Political Agents, the civil surgeon and the Missionary, all married. The total European residents of Rajkote numbered from 25 to 35, but these were periodically augmented by district officers, assistants in charge of prants, etc.

In the southern or Sorath Prant station, called Maneckwarra, resided Colonel W. W. Anderson, superintendent of the Gaekwar contingent, a body of very irregular horse, designated sowars, maintained at the expense of H.H. the Gaekwar of Baroda, according to treaty arrangements, for use as escort, and in other official capacities by the agency. The force numbered about 800, of which 500 to 600 were retained as a reserve at Maneckwarra headquarters. There was no distinctive uniform; each sowar dressed according to his fancy; and not only were the horses of any colour naturally, but not unfrequently a sowar, with a turn for art, would stain his steed's mane and tail in variegated bands, or paint rosettes of colour on his neck or haunches, and twine heavy strings of shells or coins around the animal's neck; there was no attempt at grooming, and the manes and tails were allowed to grow their full, which was convenient, of course, for switching off flies.

Each sowar, when on duty, carried his entire domestic impedimenta on his horse's back. Over a thick woollen nambda or saddle cloth of variegated colours was laid the padded cushion which usually formed his bed, while fore and aft were fastened his other possessions and a cooking pot or two, while seated in the midst with bare feet thrust into red or brown slippers, a heavy cummerbund (waistband) stuck full of knives and daggers, a long sword swinging on one side, and a satchel of canvas for food and opium suspended from the other, the ends of his moustache twisted upwards, and a brilliantly-coloured puggree ornamenting his head, the Gaeky mounted sowar presented, if not a particularly soldier-like, at any rate a somewhat picturesque object.

As a matter of form, the force was paraded once a week for inspection and put through a course of drill, which sometimes proved an amusing fiasco to watch. The animals, which were indiscriminately horses, mares, and geldings, would occasionally, during drill, engage in a free fight, and presently a number of the riders would be ornamenting the parade ground mixed up with saddles, bedding and puggrees, while their happy steeds would stampede in freedom for their lines.

But the Gaekwar sowars were not expected, nor intended to be brilliant soldiers. Fierce-looking and picturesque as they were, actual fighting not was a game they would be likely to take any serious part in, they did the work they were intended for well, and in their own way were very useful. All of us agency officers had a fixed number allotted to us for our personal escort and service, official or otherwise. They were excellent puggies and some of them shikaries, and I have many recollections of long day and night rides when but for my faithful Gaekwari escort I would not have fared so well as I did, one carrying my rifle, another my food and liquor.

The Gaekwari contingent no longer exist; they were disbanded some years ago to make way for the new agency police, and they only remain as one more memory of the good old days in Kathiawar.

Colonel Anderson, subsequently political agent, was famed far and wide for his hospitality at Maneckwarra. His appointment as superintendent of the Gaekwar Horse was, as may be inferred, almost a sinecure, and one of the best paid ones in the Presidency. He kept open house for all comers, and during the fair season his bungalow was usually full of visitors, while half-a-dozen tents would be rigged up under the trees of his fine gardens to accommodate friends from distant places, and picnics, excursions, shoots, etc., were the order of the day.

The assistant political agent, Captain Phil Le Geyt, who was Colonel Anderson's nephew, and resided near by, together with a subaltern from Rajkote, represented, in addition to Colonel Anderson's family, the only European residents of Maneckwarra, which was some seventy miles distant from Rajkote.

On our arrival at Rajkote we found all the European officers from the districts assembled at headquarters, as well as representatives from most of the principal states, this being what is called in up-country parlance "the week," when official matters for the past and coming year would be discussed during the day, and the mornings, afternoons, and nights would be devoted to social functions, entertainments, and sport of every kind, so we had an opportunity of knowing everybody there was to know at once, as well as to become acquainted with the native state officers.

Colonel Keatinge, who was a great advocate for object lessons, had just got sent up to Rajkote some pumps for lifting water from wells and rivers by steam power, and he had invited cultivators from the surrounding districts to come and see them at work. The exhibition was a very good one, but I am afraid it did not impress the native mind to any great extent; "Where were they to get the engine? What was the cost? How would they pay for it? If it went wrong how were they to mend it? The pump drew up the water too quickly for their experience," and so on. No! it was Sahib's kāl (play), and gave no further thought to Keatinge's Sahib's "tamasha," and departed to their homes.

On this occasion also Colonel Keatinge had brought up some English ploughs and other farm implements, and had trials made for the edification of the farmers, but they met with a similar fate. The Sahib had much "merbhan" (kindness) for them and it was a "Bhot acha tamasha" (very good entertainment), but there it ended. The ploughs and harrows Colonel Keatinge presented to some of the Durbars, who promised that they would give them a trial with their people, and they carried them away, much pleased with their gifts.

Years after, when visiting some native chief, he has shown me as a great curiosity the English plough given him by Keatinge Sahib, which he had carefully preserved in a conspicuous place in his Durbar hall. They can still be seen, I have no doubt, but no English plough has yet superseded the native one, which has been in use for ages among the Kathiawar kumbies, who, as farmers, are, I think, second to none in the universe.

The life at Rajkote was enjoyable, and Mrs. Keatinge was an excellent head of the station society. We were all up early, not later than six o'clock, when, after the usual chota hazri, we went out for the morning's work, exercise, or recreation as the case might be, home at nine for bath, and breakfast, office till lunch at two, office again till four or five, then tea, dress for the evening's drive or ride, or to the gardens, where croquet was played, and where the regimental band appeared once a week. Dinner was usually half-past seven or eight. (Badminton and tennis were not invented till the 'seventies.) The country abounded in game, and all was free to Europeans.

After staying nearly three weeks at the Kothie, I secured a bungalow in the military lines, and got it roughly furnished, purchasing most of what we needed from the effects of an officer, Colonel Gray, who had lately left the station.

I purchased a saddle horse, or rather pony, and Colonel Keatinge presented me with another splendid animal, one of those famous Kathi horses, dun colour, with a dark stripe down the back and black points. He was a weight carrier, and could do his forty to fifty miles a day with ease.

My first duties were, of course, connected with road surveys and construction, which were soon in full swing, and for a considerable time I was able to retain my office and headquarters at Rajkote, which was centrally situated, and from whence I made trips to the scene of operations as necessary.

The charge of the Imperial buildings of Rajkote administration were now handed over to me by sanction of Government at the political agent's request. At Rajkote these comprised jails, hospital, and Government offices, besides the official residences and civil station roads. The outstations were Wudhwan, Maneckwarra, and Songhud, where similar charges existed but of a less extensive nature.

Maneckwarra and Wudhwan I have already referred to. At Songhud, the official headquarters of the assistant political agent of Gohelwad Prant, then resided Captain John Watson, and with him, on special political work, was Captain Lechmere Russell. I soon had an opportunity of meeting them both at Songhud, and they were amongst my earliest friends.

Both were keen shikaries, and the district surrounding Songhud abounded in all kinds of small and big game.

Songhud Station was built on an elevated narrow ridge, with a deep river bed passing on one side. The bungalow occupied the highest part. At the furthest point of the ridge, Watson and Russell had erected a comical-looking structure which they termed the Star of India Bungalow. The lower story of this building was used as a smoking room and library, while the upper portion, which was in the form of a small circular tower, was provided with a lantern head in which an oil lamp was lit during the night as a beacon to guide Watson and Russell home when they were out late in search of panther, etc. Like much that belonged to what we veterans call the good old days (and they were for us the best) the Star of India Bungalow of that time has disappeared, and a modern district dispensary, I think, occupies its site.

Among the non-political residents at Rajkote was one which I must specially mention, as he was my friend and frequent companion for many years. This was Captain McDougal Gleig. He had recently been invalided from the army on account of his great and increasing weight—at this time nineteen stone—but he was still fairly active, except at riding. He was a keen shot and fisherman, and a first-class whip. He owned a pair of splendid Kathies, which he drove in a high dog-cart of great strength. Indeed, his was, I believe, the first vehicle of the kind brought into Kathiawar, and Gleig cared little over what kind of ground he took it; he would have scorned roads were there any to scorn.

He had invested any means he possessed in modern farm implements, and took a small farm, a portion of the civil station lands, but it proved a bad speculation. Gleig could not compete with the native kumbi, and after a few years he was obliged to give up his farm and sell off his stock and plant at a ruinous loss. After a time he obtained the appointment of inspecting postmaster of Kathiawar, and no doubt the heart of many a district P.O. official quaked as he heard the rattle of Gleig's cart and pair crossing the plain for an official visit.

Captain Gleig was a particularly able man, and had he entered the Civil Service he would have made his mark. He was also an excellent musician. His father was Chaplain-General to the British Army.

The civil surgeon at Rajkote was Dr. E. Butler, at this time on leave, and Dr. Christopher Joynt was acting for him. The latter was an Irishman, and very popular were he and his wife. Another political I met here then and frequently in after days was Colonel Lester, and there was for a time Mr. Aitcheson, of the Civil Service, who, I recollect, was a great gardener, and had charge of the station gardens and recreation grounds.

I think I have now mentioned all the political officers of the agency at the period of my joining the staff.

The Province of Kathiawar is divided nearly at its centre by a great watershed passing from N.W., to S.E., the highest point of which is the range of hills running *via* Choteela, Anandpur Palyad, etc., and from which the principal rivers take their rise.

The geological features of the country on either side of this watershed are nearly totally different, that upon the N.E. being of aqueous and aerial formation, while the other is distinctly volcanic. The river courses to the north and east present the nearly invariable characteristic of a bed of fine quartz sand, and the country abounds in shale and sandstone.

In these sandy river beds, a pretty constant stream trickles over the surface or beneath it all the year round, providing water for domestic use for the adjacent villages, but within twenty miles of their outlet the water becomes brackish (salty), and the population are dependent upon their tanks, the usual appendage of every village along the east-coast, and to the north.

These tanks vary from five to ten feet in depth, and from five to twenty acres in area, and are formed by excavating, and throwing up a bank on the lower side, while on the upper a catchwater drain may extend some distance as a lead for the rain water which flows off the surface. In these tanks the inhabitants and their animals drink, wash, and bathe in common, the water being all they have to look to for supplying their several wants, and not unfrequently, in years of scanty rainfall, the hot season brings drought, and the tanks do not hold out till the monsoon rains replenish them, and the unhappy villagers have to seek a temporary home in some other neighbourhood.

As we approach the south the water supply improves, and the land is more fertile. The brackish water and arid tracts of quartz and sandstone give place to sweet water, arable land, granite, trap and limestone.

Although for a very long period, centuries no doubt, almost nothing was done towards improving the water supply by retention and storing of monsoon floods, there are evidence that at some remote period this was not the case. There are found many remains of what must have been fine artificial tanks constructed at great cost and labour, all now in ruins, with the exception of those to be met with in the form of ornamental reservoirs in the gardens of some of the durbars.

Wells are plentiful in all parts, and these supply water for irrigating small patches of land and gardens during the fair and hot season, as well as for potable purposes ; but if the rainfall is insufficient many dry up just when most needed, entailing much loss in crops and cattle. In a flat country like Kathiawar the water raised from wells is only that which has percolated from the surface during the monsoon, and has been retained by impervious strata of clay or stone at no great depth.

Towards the south the larger rivers run during the entire year, and the water level is sometimes raised by means of bunds. Wells are formed at either bank, which are kept supplied by channels from the river, and the water is drawn up by koss, an arrangement of pulleys and leather buckets worked by bullocks from the top of the banks.

During the last twenty years much has been carried out through government agency as well as by some of the Chiefs, in works for the storage of monsoon rainfalls, some of the principal of which I will refer to.

CHAPTER V.

CAPTAIN LLOYD—LIEUT. HANCOCK—WORK AT LIMRI MANECKWARRA — FISHING — FLORICAN AND OTHER SHOOTING—VISITATION OF LOCUSTS—PANTHER HUNT—BUCK SHOOTING—PARLIAMENT WEEK AT RAJKOTE—THE MONSOON.

I mentioned in the previous chapter that the young chiefs of Rajkote and Limri were minors and wards of the Agency and their states were in charge of a Political Officer, Captain Lloyd.

Limri was 75 miles distant from Rajkote and stood on the bank of the Bogava river, a wide sandy bed with a shallow stream, except during the monsoon, when it often became a torrent 800 feet wide. The city was fortified with walls and bastions of brick, many parts crumbling into decay. The streets were narrow and circuitous, the houses for the most part were built of mud and sun-dried brick, but there were a few residences of merchants of some architectural pretentions. The durbar, with zenana and official buildings, occupied the centre of the town, and was completely walled in. There was no attempt at drainage, and offal and garbage were thrown by the town-sweepers into the nearest ditch. Captain Lloyd offered me the post of State-engineer in addition to my own duties, but separate pay was disallowed, the State being under agency charge. My first action was to make a complete detailed map of the city and suburbs with levels laid down throughout, and this I did with my own hands. I recollect what a very unpleasant occupation it was working a theodolite and level and taking measurements in those narrow unsavoury streets, but I finished the survey in three weeks, working at it for three or four hours in the early morning every day, while it was cool. Then improvements were laid out, school buildings, thana, hospital, jail, post office, etc., were designed and built, and the streets were improved and drained where most urgently needed. A considerable slice of land was reclaimed from river depredations above the city by a river wall, wells were sunk or improved, and I designed a movable timber tramway to assist traffic over the sandy river bed. This was formed of a teak 12 in. by 3 in. plank, in lengths of 10 to 12 ft., made to connect end to end, laid a few inches below the surface, and covered over with straw sweepings or kachra. It proved a great success and a great ease to the poor animals who had originally to drag the laden carts through the soft sand, and not infrequently lay down from exhaustion and died under the ordeal and the brutality of their drivers.

Altogether it was a very interesting charge and the first of its kind I had undertaken. In future years, after the young Thakore (one of the first pupils of the Rajkumar College) succeeded to the Ghadi (throne), I carried out many important works for him, some of which I will refer to.

Wudhwan city and civil station were 15 miles north of Limri, and the A.P.A. now in charge there was Colonel W. C. Parr, of whose genial friendship and hospitality I have many pleasant recollections. I had engineering charge of the civil station and was now erecting a court-house, thana, and police buildings, and laying out new roads, but a principal work in that neighbourhood, just now, was the construction of a bridged and metalled road from Wudhwan towards Ahmedabad, so far as the Kathiawar boundary.

The country was absolutely flat, without any defined river channels. At each village, two to four miles apart, rain-water was collected and saved in tanks formed by excavating and banking up on the lower side. These basins, sometimes of considerable area, and from 6 to 10 ft. deep, would, after a favourable rainfall, hold a reserve of water till the following monsoon, otherwise wells would come into service.

The tank water was used for all purposes; cattle and people bathed and drank in common, and in it the villagers washed their clothes. It was marvellous how the water remained wholesome. During the cold season these tanks swarmed with wild fowl, duck, widgeon, and teal, while their sedgy borders abounded with snipe. One day I recollect killing, in company with Captain Stace, over 200 head of duck, between three small tanks.

From Captain Lloyd, who was selling off the durbar stud, I purchased a fine white Katty mare, which my wife used to ride, so I possessed three excellent saddle-horses, and all our journeyings were made on horseback, while the youngster was sent ahead in a covered bullock cart with his own attendants.

Another interesting piece of work I carried out at this time was the fixing of the watershed of the Anandpoore hills, near Choteela. This was a dispute lasting over forty years. The watershed was laid down as the boundary between Anandpoore and the neighbouring state, Bhimora, but they never appeared to be able to arrive at any mutual agreement as to the precise position of the (pāni dhāl) watershed, and the boundary-line fixed by successive native surveyors, ran across watercourses and otherwise where it should not go. I recollect how very difficult I found it to make the combatants understand what a watershed really was. Indeed, I don't think I did make them understand, but I laid down the boundary over the five miles and delineated it with pillars. The work was thus finally settled.

I mention these items to show the varied description of work I had to undertake within two years of joining my appointment.

As successor to Captain La Touche, a young staff officer—Lieutenant G. E. Hancock—was now appointed to the Kathiawar agency.

My first meeting with him was when riding one morning, to Choteela. He was cantering along, pig spear in hand, sitting his horse like a young centaur, and looking as if the province belonged to him. Nearly his entire political service was subsequently spent in Kathiawar, and he was connected not only with much of the progress of the province, but perhaps no man of his time was more popular or a keener sportsman all round, or is there a name which will longer be remembered than George Hancock. It was at this time that badminton and tennis were introduced, but the manner of playing was very different from now. The first tennis court was enclosed within low mud walls, with a central wall to play over; nets were not employed. Badminton was played in the open air, a kind of shuttlecock and battledore. Cricket, rifle shooting, pigeon matches, and racquets formed some of the other station amusements; the old game of croquet was now dying a natural death. Lieut. Hancock was the life and soul of Rajkote sport; everything was organised and carried out by him.

In those early days field sport of every kind was plentiful and free to all Europeans. The jungles were full of panther, antelopes fed in hundreds over the plains, Neilghai (a large kind of deer) were common in most districts; partridge, grey and painted, abounded, also quail, snipe, wild duck, rock grouse, bustard, hares, and florican; and in the Gir jungles were to be found the only lions in India, also sambur and cheetul. Kathiawar was an ideal land for the sportsman. In our movements through the district we lived on game and could select any variety

During the monsoon of 1868 we stayed at Maneckwarra. Colonel Parr, acting-superintendent of the Gaekwari contingent, with Captain Phil Legeyt and his wife, were the only other residents, and we were a very happy party.

Captain Legeyt was a keen fisherman, and his love of the sport infected us all. The rivers and streams abounded with fish, the best description of which were murrel, a kind of pike and very good to eat. These were often caught from 6 lb. to 10 lb. in weight; there were also various kinds of tench and eels, pari and singhara.

The fishing season was during the rains, and every favourable afternoon, when work permitted, saw us all off in tongas or on horseback for some fishing locality. The baits were worms and frogs, and the programme was, in comparison with fishing generally, a very luxurious one. Selecting a favourable spot you sat down on the bank on a chair and cast out your bait, to which a float was attached. If the sun was hot, an attendant squatted behind holding a large white umbrella over your head; another presently fetched a whiskey and soda, or tea, and if the sport was not very exciting you read a book. When the bait was nibbled away, as frequently happened, another attendant replaced it. The taking of the bait by a large fish was easily detected; the float went under at once steadily and deep; then you struck and the fun began. I have frequently played a large murrel or singara half an hour before he could be landed. Some evenings we would bring home 50 to 100 pounds weight of fish among five rods.

We had also florican shooting in the great grass bhids (meadows.) They are beautiful birds, visiting the plains only during the monsoon, except in rare instances. The cock is black and tawny on back, wings and neck, with some white streaks, and carries a plume on his crest; the hen is all brown, somewhat larger than the cock and very gamey looking, not unlike a hen pheasant in colour and size. In seeking them it is usual to send out men in the very early morning, who station themselvs on some rising ground from whence a view of the bhid is commanded. Presently the call Kr-rk-rk of the cock will be heard, and the bird will be seen rising a few feet and then immediately dropping.

When his position is thus fixed, the sportsmen walk him up. The hens do not rise as above, and so are sought for by beaters in line. When the cover is scanty the birds are wary and difficult to approach, and when the grass grows high, it is almost impossible to put them up; florican shooting, therefore, lasts only a short time. The birds are partial to the Spanish or blister fly, which arrives in great quantities towards the close of the rains, and when they begin to feed on them they are not considered safe to eat.

It was in the autumn of this year that Kathiawar was visited by a great flight of locusts, and the district we were then in was one of those laid waste, so we had an excellent opportunity for observation. I had gone to Rajkote a few days before, riding through miles of country, rich in waving fields of bajri and jowari, bending under their weight of grain, cotton, young wheat, chillies, lucern, etc., a splendid prospect for an exceptionally rich and luxurious harvest. On my return, when arriving within six miles of Maneckwarra, I was astounded to find the same country transformed into a brown waste, as if it had been covered with dry mud, or as if a coir carpet had been spread over it. Every tree was bare of leaves, the grass was eaten to the ground; the splendid fields of native corn were stripped of leaf and grain, and only the brown stalks remained. It was the same as far as the eye could reach. A little further the ground was thickly covered with locusts, gorged and stupid, and unable yet to rise. For the next few miles the locusts were busy feeding; not an inch of space was free of them, and when they had gorged they would drop insensible for a time, then rise in a cloud and settle again on fresh ground. The flight covered about ten miles in width and took a direct line of 200 miles from the N.E. to S.W. coast, where, on arrival, the locusts disappeared into the ocean. For many weeks all did not leave the locality; although the bulk went southward, small batches or clouds of them remained till absolutely nothing in the way of vegetation was left. It was a terrible visitation, and entailed great loss to the States concerned and to the cultivators and the poor who were dependent for their daily food on the grain which the locusts had consumed. Along the coast millions of dead locusts continued for a time to be washed ashore with every tide, and the lower-caste natives would collect and cook them for food.

In 1870 two other important States came under charge of the agency. These were Bhavnagar and Gondal. Mr. Percival, C.S.I., and Mr. Gowrishanker, one of the State Ministers, were appointed joint administrators of the former, and Colonel Parr of the latter. Separate engineering establishments were started in both. At Bhavnagar, Mr. Proctor Sims, formerly in charge of the Backbay reclamation at Bombay, was one of my first friends; while at Gondal the department was placed under the charge of Mr. Ganesh Govind, my head surveyor, who had rendered himself fit for the charge and promotion.

An amusing experience occurred at Gondal one day at this time. I had ridden there from Jetpur on an invitation from Colonel Parr and Hancock to join them in a panther hunt. Hancock had "kubber" that a panther was lying up in a sugar-cane field three miles from Gondal, and he was engaged organising a hunt. The sugar-cane was fully grown, 6 to 8 ft. high, and of some acres in extent, and so thick that one could with difficulty force a way through it. Hancock had two avenues, six feet wide, cut clear from side to side, and the idea was to drive the animal across one of these, when he could be shot as he passed over. Colonel Parr and I were placed in trees, each commanding an avenue, and seated on native cots fastened in the thorny branches, while Hancock occupied the howdah on an elephant with about fifty beaters on foot to drive. Hancock had with him a breech-loading gun and rifle, the first of the kind brought into the province, and, of course, quite new and strange to me who had only used the muzzle-loader.

When I had climbed up into my thorny nest Hancock slung up to me one of the breech-loaders and some cartridges, so that I could place them in the gun myself. I did not understand this, and was under the impression that the gun was loaded when he passed it up.

The drive commenced, the beaters making an unearthly row with crackers, firing off native guns, shouting, etc., and presently the panther broke cover, right under my tree, and as he slunk across the avenue within ten yards of me I fired, or rather snapped right and left at him. The gun was empty! I do not at this distance of time recollect the precise language that emanated from the howdah on the occasion, or from the babul tree, but I believe it was forcible.

It was the only proper chance we got at the panther that day. He was wounded subsequently from a snap shot, but we did not get him.

Hancock and I started for Rajkote the following morning in an improvised cart, to which we attached a durbar horse, and fortunately arrived the same afternoon, whole.

Some days after this we went buck-shooting in the same direction, having noticed many herds on our way from Gondal. Riding to a village, Ribra, 12 miles from Rajkote, we procured a bullock cart and driver, this being the most approved method of stalking black buck. On approaching a herd, the cart was driven slowly towards them while we walked at either side. If we were lucky enough to get within range—50 to 100 yards—one was to take first shot and then both do their best.

By two p.m. we had bagged six fine buck, and being hungry, tired, and hot, we lay down under a large peepul tree by a well for rest and refreshment. Here we fell asleep, and must have remained so for a couple of hours when we were roused by a horrible feeling of being bitten all over our bodies. Stripping to the skin, we found ourselves covered with hundreds of red and purple spots, some painful, swollen, and intensely itchy, and discovered that we had been attacked by burrs or cattle tics. We were *hors de combat* for that day, and it was with difficulty we contrived to ride the twelve miles into Rajkote.

Early in 1870 we had moved into another bungalow at Rajkote, where my office was established, and from whence we made raids into the districts as occasion demanded, but I was now busily engaged on the College buildings. My brother came up from Bombay to see us, and stayed a few weeks for the shooting and station gaieties. It was our first monsoon at headquarters, and the entertainments and amusements were, as usual, fast and furious, especially during the "Parliament week," when all the district officers were called to Rajkote to meet the Political Agent and State representatives for discussion of official matters for the coming year. Colonel Anderson, as was his custom, kept open-house, and a considerable number of guests from outside the province would come to Rajkote for the week.

The rains usually commenced about the 20th of June, and the first fall was longingly looked for after the fierce heat of the previous two or three months. During this period one had to be housed by 9 a.m., with all doors and windows

DUCK SHOOTING ON NAL BAULI.

(*See page* 41.)

closed to keep out the heated air, and inside one could only exist under a punkah. The thermometer usually registered during the day from 98° to 110°. Fortunately the nights were fairly pleasant, and a single sheet to keep off mosquitoes was sufficient covering. The early mornings up to 8 or 9 o'clock were fresh and pleasant. In India few trees lose their leaves during the dry season; it seems to be a dispensation of Providence that many trees during the great season of heat put on their most luxuriant clothing, so as to provide shade for animal life. But the ground becomes dried up and hard, and the strong S.W. winds that blow during the day raise clouds of blinding dust. As sundown approached the wind would fall and the air rapidly cool, when everybody would emerge for the evening drive, ride, or amusement.

The first fall of rain would generally be ushered in with a violent storm of thunder and lightning in the afternoon, and after the rain came down and gave the thirsty ground its long-expected bath the feeling of relief was bliss itself. The whole of nature seemed changed. The sweet scent from the freshly watered earth was delightful, and almost instantly a green tinge spread over the landscape, everything was waiting to bound into life and joy.

I will close this chapter with a reference to one of my many shoots at Nal Bauli.

The Nal is a fresh-water lake, at the head of the Gulf of Cambay, some 14 miles long by 10 wide. It is shallow, with numerous islands and a great extent of reedy shoreland. It and the neighbouring tanks are the great resort of sportsmen during the cold season, for the numerous quantities of wild duck, teal, geese, and snipe to be found there. We pitched our camp near the little village of Bowli, in the territory ot the Thakor Sahib of Limri, who kindly sent us a boat and paid us more than one visit. A usual plan for sportsmen to navigate the Nal is by means of what are called trappas, made of large bundles of reeds tied together, forming a kind of raft 15 to 20 feet long and 3 to 4 wide. The sportsman squats on the top, and the trappa is propelled by one or two men with long poles. I have used the trappas more as a means of transport from one part of the Nal to another than for actual shooting purposes, as in the open water their unusual appearance startles the birds, and it is not easy to get within shot. The sedges, which extend for miles, are of great width, and abound in snipe, and I have often shot 20 or 30 couple in a few hours at the beginning of the season, but the walking is occasionally very severe, being through liquid mud and tangled weeds and reeds, often knee deep. The pleasantest shooting is around the small tanks in the vicinity of the Nal—two or three guns are placed around under cover, and a number of beaters sent into the water. The ducks fly in all directions and return over and over again to re-settle. We got many large bags in this way.

We generally stayed out all the day, the ladies having a good twelve o'clock breakfast and lunch combined sent to us, at which they joined.

The dear old Nal. I have had many a jolly Christmas week with you—amongst old and good friends—some of them gone to better hunting-grounds, and all dispersed, but it is pleasant to live the life over again in memory.

CHAPTER VI.

BRIEF NOTES ON THE INAUGURATION AND PROGRESS OF ENGINEERING AND EDUCATION, 1865-99, WITH REFERENCE TO SOME OF THE PRINCIPAL STATES WHO WERE LEADERS IN PROGRESS AND REFORM.

Up to 1866, as before remarked, Kathiawar possessed no made roads, and the headquarters, military and political, were, during the monsoon, not unfrequently cut off for days or weeks from communication with the outer world.

The original bullock cart track consisted of a pair of ruts, which took in the wheels of the country cart, and in which the bullocks which drew them walked. These tracks were, in many parts, impassable during the rainy season, as they sometimes followed the bed of a nallah, dry during the fair season, but a rushing torrent during the rains, or passed along a deeply worn channel in the black cotton soil, which, during and after rains, became a ditch of sticky mud. For this reason it was customary for the cultivators to lay their carts by for the three or four monsoon months, and so it may be imagined that without baggage conveyances it was very difficult for any person to move from one place to another during that period. Horseback or light bullock shigrams were employed when the weather was at all favourable, but to start on a district journey of any length in one of the latter conveyances was not unlikely to prove a disastrous experience.

There were two postal lines on which the mails were carried by runners. One was from Ahmedabad *via* Veramgam and Wudhwan, the other left the railway line at Surat, crossed the Gulf of Cambay in a ferry boat to Bhavnagar, from thence proceeding by the country track to Rajkote, 120 miles. The time occupied in transit during the fair season was about two days, but during the monsoon the mails were not expected till they arrived, and a week or ten days' delay was not an uncommon occurrence. Formidable obstacles were, of course, the large rivers, over which, when in flood, the mails were conveyed by expert swimmers, who carried the post bags strapped on their shoulders when the floods were not too high to venture safely. Huts were constructed on either bank, in which the swimmers lived.

But it was not only during the monsoon that transit was difficult; the crossings over the river beds were either rough and rocky, or vast extents of fine quartz sand. It was no uncommon occurrence to see a train of laden carts delayed for two or three days at one of these sandy beds, the crossing of which could only be accomplished by the part unloading and reloading of the carts and yoking the bullocks of two or three carts to each one in succession, when by dint of screaming, praying, twisting of tails, and belabouring the wretched animals, each pair of which would often persist in taking a line of country, or rather sand, directly opposed to that they were invited to do, they would succeed in extricating one conveyance. The second would be more difficult. The bullocks would be tired and more obstinate to deal with, and at the stiffest point might give in entirely, when the only resource would be to camp for the day.

To Colonel Keatinge is due not only the first impetus given to road-making in Kathiawar, but with such material in the way of native assistance as was procurable, he himself laid out and constructed the first road of thirty miles from Rajkote to Choteela.

The actual funds at Colonel Keatinge's disposal amounted to Rs.7,000 per annum, being a charge of one per cent. on the tribute, and at the time I refer to, some Rs.20,000 had accumulated. With this sum he commenced the above road and completed a portion of it at a cost of about Rs.1,400 per mile.

It was an unbridged road with cuttings leading in and out of the nallahs. Over low lying land the road was carried on an embankment, high enough to raise it above flood level, covered with a layer of moorum.

Although simple and primitive, the road was a vast improvement on the original native track, and was available for traffic when the latter was not.

Having thus made a commencement with Imperial funds which he trusted would be an example for the chiefs to follow, he convened meetings with the State representatives, at which he set forth the advantages to be derived from the formation of roads to develop the resources of the country, and, as with Colonel Keatinge to undertake was to accomplish, he succeeded in obtaining from the States promises to pay for three great lines of roads, branching from Rajkote —namely, to Jamnuggar, 52 miles, to Bhavnagar 120 miles, to Jetpur 34 miles, and the completion up to Wudhwan of the road he had already commenced 61 miles.

It was not, I fear, at that time due to any real appreciation of road communication on the part of the States that they gave the funds asked for. The more impassable the country the more to their taste: they were more secure from attack from their neighbours; and what was good for their fathers was good enough for them! The time, however, had arrived for the breaking down of such ancient traditions, and those who ruled in the Durbars knew it too well to show disinclination to advice from the representative of Government who was determined to carry out what was necessary for the prosperity of the Province.

The question of the extension of the railway from Ahmedabad to Wudhwan was much agitated by Colonel Keatinge, and he induced Government to cause a survey to be made. Being unable, however, to get the railway actually commenced by Government, he determined to make a beginning without them, by inducing the chiefs whose territories lay adjacant to the Kathiawar portions of the proposed line to promise funds for the construction of a first-class carriage road to the Kathiawar boundary, 29 miles, on the understanding that when Government decided to make the railway the road would be repurchased from them for what it had cost to construct.

The scheme was carried out after Colonel Keatinge left by the A.E. Dept., under Colonel Parr, acting assistant Political Agent at Wudhwan, but the whole burthen of the expense was not thrown on the Jalawad chiefs alone; some of the other wealthy chiefs in the Province contributed their quota in a public spirited way for the general good.

By the end of 1870, 22 miles of this road were completed. Then the railway was decided upon, and the road embankment and all works constructed were taken over at their cost price of Rs.90,000, which was refunded to the States who had subscribed it. The half of this sum was subsequently returned by the chiefs to pay for the bridging of the Choteela Wudhwan road, to be expended at the discretion of the Political Agent.

Colonel Keatinge's attention was also directed to the improvement and formation of the harbours, and he induced H.H. the Nawab of Junaghudh to engage the services of a Civil Engineer, Mr. Baliol Scott, to draw up plans for the improvement of his port of Verawul on the south coast. Ports and Harbours will be referred to in a subsequent chapter.

For the four great road lines arranged for by Colonel Keatinge, the construction was in the first instance to be similar to that already adopted on the Choteela Rajkote line, but they were to be laid out with a view to future bridging and metalling, when funds became available, and the entire works were to be in charge of the author. Surveys were speedily put into hand, work was started simultaneously on all, and in the course of the first year a considerable amount had been completed.

The formation of roads upon the principle laid down by Colonel Keatinge continued steadily to progress. The Navanagar, Jetpur, Bhavnagar and Wudhwan roads were nearly completed by the year 1870, besides various other shorter lines.

In 1870, the Thakor Sahib of Bhavnagar dying, the State was placed under British management during the minority of the young heir, and one of the first acts of the new administration was to organise a department of Public Works under a European Civil Engineer, Mr. R. Proctor Sims, M.I.C.E., under which the formation of roads amongst other improvements was vigorously pushed ahead.

Again, a similar occurrence taking place at Gondal, then a second-class but wealthy State adjoining Rajkote, an engineering department was organised under a superintendent of Public Works, Mr. Gunesh Govind, who was transferred thence from his office of head surveyor to the Agency Engineer.

Morvi, Limbdi, and Rajkote also worked creditably. They were like the others under British agency, but their finance did not admit of their entertaining separate engineering departments, and such work as they projected were principally conducted under the Agency Engineering Department.

With the exception of those I have referred to little worthy of mention in the way of road-making was carried out by any of the other States.

Indeed, owing to the natural apathy and passive resistance to improvement, the roads already made by the agency commenced to suffer in no small degree.

To induce the Durbars to furnish funds for making the roads in the first instance was difficult enough, but having furnished so much, they considered there was an end to the matter, and that a road once made was to last for ever without further expenditure. In this they were naturally disappointed when they discovered that they would be called upon to pay annually for the maintenance of the roads they had made. They then asserted that they could repair the roads themselves at a much smaller cost than if the work was carried out under the Agency Engineering Department, and they applied to Colonel Anderson, the then Political Agent, and obtained permission from him to take over charge of all the road maintenance.

It proved bad policy. The roads were utterly neglected, the repairs being let at a merely nominal rate to contractors, and some of them became in a short time as bad as the original country tracks, or else entirely disappeared.

In such manner did road-making progress until the latter end of 1873, when Colonel Anderson went home on furlough, and Mr. (late Sir) J. B. Peile, C.S., was appointed to act for him. Mr. Peile's advent in Kathiawar at this time was very opportune, and the construction of roads and their proper maintenance became one of his first cares. He proposed asking the chiefs to subscribe to a permanent road fund, to be under the sole management of the Political Agent, and to be utilised in bridging, metalling, and otherwise improving and maintaining the existing lines of communication, and for the construction of new lines as the funds permitted. As might be expected, the idea was not a palatable one, and unfortunately Mr. Peile was not long enough in the Province just then to mature and carry out his scheme.

Upon the return of Colonel Anderson, in November, 1873, the project met with very serious opposition, and every endeavour was made to set it aside; even Colonel Anderson himself expressed it as his opinion that the measure could not be carried out; and the roads upon which so much time and money had been expended remained in the same neglected condition for another year.

During the monsoon of 1874, a considerable portion of the Rajkote-Wudhwan road, which had been in charge of the States concerned for years past, gave way in part and became a mire of mud, stopping all traffic for days together, and to all appearances it was the intention of the Durbars to allow all the roads to fall into a similar condition.

Mr. Peile, however, arrived, and was confirmed as Political Agent in November, 1874 (upon the retirement of Colonel Anderson), and by the close of the same year he successfully carried his road scheme into operation.

The chiefs of first and second class agreed to subscribe Rs.64,000 annually for the construction and maintenance of trunk roads passing through the lands of minor Talukdars under the sole direction of the Political Agent, as well as to pay for the construction of all such lines of communication within the boundaries of their own States.

Operations were immediately commenced, and by the first of June following twenty-four miles of road were completely bridged and metalled, under the Agency Engineering Department alone, while extensive road construction was put under weigh independently by some of the principal States, among whom may be mentioned Bhavnagar, Gondal, Jamnugger, Dhrangadra, and Junagad. From this point the construction of roads progressed speedily.

At the close of the year 1878 Kathiawar possessed the following main roads :—

BRIDGED AND METALLED.		CONSTRUCTED BY.
Rajkote and Wudhwan, 65 miles	..	A.E. Department
Rajkote and Gondal, 25 miles	..	A.E.D. and Gondal
Gondal to Virpur, 9 miles ..	..	A.E.D. and Gondal
Virpur and Jetpur, 9 miles	..	A.E. Department
Jetput-Junaghad, 10 miles ..	..	Junagad
Jetpur-Junaghad, 5 miles ..	..	A.E. Department
Tankara to Morvi, 24 miles	..	A.E. Department
Kandorda to Porbandar, 13 miles	..	A.E. Department
Mova to Kundla, 35 miles ..	..	Bhavnagar
Mova to Bosrad, 3 miles ..	..	Bhavnagar
Bhavnagar to Dhasa, 45 miles	..	Bhavnagar
Songad to Manekvada, 11 miles	..	Bhavnagar.
Bhavnagar to Sirsai, 3 miles	..	Bhavnagar
Bhavnagar to Boodal, 6 miles	..	Bhavnagar
Bhavnagar to Gogo, 10 miles	..	Bhavnagar
Wudhwan and Limbdi, 9 miles	..	A.E. Department
Wudhwan Camp to City, 3 miles	..	A.E. Department
Dhrangadra and Camp, 12 miles	..	Dhrangadra
Jetpur and Dhoraji, 3 miles	..	Gondal
Jetpur and Dhoraji, 5 miles	..	A.E. Department
Dhoraji-Junagad, 4½ miles ..	..	Gondal
Navanagar, 3 miles	..	Navanagar
Total .. 322½ miles.		

Of which Bhavnagar carried out within their own State, 113 miles; Navanagar, 23 miles; Gondal, 28½ miles;

Dhranagadra, 12 miles; and the Trunk Road Fund in other States under the A.E.D., 156½ miles. Total, 322.

MOORAMED ROADS.

Road	Supplied by
Rajkote to Dhasa, 60 miles..	.. A.E. Department
Rajkote to Navanagar, 52 miles	.. A.E. Department
Morvi-Vavania, 24 miles ..	.. Morvi
Jetpur and Dhoraji, 4 miles	.. A.E. Department
Gondal towards Dedki, 6 miles	.. Gondal
Jetpur-Junagad, 6 miles ..	.. Junagad
Dhoraji-Upleta, 3½ miles ..	.. Gondal
Dhoraji-Navi Bandar, 11½ miles	.. Gondal
Supedi-Bhayavadar, 12 miles	.. Gondal
Kandorna-Porbander, 10 miles	.. Porbandar
Jetput-Manakvada, 25 miles	.. A.E. Department
Manakvada-Bilkha, 15 miles	.. A.E. Department
Manakvada-Bagasra, 8 miles	.. A.E. Department
Total .. 237 miles.	

Of which Gondal supplied 33 miles; Morvi, 24 miles; Porbandar, 10 miles; Junagad, 6 miles; A.E. Department, 164 miles, thus making a total of 559 miles of road within the Province of which about two-thirds were completely bridged and metalled within twelve years, and the work has still been steadily increasing.

EDUCATION.

Previous to 1865, Kathiawar possessed but two schools where English was taught, one at Rajkote and one at Bhavnagar.

In addition to these, a very few vernacular schools existed in the principal towns, but they were of an exceedingly primitive nature; in fact, the masses of the people from the chiefs downward were in a deplorable state of ignorance, and possessed no means of bettering their condition.

Colonel Keatinge proceeded to organise an Educational Department under the supervision and inspection of the Government Department of Public Instruction, but subject to the control of the Political Agent, as President of the central Educational Committee, subject to which, again, were four divisional committees.

The Central Committee was to consist of the Political Agent (President), the Agency, and Educational Officers, and the representatives of the Chiefs. The Divisional Committees were to be composed of the Political Assistants in charge of Prants, and other Political and Educational Officers belonging thereto.

The latter were to meet periodically to discuss educational matters connected with their districts, and report proceedings to the Central Committee, who retained the general direction of all educational matters and proposals.

At Rajkote two institutions for the general benefit of the Province were to be organised—namely, a training College for preparing masters and teachers, supported entirely at the expense of the States, and an Anglo-vernacular and Kathiawar High School, maintained partly from the interest of certain funded moneys and partly by annual contribution from the States.

Through the agency of the Divisional Committees the chiefs were to be further induced to set up schools in the principal villages and towns in their talukas, supported directly by the respective Durbars, and superintended by masters from the Rajkote training school.

The inspection of such vernacular schools was for a time to be entrusted to the Head Master of the Rajkote High School, and subsequently to be placed under charge of a separate officer.

There was also organised an engineering and surveying class, in 1866, to be recruited from boys who had studied in the Rajkote High School, and this Institution was placed directly under the supervision of the Agency Engineer, it being intended that young men receiving a technical education here would be preferred for employment under the Engineering Department of the Agency, as well as in the States, as appointments became available.

By the 30th June, 1865, the following schools were organised :—

High School	1
Training School	1
Primary Vernacular	43
Girls' Schools	8
Persian	1
Sanscrit	1

and the aggregate number of pupils receiving instruction was 3,703.

On the 30th day of October, 1870, the following schools were in existence :—

High Schools	1
1st Grade Anglo Vernacular	2
2nd Grade Anglo Vernacular	12
Training Colleges	1
English Class	1
Primary Vernacular	226
Girls' Schools	41
Persian	2
Sanscrit	7
Surveying	1

and the number of pupils receiving instruction was 17,000. On the 31st March, 1878, the record stood as follows :—

High Schools	3	Bhavnagar, Rajkote, Junaghad.
Training College	1	Rajkote.
Anglo Vernacular	8	Limri, Wudhwan, Morvi, Navanagar, Gondal, Vala, Drangadra, Mahuva.
State Ditto	2	Vala and Drangadra.
Vernacular Schools	472,	for boys and girls.
Persian & Sancrit	9.	

And the number of pupils receiving instruction—23,000.

On the 31st March, 1899, the following statement shows the progress of education as it stood on that date :—

	No.	Pupils.
Arts College Rajkote	1	133
Rajkumar College, Rajkote	1	44
Girassia College, Wudhwan	1	62
Anglo Vernacular Schools	44	3,694
Girassia College, Gondal	1	43
High Schools, boys	7	2,671
Vernacular Ditto	839	59,121
Night Schools	61	1,117
Aided Ditto	15	1,566
Girls' Ditto	90	8,190
Industrial School	1	64
Male Training College	1	52
Female Training College	1	25
	1,004	76,813

In addition to the above there were 1,331 indigenous or unrecognised schools with 11,688 pupils, not in connection with the Government Education Department.

The expenditure of the States on the educational expenses and the buildings of the District Schools alone amounted to:

Expenditure of education	Rs.9,14,665
Buildings	Rs.1,86,000
Inspection charges	Rs. 35,542
	Rs.11,36,207

For the foregoing figures I am indebted to the late Rao Bahadur Gopaljee Surbhai Desai, for 30 years Educational Inspector in Kathiawar.

But the above was apart from the large expenditure incurred by the State during the period under reference, in the construction of the fine, and in some instances palatial, institutions erected for educational purposes both in some of the principal cities and at Rajkote.

Amongst these may be mentioned (1) the Alfred High School at Rajkote, built in 1872 at a cost of Rs.70,000, presented by H.H. the Nawab Sahib of Junaghadh, to commemorate the visit to Bombay of H.R.H. the Duke of Edinburgh in 1870. H.H. the Nawab Sahib, the senior Chief of the Province, had already subscribed handsomely towards the projection of public works in his State, and now spontaneously expressed a desire to commemorate the Duke's visit by some token of loyalty at the headquarters of the Province. This, under the Political Agent's advice, took the form of a commodious building for the accommodation of the Kathiawar High School, which was fast outgrowing the limited quarters it had hitherto occupied in the civil station.

On the occasion of laying the foundation stone in February, 1872, the wishes and object of H.H. the Nawab Sahib were explained by the State Vakeel, Mr. Bhanji, who read a letter from His Highness, and addresses were made by the Political Agent, Colonel Anderson, and by Mr. Uttumram, head master of the Kathiawar High School.

The building was opened on January 4th, 1875, by H.E. Sir Philip Wodehouse, Governor of Bombay.

It was designed and carried out by the Agency Engineering Department. The accommodation provided comprised a central examination hall, 56 ft. by 36 ft., twelve class-rooms, each 25 ft. by 20 ft., four tower-rooms, and a main staircase leading to a gallery over the hall and to the upper verandah, with smaller stairs in the end towers. Ten years later six class-rooms were added at the north and south ends.

ALFRED HIGH SCHOOL, RAJKOTE.

(See page 52)

Baha-ud-din Bhai, C.I.E., late Vizier Junaghud.

Azum Harridas Veharidas, late Dewan Junaghud.

(*See page* 53.)

In 1879 H.H. the Nawab Sahib had built in his capital of Junaghud a high school building of the same dimensions and of nearly similar design. The architect was Mr. Khanji Mackanji, state engineer (formerly of the A.E.D.). The cost of this building was Rs.127,240. It is named after his late Highness Sir Badurkhanji.

Some years later was commenced the construction in the same State of one of the finest educational buildings in the Province—the Bahauddin College, named after the Vizier Sahib Bahauddin bhai Haran bhai, C.I.E. The cost was over 2⅛ lacs, of which Rs.60,000 were raised by the admirers and friends of the Vizier Sahib Sir Rasalkhanji, K.S.C.I. The building was designed and built by the State Architect, Mistri Jetta Bhaja, and finished under Mr. Ribeiro, L.C.E. Sup. G.W.O. of the State.

The college was opened in 1900 by H.E. Lord Curzon, Viceroy of India.

HISTORY OF THE FIRST INDUSTRIAL SCHOOL IN KATHIAWAR.

Early in 1872 the Thakor Sahib of Palitana, following the public-spirited example of some of the other chiefs, presented the Political Agent, Colonel Anderson, with Rs.10,000 to be expended on some approved work of public utility at Rajkote. On Colonel Anderson consulting the author, the latter begged that the money might be applied for erecting and furnishing a workshop in connection with the engineering department, to form the nucleus of a future industrial school. The request was agreed to.

At this period Rajkote did not possess a single workshop where it was possible to get a piece of furniture made or mended, except in the roughest manner. All the furniture the station possessed had been originally imported from Bombay, and it was bandied about from bungalow to bungalow and from dealer to dealer, over and over again, till the wretched articles could barely support themselves, much less anything upon them, and when they gave way beyond hope of future service, the Parsee or other dealer would import a fresh consignment of cheap and rickety goods from Bombay Bazaar. These it was his custom to rent to officers, charging them such exorbitant prices as would repay him many times the original cost; and the new arrival, who would most likely be only a temporary resident, had no option but to take what he could get and for what he could get it.

It was the same with every branch of industry. Bombay was the nearest market, and considering the difficulties of transit and length of time occupied in carrying on any kind of business transactions from so out-of-the-way a place as Rajkote the residents were perforce obliged to content themselves with resting in the hands of the local dealers and agents.

It was the author's object, in the first place, to construct and furnish a workshop in connection with his own department, and employ expert artisans from other localities. Then he proposed that the States should send pupils to serve a certain time in the Karkhana, learning and working at some special trade; and he intended (following the system of Government industrial schools at Jubbulpore, etc.) to introduce carpentry, iron work, carriage building, tent and carpet making, weaving and basket-making, etc.

As the sum in hand would not be sufficient to start the scheme properly, he laid the matter before Mr. Peile, the newly arrived Political Agent, who not only approved of it, but obtained further subscriptions—notably from Mr. Percival, Administrator of Bhavnagar—which raised the total funds to Rs.30,000.

Extensive workshops and sheds were erected and furnished with all needful plant. In the iron department forges on the English system with anvils, lathes, boring and drilling machines, worked by steam or hand, while the same power drove a saw mill where the round imported logs were cut up into scantlings. In the weaving department frames were set up for the making of tent cloth, carpets, tablecloths, and napkins, and expert teachers were procured through the courtesy of the Superintendent of the Jupplepore School of Industry, while in other departments competent foremen were placed in charge.

A committee was formed consisting of Colonel Law, (president), myself (secretary and manager), with four members—Mr. M. A. Turkhud, Vice-Principal Rajkumar College; Mr. Khrisanjee Luxman, Station Magistrate; Mr. Bhanji, Dewan of Junaghud; Mr. Santokran, of Bhavnagar.

The States were invited to send boys to be taught at the institution, but in only one case, Bhownagar, was there any response. This State sent two pupils. After waiting a time in vain, the author decided to seek pupils nearer home, and invited the poor lads of Rajkote City and Bazaars to come and be taught; but this they could only be induced to do on payment of Rs. 2, a month and free schooling. A room was set apart where school was held for two hours daily, and the rest of the time was passed in the workshops. The boys proved particularly smart and quick at learning, and in many instances their progress was so satisfactory that it was found remunerative after a time to increase their wages.

Work went on briskly and orders increased; the pupils numbered between 30 and 40, while 60 to 80 hands were employed in the various branches of industry.

For nearly three years the work proceeded, and the principal object of the Institution had been accomplished. The head foreman, Pitamber Vasta, a remarkably intelligent and able, although uneducated, man, left and started a carpenter's shop in the Bazaar in opposition to the school, and his example was followed by several others, so that in the course of a year there were a score of artisan's workshops established in the Station and City Puras, all prepared and ready to undersell the School of Industry and compete among themselves.

The only branches which were not competed with were those in the weaving and tent-making line. In these industries it was found that owing to the absence of free prison labour, such as was available in the Government workshops, we could not compete in price with Jupplepore and other similar institutions, and after a time the work was permitted to drop.

Pitamber Vasta's and other workshops, emanations from the Rajkote School of Industry of 1873–76, are in existence this day, and with their establishment much of the old ways vanished. The Rajkote Karkhanas for cabinet work, furniture, carriage building, and iron work in all its branches are to-day as famous through the Presidency as are the artisan carpenters and masons of Kathiawar.

As an instance of natural ability and intelligence, I may mention that Pitamber Vasta, above referred to, actually made with his own hands a complete miniature portable steam engine, which he copied from the one in the School of Industry and used in his own workshop.

For some little time the Industrial School was continued in the form of a simple engineering department workshop, but this eventually ceased, it being found more economical and equally satisfactory to give out the work under the department by contract.

Industrial or technical schools were started at Gondal, and some of the other principal States, but their histories were more or less similar to that of Rajkote.

GIRASSIA COLLEGES.

WUDHWAN COLLEGE.

Although the term Rajkumar means eldest son and heir of a ruling chief, it was not found convenient or desirable to limit the services of the institution only to such. It was made open to all the nobility and relatives of reigning princes, who possessed the condition and means to pay the college fees, subject, of course, to the approval of the College Committee.

Amongst these were from time to time wealthy girassias, petty landlords who had acquired their "giras" (lands) for some ancient service rendered to their State, and some of these were allied by blood or marriage with the ruling family.

But as time went on it was found that many of the girassia class, while not possessing the means or social standing to render them eligible for acceptance as pupils at Rajkumar College, were yet averse, or of too good position, to attend the schools of the lower middle and poorer classes, and hence arose the introduction of a college especially designed for the education of the girassia class, or rather of such members of it as were not entirely eligible for the Rajkumar College. The first girassia school was established at Wudhwan in the early 'eighties, chiefly through the instrumentality of Major Stace, then assistant Political Agent of that Prant, and was intended principally for the girassias of Jallawad, whose chiefs provided the funds. It was established on a similar principal to the Rajkumar College, but on a less pretentious scale, and has been conducted since its opening with eminent success by the headmaster in charge, Mr Strip. The institution is open to girassia boys throughout the province, and is under agency management and control.

GONDAL.

In 1895 H.H. the Thakor Sahib of Gondal, one of the leading chiefs and successful students of the Rajkumar College, finding that the means of education already established was not being taken the advantage of that it should be by that very exclusive class the girassias of his own State, decided to give them a leading hand, and established further a college at Gondal itself under his own immediate control.

GIRASSIA SCHOOL, WUDHWAN, MAIN BUILDING, 1880.

(*See page 56*)

Girassia College, Gondal.

(See page 56)

H.H. Sir Bhagwatsingji, K.C.I.E., LL.D.,
Thakor Sahib of Gondal.

H.H. Sir Waghji, K.C.I.E.,
Thakor Sahib of Morvi.

(See page 57)

This college, which was designed by his State engineer, is a remarkably fine piece of architecture, and a credit not only to its designer, but to the State, which is one of the leading ones in Kathiawar in every kind of public improvement or the benefit of its people.

The present ruler of Gondal, H.H. Sir Bhagwatsingji, was one of the first pupils of the Rajkumar College, and during his minority the State was administered in succession by the British Officers, Major Phillips, Major Nutt, and Colonel Scott. On completing his education at the college, the young chief made a tour through Europe, under the guidance of Colonel G. E. Hancock, and spent some four months in England. During his travels he kept a diary, which was subsequently published, and proved how much he was interested and benefited by the experience of the countries he visited. He assumed charge of his State in 1884, after for a time being associated with the English administrator. In 1887 Her Imperial Majesty the Queen-Empress raised him to the rank of 1st class, and he obtained a G.C.I.E. His Highness is a fellow and member of numerous learned societies in Great Britain, and a fellow of the Bombay University.

Her Highness the Rani Sahib frequently visits England with His Highness Sir Bhagwat. The State possesses, or did ten years ago, upwards of eighty schools and colleges, and up to the close of the last decade of the century had expended three lacs. of rupees on Educational institutions alone. This is marvellous progress for a single State, which twenty years earlier possessed scarcely any means of education.

In addition to the railways hereafter referred to, there were at the beginning of 1900 in this State over 100 miles of metalled and bridged roads where none previously existed.

One of the finest hospitals in the province was erected at Gondal in 1874; this building was designed by and carried out under the supervision of the State Engineer, Mr. Ganesh Govind, to whose ability and energy the State owes much of the remarkable improvements effected during the administration and for some years after.

Altogether, including the period of British Administration and up to 1899, this State had expended upwards of £1,000,000 on public works and general improvements.

BHAVNAGAR.

The State of Bhavnagar also took a very leading part in public welfare, first under the administration carried on during the minority of the late Maharajah Sir Takhatsingji, under the late Mr. Percival, C.S.I., and Mr. Gowrishanker Owdishanker jointly, and subsequently under the chief himself.

The improvements and developments of the Bhavnagar State have been on a par with its wealth and importance. The State was fortunate from the beginning of the administration 1870, in securing the services of the late lamented Mr. Proctor-Sims, previously of the Bombay reclamation works, as State Engineer. There is scarcely any improvement in the State to-day which is not due in some measure to his far-seeing zeal and great ability. The port, which he may be said to have created, the railways, roads, magnificent public buildings, gardens, schools, and works, too numerous to mention, in the city and throughout the State, are lasting memorials to a name which can never be forgotten.

Mr. Proctor-Sims came home in 1899, hoping to retire and take the rest he had so well earned after a long and arduous service, but the breaking out of famine and plague led the Durbar to ask him urgently to return to duty for a while. He would not refuse, and although his health was not such as to justify his going back to India, nothing would stop him. A few months after his return he died of cholera.

MORVI.

The Morvi State is another which, especially since the young chief H.H. Sir Waghji, K.C.I.E., was placed on the gahdi, has made the most marvellous progress.

While the State was under management his Highness, then a minor and ward of the Agency, was educated at the Rajkumar College. Before assuming the Government he made a tour through Europe and America, under the charge and guidance of Mr. W. H. White, M.I.C.E., late of the Bombay P.W.D., and then appointed his State engineer, and herein he was eminently fortunate. His Highness was one of the representative chiefs at the Victoria Jubilee in England in 1887. During his tour in America, he purchased 60 miles of permanent way for a metre gauge railway, to run from the B.B. and C.I. terminus at Wudhwan to Morvi and Rajkote *via* Wankaner, partly through the lands of other States, and after his return got the Bombay Government to sanction it, which they did, and the railway was carried out under Mr. White. The chief next constructed a tramway to connect his capital with the port of Wawania, 24 miles distant.

In the course of 15 years the young chief carried out works of public improvement over his entire State,

The late R. Proctor-Sims, M.I.C.E., State Engineer, Bhavnagar.

H.H. Sir Takhtsingji, G.C.S.I., Late Maharajah of Bhavnagar.

(See page 58.)

comprising roads, jails, schools, libraries, bridges, water schemes, etc. He is a pattern chief who only leaves his charge for the purpose of seeing how he can better the position of his subjects, and no chief in the province has succeeded in doing more, or doing it better. Shortly before I retired he invited me on a visit to his capital, and no one who had not known and worked in Morvi more than thirty years previously, as I had, could have appreciated the immense changes made by his Highness Sir Waghji, with the advice and assistance of his friend, Mr. White, and subsequently of his brother, Mr. T. White, C.E., who was in executive charge of water schemes and other important undertakings.

Jamnugger also made commendable progress in education and public improvements. In 1878 a P.W.D. was established by the grandest of the old chiefs, H.H. the Jam Sahib under the control of the late Mr. Walter McClelland, M.I.C.E., after the death of his Highness, which took place in 1896, the State was for some years under agency administration, during which time the progress was well maintained. To Mrs. McClelland is due also great praise for her indefatigable exertions in the cause of education.

Porebunder is another of the first-class States in which in course of time a P.W.D. was formed, under the administration, and a European engineer, Mr. Benson, M.I.C.E., was appointed in charge, and the improvements commenced under the Agency Engineering Department were continued, and many new and important works in connection with the harbour, river navigation, and reclamation were carried out.

JUNAGHUD.

I have already referred to this, the premier State, which was always foremost.

The States of Drangodra, Limri, Palitana, Wudhwan, Vala, Jusdun, etc., were not behindhand.

The latter led the way in irrigation schemes, as referred to in another place, and all so far as their means permitted furthered and helped projects for the general good.

I have no space here to refer in any detail to more than a few of the chiefs who after assuming their own Governments took a leading part in the welfare of the province as a whole, in addition to that of their own States.

The next chapter will be devoted to a history of what was Colonel Keatinge's greatest idea for the future happiness and regeneration of Kathiawar—namely, his conception of the Rajkumar College.

CHAPTER VII.

HISTORY OF THE RAJKUMAR COLLEGE, 1866 TO 1899.

The year 1865, and the advent of Major (late General) Richard Hart Keatinge, V.C., C.S.I., I.C.S., as Political Agent in Kathiawar, mark the commencement of the improvements which have since so rapidly and steadily developed in that province. Where, in 1865, there was not a mile of made road, there are, to-day, upwards of 2,000 miles; where no railways existed, the province is now intersected more extensively than perhaps any similar area in India. Where were no schools or system of education, and the population from the chiefs downwards were in a deplorable condition of ignorance, there are to-day over 1,000 recognised schools and colleges established for the use of all classes, in which some 80,000 pupils receive instruction, and this does not include the small local schools established in every village, which number many hundreds.

Where public works in any form for introducing modern science and improvements were unknown, waterworks, irrigation, drainage, harbours, etc., have for years been receiving the attention they demanded.

And while to General Keatinge is due the honour of having given the first impetus to all that has taken place since 1865, doubtless his grandest idea, and the one which had the greatest and most enduring effect, was that of educating and training the young chiefs themselves in a manner which would fit them eventually to rule their States with intelligence and wisdom. Major Keatinge had some correspondence with the Bombay Government on the subject, but had only obtained permission to employ a small amount from the local funds to assist the project in case it was supported by the chiefs.

He proposed to erect at Rajkote what he termed a Talukdary school which would consist of a certain number of classrooms, libraries, etc., with residences for a principal and staff of masters. The heirs of the States were then to be transferred to Rajkote and placed under the charge of a trusty European officer, where they would be freed from the subtle influence of their courts and satellites, and receive a liberal education, somewhat on the principle of an English school.

THE LATE GEN. RICHARD HART KEATINGE, V.C., C.S.I.

(*See page 60.*)

THE LATE CHESTER MACNAGHTEN, M.A.

On the completion of their studies they were to be sent to travel in foreign countries, under competent guidance, till they became of age and were considered fit to succeed to their hereditary possessions and government.

This was a general outline of Colonel Keatinge's scheme, and the first persons called by him in consultation were Captain Hebbert, A.P.A., Sorath, Captain La Touche, personal A.P.A., and the author, to whom was entrusted the preparation of designs and estimates for the necessary buildings.

Then came a real difficulty; funds were required, and for this special purpose it did not appear likely that they would be produced without considerable trouble. The removal of the young chiefs from the influence of their homes would be laying the first blow of the axe to the root of practices so long established and so dearly cherished by those who had the chief power to thwart the movement.

Ere long, however, through the influence of Captain Hebbert, H.H. the Jam Sahib of Nawanagar took the initiative and came forward with the first handsome offer of 30,000 cowries. Thus a beginning was made, and it is something for the descendants of these men to remember with pride, that to them was due the primary impetus given to the erection of the first college established in India for the education of chiefs.

At this juncture, June, 1867, Colonel Keatinge was obliged to proceed to England for three months, and Colonel W. W. Anderson, Superintendent of the Gaekwar Contingent, was appointed to act for him. So matters relating to the College project perforce remained in abeyance for the time being.

It was early in June, 1867, that I rode with Colonel Keatinge part of the way to Wudhwan, on his homeward journey. We (my wife and I) were staying at Bamonbore traveller's bungalow, 18 miles from Rajkote. Colonel Keatinge breakfasted with us and then we rode together to Choteela, where after a mid-day meal of a very rough description, I spread out on a native cot the drawings of the Rajkumar College as it stands to-day. The heat was stifling, and we were without coats or vests. Colonel Keatinge used a pencil freely in crossing out a deal of my elaborately prepared drawings, which he termed needlessly palatial and expensive. He did not consider it wise to make a first move in such a direction too costly.

Privately I did not agree with him. I could not help feeling that such an Institution as a Chief's College ought to have a home in buildings worthy of the object in view, and that anything cheap or mean would serve in some way to mar its success. I was young and sanguine, and the Political Agent's decision was disappointing. That evening he laid out the Choteela Thana buildings for which I had prepared designs, and he had the Kathi Baghedars in for some wholesome advice.

The following morning we rode over the new road to Dholia, 14 miles, where a bullock shigram from the Muli Durbar was waiting to convey him to Wudhwan civil station, where Colonel S. C. Law was then in charge, and on to Ahmedabad, 75 miles.

It would be strange to-day, to see the Political Agent of Kathiawar leave the province stretched full length in his shirt sleeves in a native bullock dumny, with a single gaekwari sowar as escort. Now, luxurious private saloons on the railways or well-appointed horse-carriages, with outriders and relays, would be the order of the day.

In November following, Colonel Keatinge returned to India, but to take up another appointment as Governor General's agent in Rajputana, and Colonel Anderson continued to act for him in Kathiawar.

In the following month—December—another most unfortunate and sad occurrence took place, in the deaths of Captains Hebbert and La Touche, while engaged in action against the Wagheer outlaws in the west of the province. Thus the scheme was again delayed, and indeed it now seemed as if it was doomed to die in its infancy; its originator gone to another appointment, unable to act further, and his two assistant promoters dead.

Colonel Anderson, however, was now confirmed as Political Agent, and in the hope that the college scheme would be revived by him, I laid the plans and particulars before him.

Colonel Anderson took up the work keenly. Various subscriptions were raised from the States throughout the province to augment those already promised, until a sum of some Rs.50,000 was available, and the Bombay Government, on the original application made by Colonel Keatinge, approved of the transfer of Rs.20,000 from the infanticide fund. Orders were thereupon issued to commence work, in the expectation, subsequently fulfilled, that further funds would be subscribed as required.

A site for the buildings was selected, south of the Civil Station, and on the 28th April, 1868, the foundation-stone was laid by Colonel Anderson in full Durbar before the assembled representatives of the chiefs of Kathiawar.

The works progressed speedily, and in the following year a further subscription of Rs.50,000 was gathered from the chiefs, and eventually a third; and by the close of 1870 the main building, with its two wings, and a pair of residences for a principal and vice-principal, with gardens and grounds, were all completed, and to crown the whole, H.E. Sir Seymour Fitzgerald, Governor of Bombay, expressed his willingness to come to Rajkote for the purpose of opening the Institution.

Captain Lloyd, who was in charge of Rajkote and Limri, was now transferred to Gondal, and Lieutenant Hancock acted in the former appointment. As it was intended that the young Thakors of Rajkote and Limri were to be sent to the College, Lieut. Hancock, who was now in charge of Limri and Rajkote, applied for two residences to be built for them, and these were under construction with the rest of the College buildings; but they were the only separate residences ever constructed, because, as will be referred to hereafter, it was decided that no pupils should live outside the College precincts, and these two buildings became the permanent residences of the principal and vice-principal.

It appeared in this as in many other instances during the carrying out of the College project, that there was a Providence directing the undertaking, and whatever was done seemed at last to fit into its place as if it had been the place intended for it from the first, whereas it was impossible for anyone then connected with the project to form an opinion with any degree of certainty, whether the works being carried out would be appropriated eventually for the purposes they were intended for. The whole thing was an experiment, and it appeared to most people during its infancy to be a very risky and dangerous one.

And in no way perhaps was the guiding hand of Providence more apparent than in the finding of a principal fit to assume the charge and direction of this undertaking.

The intended visit of Sir Seymour Fitzgerald to Kathiawar would be historical and remarkable in two ways :—

It would be the first occasion on which a Governor of Bombay had visited the Province, and

The invitation issued by the Bombay Government for the Chiefs to meet the representative of her Majesty the Queen at Rajkote would necessitate their crossing the boundaries of the respective States for the first time on a peaceful mission.

Consequently, every effort was put forth by each State individually to make the reception, in dignity and Oriental display, worthy of the high occasion. Gorgeous camps were erected by the Durbars, round Rajkote. A new race stand was built, and the course was lined with magnificent pavilions and marquees, a blaze of flags and decorations.

The preparations occupied two months, and on a day or two previous to his Excellency's arrival, the Chiefs were awaiting him in their respective camps.

The Governor travelled by way of Jamnugger and approached Rajkote by easy stages. A road had been constructed over most of the distance during the past five years, and the Durbar possessed a few horse carriages, but such conveniences were, as yet, rare in the Province, and on this special occasion it was decided that the traditions of the States would be most appropriately represented by having everything conducted in the original Oriental style, consequently every Durbar arrived at Rajkote accompanied by his fullest retinue of elephants.

The procession which received the Governor, three miles from Rajkote, was probably one of the most magnificent of its kind ever seen in that land of gorgeous pageants. It extended for two miles, and was entirely composed of elephants, either carrying howdahs or drawing cars. The car upon which his Excellency rode in company with the senior Chief, H.H. the Nawab of Junaghudh, and attended by an escort of Lancers, was an enormous and gorgeous structure on four wheels, and had to be mounted by a ladder. It was a blaze of cloth of gold and Oriental devices; the monster pair of elephants attached abreast to it were clothed in gold kincob nearly to the ground, with necklaces of jewels and anklets of gold and silver. It was estimated that the value of their trappings alone was upwards of £30,000. Following this, the other Chiefs, on elephant cars or howdahs, proceeded according to their rank, each escorted by a political or military officer, and attended by their respective bodyguards, while detachments of cavalry and infantry preceded or followed.

The road was lined with flags and spanned by many arches a blaze of tinsel and bunting.

On arrival at the Kothie (chief residence) each Durbar with his principal officials was received by his Excellency and then departed to their respective camps.

RAJKUMAR COLLEGE, RAJKOTE, KATHIAWAR (WEST FRONT).

(*See page* 65.)

A banquet was held that evening, at which all heads of departments were invited to meet his Excellency. The following day was devoted to receiving visits from the Chiefs. The Governor, attended by the Political Agent, and other State officials, sat on a throne in the large Durbar pavilion, and each Chief, under the salute due to his rank, was led up to the throne by a Political Officer and introduced to his Excellency, to whom he presented a Nuzzur, or formal present, in token of his allegiance, which his Excellency touched and returned. He then took his seat at his right hand. A few words of conversation by means of the Government Interpreter took place, followed by officials carrying silver trays on which were placed the Supari (betel nut) rolled up in small gold paper packets, attar of roses in a tall golden vase with spray, and garlands of flowers. A principal official sprinkled some attar on the Chief's robe, presented him with a packet of betel nut and a bunch of flowers, and placed a garland round his neck, on which he immediately rose, shook hands with his Excellency, and departed as he had come, under a salute. This ceremony had to be repeated in the case of all the Chiefs up to, I think, fourth class, and occupied the greater portion of the forenoon with the expenditure of a great deal of powder.

In the afternoon, the Governor in person returned the visits of the 1st, 2nd, and 3rd class chiefs, the same programme being followed.

The next day a grand Durbar was held, at which all the Chiefs, nobles, officials, and residents attended. This was followed by a levee.

The third afternoon was set apart for the opening of the Rajkumar College. The visit of his Excellency, which lasted about ten days, was a continual round of gaiety. Breakfasts, dinners, balls, racing, etc., succeeded each other in the usual fast and furious manner.

H.E. the Governor and Staff were housed in a splendid encampment sent from Bombay, which, together with the station, roads, public buildings, and Chief's camps, were nightly illuminated in true Oriential style and magnificence.

At the opening ceremony of the Rajkumar College on the 16th December, 1870, by H.E. Sir Seymour Vesey Fitzgerald, Governor of Bombay, before the assembled Chiefs and Officials of the Province, the following speeches were made :—

By Colonel W. W. Anderson, Political Agent :—

"Your Excellency,—The ceremony which we have solicited your Excellency to perform this evening is one which we fervently hope may be the most auspicious connected with your visit to this Province.

"It is the opening of the Rajkumar College, designed for the education of the sons of the Chiefs and Nobles of Kathiawar. It owed its origin to that most energetic and able Political Officer, Colonel Keatinge, to whose powerful impetus most of the progress this important province has made of late years is due.

"Urged by him, the Chiefs and Talukdars with characteristic willingness responded to the call and furnished the requisite funds, which subsequently had to be doubled.

"The foundation-stone was laid in 1868, and the building, you see, is now in a state of sufficient completeness to admit of its being put to the great use for which it is intended.

"In its present state it has cost a lac of rupees, but some considerable sums will yet have to be spent to provide accommodation and equipment indispensable for an academy intended for the noble youths to be lodged and brought up in a manner befitting the positions they will hereafter be called upon to hold.

"For the architectural beauty and the professional skill displayed throughout the whole, our warmest thanks are due to Mr. Robert Booth, who has constructed many useful public works in the Province.

"The present building can accommodate twenty students, the number at first contemplated as likely to avail themselves of it; but with the additions which have been provided for in the original plans, and for which funds are required, quadruple that number can be lodged within its precincts.

"In according your formal sanction to it, and declaring it open, in the presence of the Chiefs of Kathiawar, assembled around you, I would earnestly crave that you would again impress upon them the political utility, nay, the desirability of educating their sons in such an institution, common to all. The fact may not be unknown to all, that the rulers and leaders of peoples and communities cannot with safety be permitted to be brought up in ignorance or suffered even to be satisfied with what a common pundit, or even what an educated tutor can impart from books at home.

"To be properly fitted for this position, they must have what we in Europe call a manly education and a physical training, in order to make them strong and healthy and intelligent governors and administrators of the people of their ancestral dominions.

"Persons occupying their positions cannot afford to lose sight of the fact that, although education in its widest sense has, in all countries, had for its votaries the poorer portion of the population, royalty and the aristocracy have ultimately found it to be of vital interest to pay their devoirs to the goddess of knowledge, and history furnishes no example of an aristocracy or monarchy successfully holding its own by lagging behind in progress of knowledge amongst their social inferiors or subjects.

"Regarding the establishment of the College, the Director of Public Instruction, with whom I have been in communication, has secured for it the services of Mr. Chester Macnaghten, a gentleman of high and varied attainments, and master of some of the vernacular languages of the East. It is a matter of much regret that he has been unable to arrive in time to take part in this interesting ceremony of the opening, but from a communication received from him, he announces his immediate departure from Benares, and his hope of joining us by the first week in January. In the meantime, such of the assistants as can be secured will make all the preparations pending his arrival. It is a source of the greatest gratification to me that your Excellency should have so opportunely timed your visit to this ancient Province as to admit of this noble building being opened formally by yourself. The benefit which it will derive from this auspicious event will, I consider, be incalculable. The prestige of your Excellency's name is great, and your Excellency's interest in all that concerns education will, I fervently trust, be extended to this College, the first of its kind in India, and which, under Providence, let us hope, may in time emulate the fame of the Eton of the Western world. Its success will be a step in advance, and will be a pledge of future benefit to both the rulers and ruled of Kathiawar. And whereas formerly the sons of Chiefs rarely, if ever, learnt anything beyond the limits of the palace or zenana, we now hope in time to have in their place an intelligent, educated set of manly youths, cognisant of the responsibilities as well as the privileges of their rank, and burning with emulation to outstrip each other in the glorious task of elevating humanity. I now beg of your Excellency to declare the College open for its important object, naming a day when its first term shall commence, and informing the fathers of its intended inmates, assembled round you, of the arrangements made for the beginning of its work, and may Heaven's choicest blessings be showered upon it."

By his Excellency, the Governor :—

" Princes and Chiefs of Kathiawar,—The duty which you, Colonel Anderson, have called upon me to fulfil is one almost of a merely formal character, but because it is merely formal, it is not less a subject of the greatest gratification to me, because I am confident that the ceremony in which we are engaged to-day, simple as it is, in which we are this moment engaged, is one of the most vital importance to this presidency, and one which will probably, or rather certainly, if it is properly carried out, bear fruits the full value of which neither I nor any one here can rightly or fully estimate, and I must congratulate you Chiefs of Kathiawar, that we are met here to-day to complete an undertaking, which his Excellency, the Viceroy, a few weeks ago, in addressing your brother Chiefs of Rajputana, recommended as an enterprise it was important to them to commence, and thus among the princes of your own blood and race, you have arrived at the goal before they have started, you have this noble building completed before they have even begun to consider the measures necessary to enable them to carry out what you have so successfully achieved.

" You have asked me, Colonel Anderson, to impress upon the Chiefs here present the importance and the value of this Institution. It is difficult for me to do more than reiterate that which I ventured most to impress upon them in Durbar only the day before yesterday ; but I have the success of this undertaking so much at heart, that I do not hesitate very shortly, but earnestly, to repeat what I then said. I beg of them to consider what you yourself have pointed out in your address, that the object of the Institution is not merely that the sons of the Chiefs of Kathiawar should have the means of acquiring a certain amount of knowledge, but that they should acquire it in the most valuable form in which it can be attained, in a manner that shall train and discipline the character as well as the head, and strengthen them for the duties they will be called upon hereafter to fulfil. I do not doubt that information may be acquired under a tutor at home, nor would I have it supposed that under a system of private tuition moral principles are necessarily neglected, but what cannot be so obtained is the self-reliance on the one hand, and the appreciation of others on the other, which is obtained by an education in a public college among their own fellows and equals, removed from the evil influences which might counteract the benefits they would otherwise receive. It is the object of this Institution to secure this, and I look to you, one and all, by your example and by your influence, to second our efforts, and take care that no groundless prejudice, no evil influence or underhand advice shall impede the success of this great experiment. I was particularly pleased, Colonel Anderson, with one point which you remarked upon in your address, and that was, that the lads who are to be educated here will receive a good physical as well as a sound mental training ; that it is not merely in acquiring knowledge that they will be placed in competition with their equals, but that as a part of your design, space is set apart for athletic sports and manly amusements.

"I should wish the youths trained here to take pleasure in feats of strength and activity, to ride well, to shoot well, in fact what a gentleman seldom fails to obtain at a public school.

"There is one particular point to which you alluded, Colonel Anderson, which I cannot pass over, and that is, the obligation which the whole community of Kathiawar, and, as one having the interest of that community at heart, the obligation which I also feel to the gentleman who has so zealously co-operated with you in the erection of this noble building. I am sure there is not a single Chief here who, both now and hereafter, will not say that he is greatly indebted to Mr. Booth, for the care, the zeal, and the intelligence with which he has carried out the design which your predecessor, Colonel Keatinge, originated, and which you now have so successfully completed. I have now the formal but agreeable duty to perform of declaring the College open ; and in doing so, the first step is to commit the charge of this institution and building to the able public officer who presides over the education of this presidency. I now ask you, Mr. Peile, to take this institution under your fostering care, and to bestow upon it the same attention—

the same zealous attention, which you devote to every part of the department which has been entrusted to you. It will be a great object, I think, that this should be opened at an early date. Of course, it is impossible at this moment, under the circumstances that you, Colonel Anderson, have alluded to, absolutely to fix a day upon which the Institution shall be opened, but I would suggest to you and Mr. Peile that the Chiefs should be given the earliest opportunity of availing themselves of its advantages.

"I think that probably after some conversation with you, Colonel Anderson, that Mr. Peile will be able to say that the College shall be open for the reception of inmates from the 1st February next, and that will give the Chiefs full time to mature their plans, and make the arrangements they may consider necessary. And, now, having said this, it is only left for me publicly to declare that this, the Rajkumar College of Kathiawar, is from this day open.

Mr. Peile, the Director of Public Instruction, then spoke, as follows :—

"Your Excellency,—It is a matter to me of much pride and satisfaction that it has fallen to my lot to receive from your Excellency's hands this most important trust. By its ancient history, by its great extent, by the very difficulties of its administration, Kathiawar ranks as the foremost tributary of the Presidency over which your Excellency rules. In its Chiefs there have assembled to meet you here to-day, two generations, within whose experience this Province has passed through a very remarkable change. There are Chiefs here of the elder generation, who may have heard the latest story of Mulakgiri rapine fresh from the lips of actors in the scene, while these boys of the younger generation have come here to enter an institution which will differ in no essential point from an English public school. From times of which history gives no certain account, some of these houses have observed the course of events from the thrones and strongholds of this Peninsula ; but I venture to say that from the day when the Ghuznivide stormed the temple ramparts of Somnath to the day when the last Mahratta squadron withdrew from the shorn fields and smoking villages of Sourashtra, they learnt not one lesson of constitutional government from their invaders. We succeeded the Mahrattas, and I am proud to remember that from the first we entered this province as mediators. To a country distracted with internal feuds and crushed with external violence we extended peace, and that peace has never been broken. Along with peace came the opportunity of development, and, I will add, the necessity of progress. For wars and feuds are in some sense a safety-valve to national growth, which is closed by peace.

"They check the increase of population, prevent the division of old estates, and permit the formation of new ones. In guaranteeing peace, therefore, we took upon ourselves a grave responsibility that the country should not stand still. The progress made at first was slow, while jurisdictions were consolidated and rights adjusted. But in the last ten years it has been very rapid, and year by year the Chiefs have been called upon to give more and stronger proofs of their faith and trust in the British name and example. We must not forget that such faith may sometimes be hard to exercise. Although your Excellency represents the supreme power in these territories yet we did not enter them as conquerors.

"These Chiefs are not the subjects of our laws, and though undoubtedly our measures rest on the basis of superior power, yet the alacrity with which they are adopted is secured by their justice and wisdom alone.

"Your Excellency has noted the works of improvement which begin to cover this country. You have also observed with gratification the unmistakable warmth of welcome with which you have been received by the Chiefs. That this cordiality and this activity in useful works co-exist is a signal proof that the Chiefs have entered heartily into the reforms which they have been invited to accept; that they have not been led onward too rapidly, nor taxed beyond their power to adapt themselves to change. And now, Sir, you are here, the first Governor under the British Empire, who has penetrated into the heart of this Province, not backed by a Mulakgiri force to harass and destroy, but to give the sanction of your presence to a new and bold experiment for the general good, and to open a fresh chapter in the social education of those young chiefs by directing that their moral and mental training within these walls shall begin. If this is one of those cases where the exercise of faith in our purposes is hard, yet let those Chiefs who have sons believe that we press this discipline upon them, because we have ourselves experienced its tonic value. Let them believe that the men who have conquered and now administer India, that all those who rule the British Empire at home and abroad, have been unhesitatingly sent to public schools from far safer homes than theirs. Let them believe that however respectable their own lives may be, yet their children must inevitably be surrounded at home by subtle and corrupting influences, from which their safest refuge and protection is here. Let them believe that this College, rightly used and heartily supported, will become the strongest bulwark of their rights. And let them feel assured, as your Excellency has assured them, that the students of this College will not be educated to be pedants, or anglicised out of sympathy with the traditions of their fathers and habits of their people. We shall rather seek to strengthen their minds to judge broadly and soundly the practical questions which will be presented to them. We shall desire to open their hearts to a humanising influence in all classes of their people, even the remotest and the lowest, in those who differ from them, and are frank with them, or hold aloof from them, as well as those who court them and minister to their pleasures. We shall discipline their bodies in the manliness and hardihood of the English public school boy. We shall teach them to value justice and uphold it, even to their personal loss. We shall show them that it is better to collect wealth for their people than themselves. It will be our aim that they may become, and feel that they are, wiser than their subjects, and yet that they shall be prepared to respect that voice of public judgment on the acts of public men which has been likened to the voice of God. To what results the enterprise begun to-day may tend, whether these boys when grown to man's estate will be careful to perpetuate their hereditary right to govern in honourable rivalry of their mighty neighbour and protector, or whether they will elect (as I think the nobler choice) by a voluntary surrender of their isolated sovereignity, to enter the Councils of India as nobles of the Empire, time will decide. They have been fully assured by your Excellency that no privilege which they desire to retain will be swept away as obsolete or will fail to be treated with respect.

"It is sufficient for the present to enter on the work before us with the conviction that the wellbeing of the subject is bound up with the culture of the Chief; and that we hope that if much has been done with far smaller advantages or even under many drawbacks and difficulties, by the elder Chieftains who have met your Excellency here to-day, a great work lies before those future rulers of Kathiawar, who will grasp with the strength of well-educated minds the great leading principle of our political empire, that just and wise administration is the surest guarantee of the tributary throne."

On the conclusion of the function, which lasted to some little time after sunset, His Excellency was conducted to the terraced roof of the main building, from whence he, in company with some hundreds of the principal officials, chiefs, and guests, witnessed a fine display of fireworks in the west quadrangle. While this was proceeding orders were given to commence the illuminations, and by the time the fireworks exhibition was over the entire camp and city was a blaze of light. Every road was picked out with small oil lamps placed three feet apart, while garlands of lights were suspended from tree to tree or formed geometrical figures at fixed distances apart, and the verandah roofs and arcades of every building of consequence in city or camp were picked out with thousands of coloured lights. But the grandest show of all was the College itself and its surrounding grounds. On the east façade of the main building and wings, every pillar, arch, parapet, and string course was outlined with myriads of lights, and the garden of nine acres, together with the grounds subtending the east front, were a sea of light all the more effective because the trees and shrubs had scarcely yet been planted ; and the maze of walks, squares, roads and circles, as they receded, outlined in fire, presented a marvellous picture. The illumination of the grounds and garden, on which some 20,000 lights were employed, occupied, with the large staff employed, only a few minutes, and was viewed from the College roof. The night was most favourable for the display, being calm and dark.

A procession was then formed from the east entrance, in which figured carriages, elephants and bullock dumnies, and proceeded with a great concourse of followers on foot to view the illuminations, which were continued till midnight. That evening a banquet was given by his Excellency, followed by a ball at the Kothie.

Mr. Chester Macnaghten, elected to be the first Principal of a Chiefs' College in India, was a son of Mr. Elliott Macnaghten of the Supreme Court of Calcutta, and Director of the East India Company in 1841, and his grandfather was Sir Francis Macnaghten, also of the Indian Civil Service. He distinguished himself at Cambridge, but owing to feeble health was unfortunately debarred from entering the Civil Service. He went to India in 1841 for his health, and in 1866 was appointed tutor to the Maharajah of Durbhanga.

He took up his appointment as Principal of the College in February 1871, with Mr. M. A. Turkhad as Vice-Principal, and after a certain amount of official pressure five young Chiefs entered upon their term of pupilage.

As was previously remarked, it was the original intention of Colonel Keatinge that the boys should not live in the College, but it was subsequently wisely determined by Mr. Macnaghten that they should, and so be entirely under the eye and care of the Principal.

I have said under official pressure, but at least two of the boys referred to were at the time wards of the Agency, and their instalment in the College was a matter of no difficulty; with the others, however, it was different, and all watched the operation with curiosity and anxiety.

Then it was that real ability and fitness for the post were required and showed themselves in the man who was entrusted with the sole management and conduct of the Institution. He was surrounded by many eagerly watching for an opportunity to cavil, and to have an excuse for complaint against the College, and so procure the return of the boy to his home, but no such opportunity occurred.

In these early days I had the privilege of frequently observing the system adopted by Mr. Macnaghten in his very difficult and responsible charge. When the boys first arrived at the College they were accompanied each by strong escorts and armed guards, under orders of their Durbars, to watch the lads day and night. While the boys were in the class-rooms armed servants mounted guard at the doors, when in the play-ground armed sowars on horseback were stationed round the enclosure, and while they slept their bedrooms and the adjacent verandah were occupied by several of their Durbar servants.

Mr. Macnaghten took his time; he sought no aid, political or otherwise, but by tact and quiet determination he gradually reduced the attendants, until by the close of the first term it was an established rule that no armed guard was permitted within the College precincts, and each boy, irrespective of his rank, was allowed but a single unarmed servant to remain in his room during the night, and, strange to say, in not a single instance was any objection taken to the rule. It gradually became apparent to the Durbars that Mr. Macnaghten was a man who was not to be interfered with, and that the lads safety was secure in his hands. Patience, tact, kindness, and force of character won the day for him as surely as any other system would have certainly failed. He engendered love, respect, and confidence, not only from the boys themselves, but from those who from the beginning viewed the experiment with anything but friendly eyes.

The result was that within a year the number of pupils so increased that it was found necessary to procure a further grant of Rs. 80,000 for the construction of the north wing, consisting of sixteen separate suites of apartments, or private residences.

The money was obtained without any difficulty, and the new wing was completed in 1873.

In January, 1875, the College was visited by Sir Philip Wodehouse, Governor of Bombay, when a number of the principal Chiefs received His Excellency at Rajkote. At a public Durbar held on this occasion the following address was read by H.H. The Maharajah of Bhavnagar, one of the first pupils of the College :—

> "Honourable Sir,—We the Chiefs, Talukdars, and Bhumias of this Province, bid your Excellency heartily welcome to Kathiawar.
>
> "We are gathered here once more to receive, in the person of your Excellency, the representative of the Supreme Power of Her Gracious Majesty in this Peninsula ; and we assure your Excellency that we meet you with no abatement of the loyalty and devotion which we have ever tendered to your distinguished predecessors.
>
> "Since we last addressed the Governor of Bombay on this spot, many things which then existed only as projects for the future have become substantial realities. The then unopened Rajkumar College, supposed at that day to be complete, has been vastly enlarged from funds supplied by us, and its lecture rooms are now filled by our sons and our kinsmen. The railway and the telegraph line have been laid across the plains of Jhalawad, and we hope to see them carried further into the heart of the peninsula. At the instance of the British Government, and in the hope that the ends of justice may be thereby promoted, we have temporarily transferred a part of our rightful jurisdiction

to a new tribunal, empowered to decide disputes relating to ancestral lands between ourselves and our brethren, and to frame a permanent record of their rights. Again, with the advice of the paramount power, we have reformed the administration of our police, and have adopted measures which we trust to find sufficient to ensure safety in life and property to all our subjects. And we are now preparing, under similar advice, to make more permanent and more united efforts for the construction and maintenance of the great trunk roads of Kathiawar.

"Your Excellency, the country, as you will yourself see, is in a state of peace; justice is improved, commerce is increasing, factories are rising, roads and bridges are being built, schools are multiplying. While we frankly own that the great change since the days of our forefathers has been made under, and is due to the beneficent counsels of, the British Government, yet we claim what credit is due to Chiefs who have ever adopted those counsels with alacrity and have admitted their wisdom even where their adoption was hard to reconcile with the habits and associations of the past.

"We freely recognise that the supreme power to which we are tributaries is animated by a spirit of justice and benevolence, and we shall not be wanting when further occasions arise for accepting its guidance and profiting by its knowledge. We only ask in return that, as in times past, the Governors and other high officers who represent Her Majesty the Queen in this land may show themselves interested in our feelings and associations, sympathetic with our difficulties, and considerate of our ancient rights."

His Excellency the Governor replied as follows:—

"Chiefs, Talukdars, and Bhumias,—I beg you to accept warm acknowledgements of the feelings with which you have assembled in the capital of the Province for the purpose of bidding me heartily welcome to Kathiawar.

"And I accept that welcome with the deeper satisfaction, because it is accorded to me as the Governor of Bombay, and is accompanied by declarations of your unabated loyalty and devotion to the Sovereign whose servant I have the honour to be. The sincerity of those declarations I cannot doubt; and it will be my agreeable duty to request the Secretary of State to convey to Her Majesty the assurance thus renewed of your faithful allegiance to Her Throne.

"It is but seldom that one holding my present office can find an opportunity of visiting your Province, and becoming personally acquainted with its Chiefs and people, and four years have now elapsed since my predecessor, Sir Seymour Fitzgerald, enjoyed that pleasure. Since that occasion, as I am reminded by you, many things which were then only projects for the future to accomplish have taken shape and substance, and have become living realities

"You first refer with honourable pride to the Rajkumar College, and describe the means by which you have yourselves contributed to the success with which the establishment of the College has been happily crowned. To those among you who have supplied funds for the enlargement of the College buildings, the thanks of the Government are due, and equally to the Thakor of Bhavnagar, who, by his gift for an endowment, has made a valuable contribution to the permanency of the Institution. The thanks of the Government are also due to those Chiefs who have marked their confidence in the College by sending sons and kinsmen to be educated there. The Government must ever be desirous of doing all within its means to extend the benefits of the education given at an Institution over which it watches with a lively interest, and upon which it builds hopes of much future advantage, but it would be vain to dispute that the success of the Institution depends in a primary degree upon the feelings with which it comes to be regarded by native princes and their families. You have had during the last few days an opportunity of forming your own opinion on the character of the Institution and of its effects upon your children—and I may hope you are convinced, and that you will spread the conviction throughout your families, that the Government desire and encourage the education in the College of young native princes and nobles with no other aim than to promote their happiness and the welfare of the people whom they will hereafter be called upon to govern. The sole purpose with which the College has been founded and conducted is to rear and train these native princes in such a manner that they may be made by study, combined with manly exercises, active and vigorous both in mind and body, and they may gather from the precepts and examples of careful teachers the virtues which constitute a strong and upright character. You cannot yourselves fail to notice the progress which education is making amongst the people of this country, and you must be prepared for its further extension. It is manifest, then, that if your sons are to keep pace with the spirit of the age, if they are to look hereafter for the confidence of the paramount power, you will best discharge your duty as parents by taking full advantage of the opportunities freely placed within your reach for their benefit.

"Before quitting this subject, I would express the satisfaction with which I regard the example set by some among you, of completing the education of your sons by foreign travel under proper guidance; and I would also give utterance to the pleasure with which I found (upon the presence in the College of some youths who do not belong to Kathiawar) the hope that the advantages of the College are becoming more widely known, and that its future students will be drawn from the entire area of Guzerat.

"I have listened with sincere gratification to your description of Kathiáwar as a country where peace and order prevail and the administration of justice improves, where commerce extends and new factories rise, where facilities of locomotion and the means of sound education are being multiplied. And I rejoice that I have no reason to question the truth of that description. It is not surprising that you should hesitate to undertake the construction of railways without strong reasons for believing that you will ultimately receive an adequate return for the outlay. But this hesitation renders it more incumbent on you to promote every reasonable improvement of the ordinary channels of communication, and I trust the project that has been set on foot for the construction and maintenance of arterial roads will be carried forward with vigour.

"I willingly recognise the validity of the claim which you prefer to the credit of having made yourselves, in great part, the authors of the improved condition of the country, by the alacrity with which you have adopted the counsels of the British Government. That it must sometimes appear to you difficult to reconcile the adoption of counsels suggested by European judgment and experience with popular habits and the associations of the past in Eastern States, I am well aware; but I am confident that such difficulties as now beset your path will year by year diminish, while under a reign of peace and order assiduous attention is paid to the moral and material improvement of all classes inhabiting your territories. Whatever advice may be tendered to you, whatever exertions you may be urged to make, continue to rely securely on the justice and the benevolent wisdom of the Sovereign whose tributaries you are, and of the officers who are charged to execute her missions in this country. Inspired by Her Majesty's example, it is their bounden duty to be mindful of the established rights of princes and nobles, and of the rights of the humblest labourers, and to be considerate in all matters which affect the deep-rooted sentiments of ancient races. It is equally their duty to be impatient of fraud, injustice, and oppression, and to be unremitting in their efforts to better the lot of the people for whose welfare they are in any degree responsible.

"I am glad to think that from the Political Agent, Mr. Peile, and the officers serving under him, you may expect a proper sympathy for your feelings and regard for your interests, combined with a freedom from local prejudices and jealousies, a loyal co-operation with one another, and a faithful adherence to the spirit and the letter of the policy which they are instructed to carry into effect.

"It now only remains for me to thank you once more for the friendly and gratifying address which you have presented to me, and to ask you to accept the expression of my best wishes for the prosperity of the Chiefs and all other inhabitants of Kathiawar."

On the following day His Excellency distributed the prizes at the Rajkumar College, on which occasion Mr. Chester Macnaghten made a speech which is specially interesting to record, both as showing the progress and position of the college at the time, and as explanatory of the system under which the institution was conducted. He said:—

"Your Excellency, Mr. Peile, Ladies and Gentlemen.

Only a few Governors of Bombay have visited Kathiawar, yet already during our short existence two of their number have stood in this hall. In that, we feel that we are much privileged. It is good for us, Your Excellency, that you should see us, and we venture to hope that, as we have the honour of your presence amongst us to-day, so we may continue to have in the future (as we have always had in the past) the favour of your support and encouragement.

"In December, 1870, Sir Seymour Fitzgerald, standing in this place, declared the college open. But at that time we were but an embryo, existing only in hope; and hope of a not very confident kind. I think it is only true to say that in the minds of all sorts of people our birth was expected with doubt and distrust. Some thought we would never be born at all; others that we should die in our cradle; others that if we survived a while, we were doomed to a meagre and feeble existence. There was, perhaps, a good deal of reason for those unfavourable anticipations, though not so much, I believe, as was supposed. I hope that the experience of the last four years has at least been sufficient to prove that. Not that we have not had our difficulties, and have them still—difficulties not ordinary either in kind or degree. For, as Mr. Peile has said, this college cannot fairly be called a 'spontaneous offering of the Chiefs.' It is, in fact, a foreign innovation in a country which is radically conservative, and which loves its old customs because they are old, and resists new methods because they are new, with an almost religious intolerance. We knew from the first that it was necessary to the very notion of our existence that we should conflict with many things which had been established by custom and honoured by time. That we knew and for that we were prepared. We knew also that these ancient prejudices could not all be removed in a day, or a year, or even in one generation, but we believed, and believe still, that if we could establish between ourselves and the Durbars a spirit of mutual forbearance and conciliation, if we could show them by attention and sympathy that it is our desire to work with them towards what we believe to be their greatest good, so we should be able most surely and most quickly to win them to our side, obtaining first their confidence and then their co-operation.

"How far that confidence and that assistance have been already secured is not for me to say. There is, I know, much opposition to us still, serious opposition in some quarters. Nevertheless, we have many friends—especially among the political officers—and through their influence we hope and believe that the opposition is less than it was. Its complete annihilation must be a matter of time. It cannot disappear all at once; and we must deal with it patiently and kindly. Probably not in my days, not possibly in those of my successor, but hereafter, I venture to think, in the second or third generation, all opposition will have been lived down, and all the Durbars with one voice and endeavour will thankfully combine to acknowledge and extend the benefits of this institution.

"I may be allowed to say in our defence—and I wish to speak with the greatest respect of the arguments of the gentler sex—that our fiercest opponents have been those who know least about us—the Durbar ladies. Their dislike of us is so natural that, real though it is, we must forgive it. They cannot see us, or know us, or speak to us, or we to them. They only know that their innocent children, the light of their eyes, the hope of their homes, are torn from their arms to be sent to college (or as they are pleased to consider, to prison), and all for the sake of education—a thing to be easily had at home! Was ever such meaningless cruelty heard of? Surely the old ways were better than these?

"I say it is very unfortunate that we cannot ask these ladies to see us, and then to judge for themselves of the difference between a home education and ours. But, hereafter, when they have for their advisers chiefs who have themselves been educated in the College, and who, convinced by their experience, will entrust their sons to us willingly, then at last we hope and expect that these ladies will be persuaded and pacified.

That brings me to the chief part of my subject. For we have always felt from the beginning that in these boys themselves must lie our main hope of permanent success. They can understand our ways as outside people cannot; and if they cannot understand all now, we believe that they will understand more hereafter. At any rate, we must rely on them as our best exponents and advocates; and if ever this College is to be generally acceptable, it must be in the first instance acceptable to them. And of this we are not without hope. For we believe that they have many qualities that will respond to our training, but which must be fostered by sympathy not less than by discipline. To that end we have wished, so far as we may, to be boys as they are boys, to sympathise with their boyish feelings, to share and encourage their tastes and pursuits. We have wished that among us all, boys and masters, there may be one common feeling of fellowship. Such a feeling, we think, will make us all better, and will give to our society the pleasantness of friendship, as well as the strength of union. Also, we believe that this social confidence is a quality rare in all parts of India, and one which has been conspicuously rare among the Kathiawar Chiefs. And therefore we are the more pleased to think that one of the results which this College may achieve—which, in some measure, we trust, it has achieved already—is the natural creation of kindness and goodwill where hitherto there has been jealous dislike. Many of these boys' fathers would never meet one another, and now the sons of those fathers are here, finding that all that ancient distrust may be stanched by a schoolboy's friendship.

"Also we have rules. We have given the greater part of our time to systematic school teaching; but we have also paid some attention to physical development and outdoor exercise.

"In our classes we have had to contend with difficulties of an exceptional character. This College is not like other schools. We have not, nor can have, any fixed standards, and prohibitive limits, in scholarship, but are bound to admit every boy who comes of a certain social elevation. It will, therefore, be easily understood that the work of arranging our classes has not been a simple one, and that we have been seriously hampered by the necessary combination of unequal attainments. Nevertheless, we venture to hope that the general results of our work have not been unsatisfactory.

"In the hours not devoted to school we have done our best to encourage a taste for field sports and outdoor games. And in this matter we have not had much trouble, as our boys, with very few exceptions, have inherited the manly spirit of their ancestors. Small, childish faults we have easily pardoned, as common to our humanity. We have hoped to develop some *esprit de corps* as our safest guard from the greater sins. We have wished to treat one another frankly without any sign of suspicion, believing that trust on the one side will best promote truth on the other. In general, it is pleasant to add, the boys' behaviour has been very good; and for this I have mainly to thank the first class, who, as monitors, have always exerted an excellent influence over the rest.

"I have only to add, in the name of us all, our hearty thanks to Your Excellency for so kindly honouring us with your presence. This day will henceforth be one *creta notandus* in the calendar of the College ; a day to be remembered with pride, and to stimulate, I hope, to future exertions. With Your Excellency's permission, the boys will now, as usual on these occasions, recite a few pieces, and perhaps after that Your Excellency will kindly distribute the prizes."

The next important record of the progress of the College occurred in 1877, when H. H. Sir Takhatsingji Maharajah of Bhavnagar on assuming the Government of his own state, and in commemoration of the assumption of the title Kaisar-i-Hind by Her Imperial Majesty Queen Victoria, on the first day of that year, presented one lac (£10,000) for the erection of the south wing, and some other additions.

On the 19th August, 1879, a Durbar was held in the Central Hall to celebrate the opening of the above. After the Agency Engineer read a statement explanatory of the nature and extent of the works, the Political Agent, Col. Barton, addressed His Highness and the company as follows:

"Your Highness, Ladies and Gentlemen,—I have never presided on an occasion which has given me greater pleasure than the present one. We are met to celebrate the completion of two noble works which owe their origin and existence to the munificence of my friend the Thakor Sahib of Bhavnagar. You are all aware that His Highness received his education at this institution. He was one of the first to join, at a time when the efforts of Government to impart a more efficient training to the young princes who would subsequently be called on to undertake the duties and responsibilities of their States were viewed with suspicion and alarm by all who had been brought up in the exclusive and narrow system which had hitherto prevailed. But these fears were gradually removed, mainly by the admirable tact and patience of the worthy Principal of this College, our mutual and respected friend, Mr. Macnaghten. Ladies and gentlemen, the best proof I can afford you of my statement is the noble building we are to open to-day. It is a pleasing trait in the character of His Highness the Thakor Sahib, that the first act of state was to devote the sum of one lac of rupees to the improvement of his alma mater. The gift was spontaneous, and was, I believe, from his Highness's heart, as wishing to commemorate a kindly remembrance of his early days, and as showing his appreciation of the benefits he has derived from his association with this institution. It was a princely act. We all know how the memories of the worthies who built and endowed our public schools and colleges in our own native land, such men, for instance, as William of Wykeham and Cardinal Wolsey, are cherished and revered, and now that such institutions are rearing their heads in India, we may be sure that future generations will point with pride to the Takhatsingji wing of the Rajkumar College, and will say that the Thakor Sahib of Bhavnagar has erected a monument worthy of his rank and station, and one which will keep his name green and never fading."

His Highness the Thakor Sahib replied in English as follows:—

"Colonel Barton, Ladies and Gentlemen,—It is a great happiness to me to be present at these proceedings to-day. I think it is my duty as well as my privilege, to contribute so far as I can to the general good; and while, of course, my first duty will always be to my own State, I should also wish, so far as I am able, to help towards such works of public utility as the present. These two buildings here in Rajkote, which we are opening to-day, are indeed the fulfilment of the natural wishes of my heart. It is natural that as a Chief I should wish to celebrate the assumption of the title of Empress by the great Sovereign under whose sway our small principalities enjoy the blessings of peace. It is natural, too, that I should wish to increase the capacity and the influence of a college in which I spent the early years of my youth, and of which I have very pleasant and happy recollections, thanks to the care and kindness of my preceptor, Mr. Macnaghten, for whom I cannot but always have the greatest affection. That I have been able to carry out these wishes is to me a very sincere pleasure, and my pleasure is greatly increased by the very kind words which you, Colonel Barton, have spoken regarding me and my gifts, and I thank you sincerely for the trouble you have taken in kindly opening these buildings for us. I value your kind expressions extremely, and I trust I may always have the happiness of retaining your friendship and goodwill. I am glad to see in this assemblage several of my fellow Chiefs who formerly were my companions in the College, and to all the kind company here assembled I desire to express my best thanks for their attendance on this interesting occasion."

Azam Samaldas Parmanandas read a translation of His Highness's speech in Gujarati.

The Principal of the College then expressed his thanks to His Highness the Thakor Sahib on behalf of the College as follows:

"Your Highness,—I am very glad to have this opportunity of publicly thanking you, on behalf of the College, for your noble benefaction. It is not much that I can add to what Colonel Barton has already said; but it is right, I sincerely feel, that I also should try to say something. From the first, Your Highness has deserved our thanks—the thanks of all connected with this College—the thanks of myself especially. For I well remember how you yourself, of all the Chiefs of Kathiawar, were the very first to inhabit these buildings, and to set an example which has been followed by—well, you see this assemblage of students. For that, as well as for the general influence of your life in the College, we are, and always shall be, most grateful. And as we have these grateful feelings towards you, so it is also very gratifying to feel that our handsome new wing will hereafter be a memorial, not only of the munificence of the Thakor of Bhavnagar, but also of the kindly remembrance of Takhatsingji, our first pupil and powerful friend. It may well be the pride of the Kathiawar Chiefs that this College is all their own. They, and they only, are its proprietors, and on them its prosperity must always depend.

"But it is not only theirs; it is also for them; and to help it from inside by personal occupancy is not less important than to help it from outside. In both these respects Your Highness has set an eminent example to your brother Chiefs. And the same may be said, I am glad to think, of the Thakors of Morvi, and Limdi, and Rajkote, who show by their presence here to-day their abiding interest in this Institution. I am glad to see, too, our friend Harrisingh Jassabhai, Your Highness's Secretary, who has added to the credit of our College by matriculating in the Bombay University.

"Mr. Booth has told us that he feels some pride in beholding his original plan of the College now brought to completion. I am sure we can well understand his pride and share his satisfaction.

"I think we may also feel proud ourselves of him and of his excellent work; and when we remember that he planned these buildings about twelve years ago, at a time when to many the idea of a Chiefs' College seemed no more than an idle dream, I think you will concur with me in considering that the strength of his confidence—shall we say his inspiration?—was only surpassed by the facility of his design. Your Highness, with others who have lived in the College, has learnt, I believe, to admire, as I have, the remarkable suitability of its shape and structure to the purposes for which it is intended. And I like, too, to think that its external form is in keeping with the moral character of its aims. The style of the architecture is severely simple; it is also solid and sound. There is nothing intricate or tortuous about it, but plain open windows and spacious apartments, which freely admit the light and air. And herein it seems to me to stand—and with God's blessing may it stand for ever—as the symbol and substance of a practical lesson, which cannot too often be brought to our remembrance. In the manifold distractions and perplexities of life, and especially of public life, we cannot, I think, be too often reminded of that which is simple and plain, of the good old truth that simplicity and honesty are the best methods in everything. I thank Your Highness very sincerely for your kind expressions regarding myself; and once more, on behalf of the College, I beg to return you our hearty thanks, and long may you live to see your children's children enjoying the fruits of your princely bounty."

At the conclusion, the Political Agent, accompanied by His Highness the Thakor Sahib, Colonel Walsh, and the Thakor Sahıbs of Morvi, Limbdi, and Rajkote, and all the company assembled, proceeded to the centre of the south wing, and declared it open for the reception of students.

The band then played "God Save the Queen," and three cheers were given for His Highness the Thakor Sahib.

Although the idea of a Chiefs' College had been suggested by the Viceroy, Lord Mayo, anterior to that of the Rajkote Institution, the project was not yet developed, and so for several years the Kathiawar Rajkumar College remained the sole institution of its kind in India for the education ot feudatory chiefs, and advantage was taken of this to send to Mr. Macnaghten's care the young Chiefs from Rajputana, the Maharajah of Kohlapore, the Chief of Kagul, the Maharajah of Idar, Chiefs of Luniwada and Janjira, Ilol, Baria, Soonth, and others.

Mr. Macnaghten's system included a great deal besides work in the class room. The young men were educated in all manly exercises similar to those of an English public school. He organised a troop in the uniform of Probyn's Horse, under the charge of a cavalry drill officer, and every boy was obliged to attend drill and form an integral part of the College Horse. This measure responded and appealed to their feelings, for were they not the descendants of warriors? The playground formed a very important item in the curriculum; they all became cricketers, football players, racquetters, and for those whose caste permitted them to shoot game, there was plenty of sport at hand. Besides they were trained to be gentlemen in manners and conversation. An afternoon in each week was set apart for games and a reception in the College grounds, where all the European residents in the station were received by them socially.

Cricket and other matches with teams from Bombay and distant localities took place periodically. Ranjitsinhji, who has won fame on English and Colonial fields, learnt to play cricket when a pupil in the Rajkumar College, and many others, including H.H. the Thakor Sahib of Gondal and Hurbhamjee of Morvi, distinguished themselves as members of the University of Cambridge.

It would be needlessly tedious, even were it possible, in this short sketch to record all the speeches made by the eminent personages who from year to year honoured the College by their presence, and thus gave increased prestige to the institution, which continued to do good work, not only for Kathiawar itself, but for many other parts of India. All that it is possible to do, therefore, is to select a few addresses (or extracts from them) from the heads of the most important Government departments. The first of these is an extract from a speech made by Dr. Mylne, Bishop of Bombay, when he visited the College, and was as follows:—

> "Mr. Macnaghten,—It is sometimes the case, I think, that one learns more about a man and his work from small things than from great. And there was one half-involuntary remark which fell from you in the gymnasium this morning which taught me more about yourself and your work in this College than anything even in your speech this afternoon. You said that sometimes a pupil was taken

away from you just as he was beginning to be interesting; and then you corrected yourself and said, 'just as *his work* was beginning to be interesting.' And in these words, implying as they did that every pupil was interesting to you simply because he was your pupil, I seem to read the secret of your success. You spoke this afternoon, with evident feeling, of sympathy as the grand requisite for the moral training which it was one of the great objects of the College to bestow; and what you meant by that expression, I think, was this—that underneath all differences of race, of training, and of tradition, and even underneath differences of religion, there were common aims and aspirations to which it was possible to appeal, and that it was by going straight to men's hearts that one was most likely to influence them for good. If you hold the honoured place of a pioneer in the attempt to bring to bear upon the rising aristocracy of this country some of the influence of that public school life to which England owes so much, you do so in virtue of your ability to make this most powerful of appeals. But now that I am led to say a few words about the spirit of a public school life, I shall, with your permission, address myself rather to your pupils than to yourself. There are few things of which we Englishmen are more proud, or to which we attribute more of our distinctive national spirit, than the life of our public schools. We look to the frank contact with our equals which is gained by knocking up against one another at school as the cure for that selfishness and pettiness and conceit which are generated by living among inferiors, or among those who are ready to pamper one's every whim. And if I mistake not, it is from influences like these that high-born youths in this country especially require to be preserved. Many among you will be called upon in after life to rule over thousands of your fellow-countrymen, and all of you to be at least in high stations about the persons of those who so rule. And we hold that one who would rule well must first be trained to obey. The man who is called to rule others must begin by ruling himself; and it is by obeying a law from without that self-restraint is learnt. The check that must be obeyed is the check of the public opinion of your equals. These two form the constituent elements of your moral training here. And you will forgive an Englishman for saying that he believes you can receive no greater benefit than to be habituated to the same moral influences which contribute so largely to that character of which his own nation is proud. My visit to your gymnasium this morning afforded me an opportunity of seeing that the development of your bodily powers forms an essential part of your education. It constitutes the true manliness of a man that he should be making the most of himself on every side of his nature; and the recitations to which I have listened just now show that the works of some of our great poets have been exercising their formative power over your minds. I have to travel in many parts of India, and I hear recitations in many schools, but it has never been my fortune to hear any which for intelligent appreciation of the author approached what I have heard this afternoon. Both in humorous and in serious pieces there was an evident sympathy with the writer which, in a foreigner, was, to me, quite astonishing. You have spoken, Mr. Macnaghten, of some of the difficulties of your work in a way which has roused the sympathy of us all. I cannot express to you more adequately my belief in the success which has followed you in contending with them than by saying that I have seen much here to-day to remind me of the spirit of our own public schools."

Lord Reay visited the College in November, 1886. The *Times* (of India), in describing His Excellency's visit, writes:—

"But by far the most interesting function held at Rajkote was the presentation of prizes to the students of the Rajkumar College, the Eton of Western India. All our younger chiefs have been trained under Mr. Macnaghten. The scene as described by our correspondent was brilliant and impressive. The Kumars were drawn up in parallel rows in a bewildering array of gorgeous and curiously designed raiment. The remainder of the Hall was filled with a host of native chiefs ablaze with jewels, officers in uniform, and a small bevy of ladies."

His Excellency the Governor, in addressing the princely pupils, past and present, had an opportunity of which he took the best advantage.

"My first question," he said, "when a young chief or an older chief comes to me, is, Was he educated at the Rajkumar College? and my first question, when I hear a young chief is not sent there, is to ask, Why is he not sent there?"

After giving the boys some good advice, he added,

"Before I sit down, I must pay a tribute, I am sure, in your name to Mr. Macnaghten, on whom has devolved the most important task of guiding and training you. The destinies of India, the destinies of this province, the destinies of the Southern Mahratta country, and I may say of the Bombay Presidency proper, are closely associated with what you do, or what you leave undone. Therefore the task which Mr. Macnaghten has undertaken is a task which has distinctly for its object the lightening of the burden of Indian administration, by providing the country with good administrators in high places."

* * * * *

Sir James Fergusson, on his last visit to the College in 1884, said :—

"My friends,—I do feel that this College has a very great purpose ; the lives of the Princes of India are those of enormous responsibility, of immense difficulty. The Princes of Kathiawar have within their power the welfare of millions of people. They have careers of great influence, of great temptations, and, I feel, of difficulty. They have not open to them the careers that are open to men of high rank in Europe. Their lives pass within limited circles, yet they have enormous capabilities of good with great temptations to evil. It is the purpose of this College to lead them unto higher things, to fit them for their great task in life, to nerve them against the great dangers that lie before them. That it has accomplished this great purpose we have bright examples to bring forward. I glory in the fact that among the old pupils of the College are princes who are fulfilling their task in life with singular success.

"It is delightful indeed to see the gratitude that some of them manifest for the College which has done so much for them, and to see that they take the greatest pride and pleasure in it by their generous gifts. But at the outset I should have expressed some part of what I feel for the work of Mr. Macnaghten. In his presence it is impossible to say all I feel, or all I should like to say, but you, my friends, who have owed so much to him, and have now passed from under his care, and you who have the happiness to live under him at present, I am sure, would wish that I should testify my gratification from the place that I am privileged to hold, and express the gratitude which the Government as well as you feel towards him.

"It is a great gift of God to be so well fitted to benefit one's fellow men, and it is delightful I am sure to him, as it is to his friends, to see how much he has been priviledged to accomplish."

* * * * *

H.R.H. the Duke of Connaught visited the college in 1887, and before leaving made the following remarks :—

"Gentlemen of the Rajkumar College,—I cannot leave this hall without assuring you of the great pleasure it has given me to have been present here this day, and to have listened to the very excellent recitations by the pupils. I congratulate those who have recited to-day, and I think they may be proud of the memory they have got, and hope that they may keep it all their lives. The Chiefs of Kathiawar have great reason to be proud of the good work which has been done here, and I hope it will continue to be done through their liberality. I am certain that the benefits of what is acquired here, both in study and on the playground, will remain with them as long as they live. It is a gratifying sight to see here so many of the reigning chiefs of the present day who have been pupils of this college, and I am sure they will allow me to say that none of them regret the days they have spent here. Allow me to congratulate you, Mr. Macnaghten, and the college, on the very admirable manner in which you and those under you have been training the minds of the pupils; I am certain that I am expressing the feelings of the pupils of this college when I say that they thoroughly respect you, sir, and those under you, for your untiring zeal and devotion. It has been a great pleasure to me to be present here, especially after having lately visited the Mayo College, in Rajputana, and assisted at the inauguration of the Achison College at Lahore. I hope that this college will prosper, and the good work which it has already begun will continue and increase."

Extract from *Kathiawar Times*, March, 1888.

"Mr. Chester Macnaghten, our popular Principal of the Rajkumar College, left this on last Monday evening on nine months' furlough. The Kumars, in appreciation of the great kindness of their teacher, who has always been to them more than a friend, accompanied him three miles from here on his way to Wudhwan. The speeches delivered at the tea party were each and all the results of the Kumars' and the tutors' enthusiastic and deep feeling of gratitude towards the Principal. The Kumar of Mundetti said: 'You have always been so kind and affectionate to us that you have made us almost forget our homes.' The Majarajah of Kohlapore said: 'They have been very kind to all of us.' Kumar Dataji Rao said: 'For they are very kind to us and take great care of us.' The speeches of the tutors also point to their great gratitude for the very kind treatment they received at the hands of the Principal. Mr. Manecklal said: 'Wonderful are the workings of the "Maga." Fifty years ago who could have foreseen but a real seer that the rulers of this Province would entrust their sons to a stranger from the far West, and that the royal boys thus committed through Providence to his charge would be loved and cared for by that gentleman with more than fatherly kindness? But this your kindness has not been confined to the Princes alone; along with them it has been our good fortune to share it. I am sorry I cannot adequately express the high sense of appreciation and gratitude my brother assistants and myself feel towards you for your kind and very gentlemanly treatment of us all.' The words of Mr. Gokhall were to the same effect.

"The reply of Mr. Macnaghten was elaborate, comprehensive, and concise. He said: 'Though we leave you, we shall not forget you. We shall carry away a large part of you in our heart's memories.'

"His connection with the college he thus feelingly alludes to: 'You know that for the last seventeen years my whole heart, my whole life, has been given to this college, and for nearly five years Mrs. Macnaghten, as I am sure you will all agree, has devoted herself to it as much as I have.'

"His parting advice was: 'Let us each do our duty wherever we are, and then, whether it be here or there, we are sure to do well. Whether we be here or whether we be there we shall all be, as it were, joined together by the sympathy of one aim and one friendship!'

"Mr. Macnaghten's straightforwardness and kindness have earned him a name and a fame not only within the precincts of the college, but in the whole of Kathiawar."

In 1889 H.R.H. the Duke of Connaught again visited the college and gave away the prizes. The following was Mr. Macnaghten's speech on the occasion :—

"May it please your Royal Highness. The kind hope expressed by your Royal Highness when some of us saw you last May at Mahableshwar has to-day to our great joy been fulfilled, and it is with most loyal respect and pride that we welcome your Royal Highness this second time to our college. These prizes from your Royal Highness's hands will have a value for our Kumars which none of our prizes have had yet, and we are deeply conscious of the honour which your presence gives to this happy occasion. I think I need not to-day dwell at length on the aims of a special institution such as this. You know, sir, we have aimed at a training of a liberal character, the sort of training *mutatis mutandis* which characterises English public schools. We have wished, of course, that our boys may be scholars, but we wish that they may be much more than mere scholars, that their bodily faculties may be developed as well as those of their minds; that they may be practical men of the world, knowing the right and daring to do it, retaining amid the influences of Western ideas the chivalry of their Rajput ancestry, delighting (like the ideal knight) in the redress of human wrong, and reverencing conscience as their King. In all we have wished that they may be guided by the spirit of the motto, 'Noblesse oblige.' Whether or not these high aims have succeeded, whether they have been in any way approached, is not for me to say. We have had in the course of the long period during which I have been connected with this college many encouragements, some disappointments. Our course has had its ups and downs like other earthly courses, but always we have been generously supported by our friends the Chiefs and the political officers, and if this college has done something in the past we trust it may do much more in the future."

In 1890 the college was visited by Lord Harris, Governor of Bombay. After giving away the prizes his Excellency remarked that the college had well maintained its reputation from its infancy. Looking around him he could see the results of the education and the training which the college had undertaken. Several of the rulers in the province had received their education in the college, and he thought that those who had been trained in the college had shown their gratitude to it by not ceasing to take an interest in it in after life.

* * * * *

The Chiefs of Junaghad, Bhavnagar, Gondal, Morvi, Limri, and Wudhwan have in their subsequent careers shown that the training they received in the college proved so useful to them in widening their minds and in the conduct of their worldly affairs.

The following is an extract from Mr. Macnaghten's speech on the above occasion :—

. . . . "You know, sir, it has been our endeavour to make our boys practical men of the world, developed in mind, sound in body, reverent of their consciences. This kind of training can never be easy, and under the circumstances in which we are placed it has been, I can truly say, exceptionally difficult ; still, though we can never fully attain to the ideal set before us, deeply conscious though we are of the greatness of the task and our own insufficiency, yet I trust we may find in the knowledge of the past good hope for the future of this institution. Though colleges of this kind are new things in India ; though we can boast no time-honoured cloisters inscribed with the names of illustrious examples, yet I hope we have some compensation for these things—and I think we have —in the innate nobility and prestige and, I may add, the historic antiquity of the Rajput character. I can truly say that a high sense of honour and a chivalrous feeling of 'Noblesse oblige' has in general characterised those who have hitherto studied within these walls. This is the tone we should most wish to have, and may that be the tone of the college always ! I have only to wish that in after years there may be more opportunity than at present for the useful employment of the young energies imperfectly developed in this institution.

"Education does not end here, it ends only when life ends, and sometimes the Bhayats and kinsmen of chiefs who have learnt something in this college afterwards relapse into listless inactivity, for want of something to do. This is not altogether or always their fault, for there is not, in fact, a very wide field open at present for the educated energies of the youthful nobility and gentry of India. But I hope, for their own sake, that some plan will unfold itself for useful and honourable employment that would seem to be a fitting sequel to what we endeavour to teach in this college."

The College was visited by Sir George Greaves, Commander-in-Chief in Bombay, in 1891, on which occasion he distributed the prizes and addressed the young Rajahs as follows :—

"Mr. Macnaghten, Ladies, Young Princes, and Gentlemen,—When I was asked to distribute the prizes I replied in a light and airy way that it would give me great pleasure. I thought that I should just hand you over the prizes, make a few remarks, and that the business would be over; but I find that some of the most eminent men of the day have been here and have done this thing before, and that all the appropriate expressions, all the right things to say, and all the happy thoughts have been exhausted. You have had here my illustrious predecessor, H.R.H. The Duke of Connaught, who has always the happy knack of saying the right thing; you have had his Lordship the Bishop of Bombay, who is eloquence itself, and a thoroughly manly fellow; besides, you have had His Excellency Sir James Ferguson, the new Postmaster-General—and an excellent Postmaster-General too—for has he not opened the department to soldiers?—the result of his Crimean days, may God bless him; and you have had Lord Reay, the embodiment of learning and education; you have had Lord Harris here, our esteemed Governor, who is one of the best examples in the world of intellect and education combined with skill at all manly exercises, and who could show every one of you the way over any sort of country; and you have come down to me, a battered old soldier, and what is there left for me to say to you? Mr. Macnaghten has said everything that anyone did not say, and now he admits that he has eaten all his cake, and yet he is not happy; but you, young gentlemen, have many reasons for being happy. Last year I was much impressed with all I saw here, but I had military work on hand which claimed all my attention, and so I saw very little of you; but I was much pleased with what I did see of yourselves, gentlemen, and recognised the great advantages to you and the future India, of institutions of this sort, and the excellent management of Mr. Macnaghten, your Principal. I will tell you now that I think you are an extremely fortunate set of young fellows to have such an institution, where you can come and be educated amongst your equals in birth and position, and where you can practise manly exercises and become manly in your thoughts and in your ways. In olden days your forefathers were great princes, great rulers, and great warriors, who passed their lives in usefulness according to the wants of the times; but those times are past. It is not given to us now to go fighting when we feel disposed; we must learn and work if we want to get on in the world, and can only be ready for successful fighting if we practise war assiduously in times of peace; and what is true of the profession of arms is equally true of any profession. You have here the opportunity of being well educated, and of eventually taking that share in the affairs of this great and glorious India which your birth and position have always rendered you eligible for and your education now gives you an undeniable claim to. If you ask me what you should do, I would say soldier, soldier every one of you; and when soldiering in the regular army has disciplined your minds and has given you practice in that which you were born to as leading men, go back to your raj and your estates, and take your place in the government of men and in the management of your affairs. The Imperial troops will also get the benefit of your services, and remember that it is given to few men to command well until they have been themselves commanded. In soldiering you will rub shoulders with English gentlemen, and that will be good for both. We are so bound together in the future of India that the more we know of each other the better. Some of you may have been taught to think that India could get on very well without us. Some well-known Statesmen have said, no matter what they thought, that England could get on very well without India; but this is all pure nonsense. I have served off and on in India for forty-one years, going and coming back again, and I know the whole vast country from one end to the other, and I tell you that you cannot do without England. We began by fighting, but now we have grown together and must keep together. You can rely upon us; we will depend upon you; and together, no power upon earth can injure us. I advise you to be soldiers, and I observed on parade this morning that some fifty per cent. of you were so already. That is most gratifying to me, but you must not forget that military service nowadays is very different from what it used to be. Courage, nerve, and decision are just as much wanted now as they were before, but there is not, as in the good old days, the same opportunity for personal encounter or for personal glory. Like all other professions, the Army requires hard and constant labour to succeed in it ; and to give efficient service to the State, you will have to study hard and to work hard, and between whiles you will get a little time for playing hard and riding hard.

"You are lucky fellows. You have got it all before you, and with luck ought to have a good time ; but in advising you to soldier, you will understand that I am saying all this because I am a soldier and care for nothing else. Some of you no doubt will be better advised and go into the civil administration of the country. By all means do so. You see yourselves what a good service it is, and what real good clever fellows are in it, and no doubt in many ways you may learn to administer your estates better in this manner, and you will of course rise high in the civil line. All I say is, my dear young fellows, be up and doing, and don't dream any of you of going back from this excellent institution merely to lounge about the courtyards of your palaces. Give your fathers and relations and the Government of the country no peace until they have found employment for you. Only, mark my words, you must render yourselves suitable for such employment as Government can find for you, consistently with your possessions and the requirements of the State."

Mr. Macnaghten married in 1872 Isabella, daughter of the Rev. C. L. Hodgkinson, Rector of Louth in Lincolnshire. He became a widower in 1880. In 1882 he married Susan Ferrier, daughter of James Kinloch, late of Kair in Kincardinshire, who survived him.

In 1892 his health first began seriously to fail. He went home for change and rest, and was advised to retire from a charge which had been too great a strain upon his physical energies, but his inherent courage prevented him, and after two years he returned to Rajkote and resumed charge from his Vice-Principal, Mr. Waddington, who had acted during his absence. The following speech was made by him soon after his return on the 20th November, 1894, on the occasion of H.E. Lord Harris visiting and distributing prizes at the College.

The report of the past year's work of the College having been read by Mr. Waddington, Mr. Macnaghten said :—

"Your Excellency, Sir C. Ollivant, Your Highnesses, Ladies and Gentlemen,—I hope that you will consider that report to be very interesting and satisfactory. I am glad Mr. Waddington has been able to read it in the presence of Your Excellency and in the presence of the Kathiawar chiefs and others assembled to-day in this hall, many of whom are old friends of the college and some of whom have themselves been its inmates. I do not wish to add anything to it. Only, as regards Mr. Waddington himself, I am sure we must all congratulate the college on having for the last two years and a half enjoyed the great benefit of his services. Here in his presence I cannot speak so freely as I might wish, but it is simple justice to say that this college is deeply indebted to him for the admirable manner in which he managed it during the long period of my absence. We cannot but be very grateful to him, who has the good of this college at heart. I know that his future is somewhat uncertain, but I venture to hope that his personal interests may be found to coincide with those of the college which has already owed so much to his high and exceptional qualifications. Mr. Waddington, for the most part, has confined his remarks to the present internal condition of the college, but I see many 'old boys' around us to-day who remind us pleasurably of the past. I cannot forget them on this occasion, for it is a very great pleasure to me, I may add to Mr. Waddington also, to see them all again. We are glad that Your Excellency has been the happy means of bringing together and of strengthening and tightening the links of the friendship which binds us and them to their school. The proof of this friendship is, I think I may say without being very guilty of a breach of confidence, for the story is characteristic of schoolboys all over the world, that one of our students told me last week that the bigger boys, while they remain in the college, are all very eager to leave, and that then, having left, they all wish to come back. He himself has left us for nearly three years, and said he would be very glad to return. I dare say that is the case with a good many, especially with those who have nothing to do. I believe that feeling for the college grows stronger each day in those who know it, and that its *esprit de corps* is now higher than it has ever been in the past. So though the past has not been wholly barren, we may look for still better fruits in the future. Such an institution in a country like this needs time to make itself understood. I believe it is better understood now than it has ever been before. May I on an occasion such as this, and here in our old college hall, be permitted without invidious comparison to congratulate H.H. the Thakor Sahib of Gondal on the high academic distinction achieved by him in England, when last I had the pleasure of seeing him? We are all very glad to see him here to-day and to welcome him with all his honours, in these scenes which his boyhood knew so well. And others, too, have distinguished themselves—if not quite in the same degree. Besides the rulers of States, whose actions are patent to all, Kumar Shri Harbhamji of Morvi continues to benefit his fellow men by steady attention to the duty of Assistant Commissioner in the Berars; Kumar Shri Ramsingji of Bhavnagar returned to his home last January after taking a law degree at Cambridge, and being called to the Bar; and his Cambridge companion, Kumar Shri Ranjitsinhji, after greatly distinguishing himself in cricket, hopes to return to us next month as a barrister of Lincoln's Inn. But I need not now continue the list. We have had some failures as well as successes, and of the failures we are not unmindful, for light and shadows cross one another on every mortal path.

"Sir C. Ollivant, commenting, two years ago, on the wonderful adaptability of this Province to the evolutionary principle, bade us not be faint-hearted or despair of improvement; for almost any kind of development seems possible in Kathiawar. Well, sir, when we see, after twenty years' experience, that one of the ex-students of this college has become a D.C.L. of Oxford, another a LL.D. of Cambridge, and a third, perhaps most remarkable of all, a member of an English University Eleven, has not this college a right to aspire and to be sanguine of future possibilities? If these things may happen in twenty years, what may not happen in two hundred? Yet two hundred years are not a great period in the history of a school. Therefore we would look forward with hope—*petimus altiora*. I have only to add, in the name of us all, our hearty thanks to Your Excellency for the honour you have done us by so kindly presiding on this occasion. We are sure you will not forget Kathiawar, and Kathiawar will not forget you, nor shall we of this college forget that you gave us our prizes on this your last visit."

But Mr. Macnaghten never regained his health sufficiently to permit him taking his old place in the playground or on horseback, and it was well that he now had Mr. Waddington at hand to relieve him of some of the strain of these and other college duties.

Early in 1896 an event occurred which affected him very deeply—namely, the sudden death of his old friend and pupil the Maharajah of Bhavnagar, the news of which Mr. Macnaghten received as he was entering the train at Rajkote to proceed to the festivities at Wankaner, on the occasion of the marriage of the young Chief of that place, one of his former pupils. Mr. Macnaghten, on receiving the telegram, returned to his house and the festivities were postponed.

Following very soon after the above occurred Mr. Macnaghten's last illness. On Thursday, the 6th of February, 1896, after attending to his duties in the college, he was suddenly seized with an attack of peritonitis, and on the following Monday he was at rest.

After Mr. Macnaghten's demise a movement was at once set on foot to perpetuate his memory, which was joined in by the ruling Chiefs in Kathiawar and other parts of the Presidency, former students, and personal friends, and a large amount was subscribed. The form of memorial decided upon was, first a life portrait to be hung in the new College Hall, and secondly a statue to be placed in front of the east entrance of the college, on the same spot on which twenty-five years before Mr. Macnaghten himself had planted a young banyan tree to commemorate the opening of the institution. This tree had, like the college itself, so prospered since its birth that its size now rendered it dangerous, because of its near proximity to the building, and it was opportune that sufficient excuse occurred for its removal. But it was not to be totally destroyed—numerous cuttings of it were planted throughout the college grounds.

At the same time the young Chief of Bhavnagar came forward with a request to be permitted to place a marble bust of his late revered father in the south wing, built by him in 1878, as well as to further perpetuate his father's memory by presenting funds for the sometime proposed enlargement and decoration of the Central Hall and the addition of some residences.

STATUE OF THE LATE CHESTER MACNAGHTEN, M.A.

Principal of the Rajkumar College, Rajkote, from its opening in 1871 to 1896. The Statue, subscribed for by the Chiefs (former pupils in the College), is erected in front of the East Entrance, on the spot on which Mr. Macnaghten himself planted a Bhania tree 25 years previously, to commemorate the opening of the first Chief's College in India.

The above works were completed in 1898 and opened by H.E. Lord Sandhurst on November 30th of that year.

The following speeches from Mr. Waddington and Lord Sandhurst on the occasion will give a full account of the above, and will complete this short history of the Rajkumar College to that date.

Mr. Waddington said,—

"We are met here to-day for the performance of three functions, upon each of which it will be my privilege, with your permission, to say a few words. I am glad to think that H.H. the Thakor Sahib of Bhavnagar, to whose munificence we owe the Bhavsinhji Hall and the new residences of the College, is here himself to request Your Excellency—which he will presently do—to open the Hall and to unveil the bust of H.H. the late Maharajah of Bhavnagar, which he has placed in the south wing. In the meantime I am extremely glad to have this opportunity of publicly thanking him for his splendid gift, as well as for adding a tribute to the memory of his illustrious predecessor. But before doing so, I have the honour to request Your Excellency to perform a ceremony which is of very deep interest to all connected with this College, indeed, I may say to all classes in Kathiawar, and that is, to unveil the statue of Mr. Chester Macnaghten which stands before us. That is a name so well known to us here that I feel I can add but little by any words of mine to the general affection and veneration with which it will always be regarded. And it has already been my duty, or rather my privilege, on more than one occasion, to speak at greater length of the services which Mr. Macnaghten rendered to this Province during the 25 years in which he filled the office of Principal of the Rajkumar College. I do not therefore now propose to dwell at length upon those services and the character of one who endeared himself to all who knew him by his wide-reaching sympathy and kindness of heart. But if I may be allowed to repeat the substance of a remark which I have made before, I do so because I think it is apt to be overlooked. To those who only known the College as it stands before us, and the Province of Kathiawar at the present day, it is not easy to realise what the difficulties of the work were which Mr. Macnaghten was called upon to perform in the early 'seventies. Those who only see the finished achievement are perhaps apt to lose sight of the labour, the forethought, and the sympathy which made such an achievement possible. At the time when this College was first projected there was a general distrust of innovation; the idea of gathering the young chiefs and nobles of this Province into a common centre of education and training was quite unfamiliar, and even at variance with many of the most deeply rooted customs and traditions of Kathiawar; there was the ancient jealousy of different rival States to contend with; and there were then none of the railways which now bring our students so rapidly from all quarters of Kathiawar and Guzerat. Nor must it be forgotten that this College was practically the first institution of its kind in India, so that Mr. Macnaghten had no model in this country to whose history he could look for guidance or for warning. With no less tact than steadfastness he matured and carried out his designs, until by degrees the old suspicions and alarm were removed and the College acquired that established reputation which we trust still belongs to it to-day. And I think I may say that we meet here to-day to witness the erection of an abiding monument of his memory, because we believe that this statue will remain an eloquent though silent witness to the value of those lessons of singleness of purpose, of devotion to duty, of uprightness, and of honour which Mr. Macnaghten set himself all his life to inculcate, and of which his own life was a conspicuous example. For, as I have said on a previous occasion in reference to his life and work, so I may now repeat with undiminished confidence, that no more complete unselfishness and no more single-handed devotion to duty were ever shown by an officer of Her Majesty in India than by the late Principal of this College. However lasting may be the marble which here commemorates him, it will not be more lasting than the spirit of his work and influence, which will continue long after those who personally knew him shall have passed away.

"After this short, and I feel imperfect, tribute to the memory of Mr. Macnaghten, it will be right, sir, I think, with your permission, for me to give a brief account of the movement which was inaugurated after his death in 1896 to perpetuate him, a movement in which the ruling Chiefs of Kathiawar and other parts of the Presidency, as well as many other former students of the College, and personal friends of Mr. Macnaghten, unanimously joined. On the 27th of February, 1896, a public meeting was held in the Lang Library at Rajkote, to discuss measures to be adopted to commemorate Mr. Macnaghten, and to record the universal esteem and respect with which he was regarded throughout the Province. Colonel Hancock, then acting as Political Agent in Kathiawar, took the chair. The meeting, after recording its deep regret, and conveying its heartfelt sympathy to Mrs. Macnaghten in a letter of condolence, proceeded to select a committee to carry out the proposed memorial. H.H. the Thakor Sahib of Bhavnagar having come forward with a liberal donation, his example was followed by other Chiefs and gentlemen, and in a few months the Hon. Secretaries of the fund, having announced that the total of the subscriptions exceeded Rs. 23,000 it was decided at a second meeting to erect a statue in the College, to place a portrait in the College Hall, to present a similar portrait to Mrs. Macnaghten, and to purchase Mr. Macnaghten's collection of valuable botanical books for the College Library. It happened opportunely that Mr. Booth, the Agency Engineer, was at that time on leave in England, and he was there able to secure the kind co-operation of Sir Charles Ollivant and Sir James Peile in the selection of a sculptor and an artist. Their choice of a sculptor fell on Mr. Roscoe Mullins, whose work was already known in India from his busts of Sir Charles Ollivant and Sir Frank Souter in Bombay, of Mr. Woodrow in Calcutta, and his statue of General Barrow at Lucknow. The artist selected was Mr. Trevor Haddon. I believe, sir, that you will readily acknowledge that both sculptor and artist have worthily fulfilled the commissions entrusted to them, and that their works will be a real ornament to the College and the Province. The statue arrived in Rajkote about the middle of this year, and the difficult and delicate task of erecting it in its position was successfully undertaken by Mr. Booth. It was decided, after some discussion, to place it in front of the main east entrance to the College hall, a site which I think will commend itself to you as the best which could have been selected. The Statue itself is of grey Silician marble, standing on a pedestal of dark-red Aberdeen granite. This is placed on a base of grey granite from the Girnar Hill at Junagadh, and surrounded by an ornamental iron-work railing. The inscription on the pedestal is as follows:—

"Chester Macnaghten"
Principal of the Rajkumar College
From its foundation in 1871
Till his death at Rajkote
On February 10th, 1896.
This Statue is erected by his former pupils and other
friends in Kathiawar, in affectionate admiration
of his high purpose, ready sympathy,
modest and loving character, and
in grateful recognition of
his unselfish devotion
to the noblest ends
of Education.

"The replica of the portrait has been duly presented to Mrs. Macnaghten, who has written desiring that her most heartfelt thanks may be conveyed to all the subscribers to the fund for the gift, than which none could have been more acceptable or more highly valued. I should add that after the cost of the works I have mentioned had been defrayed, a balance remained of approximately Rs. 6,500, and at the first meeting of the Committee it was decided to expend this in founding in the college a gold medal stamped with Mr. Macnaghten's bust. As a prize of books and a gold medal are already given for proficiency in English composition and speaking, it was decided to award the Macnaghten Medal to the Kumar most proficient in history. Mr. Allan Wyon, Chief Engraver of Her Majesty's Seals, has been entrusted with the task of cutting the dies for this medal, which will be presented for the first time next year. It only remains for me, on behalf of the college, to express our deep sense of gratitude to the subscribers, both Chiefs and others, for endowing the college with these fine works of art, which are not only beautiful in themselves, but will always remain as honoured mementoes of one who for so many years was our presiding genius.

"I have now to ask Your Excellency and Your Highnesses to join me, as I fell sure that you will gladly do, in a tribute of sincere respect to the memory of the late Maharajah of Bhavnagar, and in our no less heartfelt thanks to H.H. Bhavsingji for the princely donation with which he has followed the example of his illustrious father. It is now almost twenty years since Colonel Barton, then the Political Agent in Kathiawar, entered the hall of the college in Durbar with Sir Takhatsingji in order to celebrate what was the first act of State performed by His Highness on his accession to the gadi, the presentation of a lac of rupees for the construction of the south wing and other purposes. You are aware that His Highness the late Maharajah was the first pupil to enter these walls; how he gained the affectionate esteem of his fellow students and teachers by his high character and noble qualities; and how in after-life he continued to be always the firmest friend and most generous benefactor of the college. The list of his benefactions is a long one. He built the entire south wing. He enriched the endowment fund. He enlarged the Principal's residence and other buildings. He presented the handsome cricket pavilion. He founded a gold medal in memory of the Governorship of Sir James Fergusson. Of the part which he played in the administration of his State and in the world at large I need hardly remind any one present here to-day. The House of Bhavnagar has long been a synonym for loyalty to the Queen-Empress and for princely liberality in all good works. It would take up more time than I can well ask you to spare if I were to relate the history of the late Maharajah's good deeds. I can only refer in the briefest way to the numerous services performed for the British Government and benefactions conferred upon his own subjects.

"Sir Takhatsingji was the first Chief in Kathiawar to come forward with an offer to maintain a corp of Imperial Service troops for the defence of the Empire. Railways, hospitals, colleges, and schools owe their existence to him. It was his enviable custom to celebrate each birthday by fresh remissions of taxation and by fresh kindnesses to the poor. The State of Bhavnagar under his rule became justly renowned as one of the most enlightened and progressive States in India. No Chief more worthily carried the high distinctions which Her Majesty was pleased to confer upon him, among others the title of Maharajah and the Insignia of the G.C.S.I. No Prince in India has been more honoured by the world at large, more respected by the British Government, more beloved by his people. And I feel that it is particularly fitting that his name should on this occasion be connected with that of Mr Macnaghten, because from the commencement of his school career down to his death, so shortly followed by that of Mr. Macnaghten himself, there subsisted between master and pupil a friendship which was disturbed by no difference of creed or race. The premature death of His Highness came as a great shock to Mr. Macnaghten, and sensibly affected his health; and among the last words which he wrote, but which he was destined never to speak aloud, were words of 'mourning and affectionate regret' for the sudden and lamentable death of his former pupil and life-long friend. Though the master and the pupil are gone, their memory remains fresh and green with us. 'Sceptre and crown may tumble down,' but we have the words of the same poet to remind us, no less than the statue and the bust which are to be unveiled to-day, that 'The actions of the just smell sweet and blossom in their dust.'

"It is permissible to speak of the dead without accusation of flattery, and I hope I shall not be accused of any such sentiment when I associate with the name of Sir Takhatsingji the name of H.H. Bhavsingji as one of the great benefactors of the College. I am not unmindful of all that other Chiefs, both individually and acting in concert, have done in time past towards founding, endowing, and maintaining this college, with which I am proud to be connected. To them collectively I have frequently been impelled to speak my gratitude. To-day we celebrate the opening of a splendjd hall, which we owe to the munificence of one, H.H. Bhavsingji, Thakor Sahib of Bhavnagar. You are aware, sir, that His Highness, like his father, was a pupil here; it is now some years since he completed his education and travels; he has more lately assumed the control of his administration. And, like his father, one of his first acts has been one of generous gratitude to his *alma mater*. We have cause to welcome him for his own sake no less than for his father's memory. And I may assure him that we who are connected with this college do welcome him and thank him from the bottom of our hearts. I cannot imagine a nobler or a better way of spending great revenues than in the foundation or the endowment of institutions which will be centres of progress and enlightenment for the years that come after. The names of those great men who have founded and endowed the famous University Colleges and schools

NEW BHAVSINGJI HALL, RAJKUMAR COLLEGE, RAJKOTE. 1898.

(*See page* 166.)

of England, those colleges and schools to which we believe is owing in no small degree the greatness of the British Empire, such names as those of Henry VI., of Cardinal Wolsey, of William of Wykeham, of Thomas Sutton, the sound of these names is pleasant to us. They resemble the names of the immortal writers and poets who in past centuries have enriched the world with the creations of their genius, formed equally to delight and to instruct their children's children so long as their mother tongue endures. We hold them in peculiar honour. We venerate their memory. And I doubt not that here so long as these walls shall stand, the names of their Highnesses Takhatsingji and Bhavsingji, who have given freely where much was given to them, will be revered by generations to come.

"It may be of interest to those present if I read a short description of the improvements to the College, including the Hall, kindly supplied to me by Mr. Booth, the architect and builder of the whole fabric from its commencement. Firstly, the formation of a new central hall, 78½ feet in length, 42 feet in breadth, and 34 feet high, in place of the old hall, which was 38 feet by 42 feet. This was effected by throwing into the new hall four class-rooms, two below and two above, each 18¾ feet by 20 feet, and two west verandahs 10 feet wide. Secondly, to provide class-room accommodation in lieu of the above, the four small living rooms in the side wings were lengthened 10 feet and the four large class-rooms at either end of the main building were increased from 30 by 20 feet to 43 by 20 feet each. Thirdly, to provide living rooms in place of those taken up for class-rooms, a new upper-storeyed block of four complete residences was built in continuation of the south wing and connected with it by a covered archway. In the new hall the old wooden gallery has been replaced by a handsome cast-iron ornamental gallery, made by Messrs. Richardson and Cruddas, of Bombay. The interior of the hall affords excellent space and light for the interesting and valuable portraits of which the College now possesses a considerable number. Amongst these I must not omit to mention the portraits of the late Maharajah and the present Thakor Sahib of Bhavnagar, painted by Miss Clara Hawkes, which was the latest gift of H.H. Bhavsingji, and have been generally admired. In other ways the hall will supply some long-felt wants. It will afford the accommodation which has often been lacking on such public occasions as that which will take place to-morrow. At other times it will be used as a playroom. In the evenings and in wet weather for purposes of drill. I feel confident that your Excellency will pronounce it to be in every way worthy of this Institution.

"I cannot conclude without a very hearty expression of thanks to Mr. Booth, in which I am sure that I shall be joined by all who have the welfare of the College at heart. I need not tell you that it was Mr. Booth who designed the original plan of this College, that it was he who made every addition to it in the course of thirty years, that it is he who has now completed what may be called his crowning achievement in regard to the College. But I dare say few of those present have any idea of what the College might have been if it had not been for Mr. Booth's confidence and energy at the time when the idea of building such a College was first discussed. As an instance I may mention that the hall, which we shall shortly visit, was originally intended to be a mere roofed entrance, into which might be driven the carriages of the young gentlemen who would come daily from their residences in the town to attend classes in the College. No system of the College residences had been seriously proposed. But, as all who know him will readily admit, Mr. Booth does nothing on a mean or sordid scale. The College was to be worthy of its prototypes in England. The design was made, and although it was twelve years before the south wing was built, that original design was ultimately carried out in its entirety, and we have to-day a range of buildings which we may well be proud of. Mr. Booth, more than all, may well feel pride and gratification in the completion of his work; and I am sure that you will all join with me in offering him our very sincere congratulation. We have, as yet, no statue, bust, or portrait of Mr. Booth within the College; but I feel that no one who enters these gates need demand any other memorial of his work than the buildings themselves—*Si monumentum quæris, circumspice.* To Mr. Proctor-Sims, the State Engineer at Bhavnagar, I must express my hearty acknowledgments also for his cordial support and assistance in this scheme of works; and to Mr. Harilal Savailal, the Bhavnagar State Vakil at Rajkote, who has been indefatigable in this, as he always is in works of public usefulness.

His Highness desires to record his appreciation of the excellent and speedy manner in which the contractor, Jiva Dosa, has carried out his task, and I am to request Your Excellency to present to him a poshak, or dress of honour, in memory of this occasion. I have to request Your Excellency also to accept our hearty thanks, for the readiness with which you have consented to honour us by performing these functions."

The speech having been translated into Guzerati, his Excellency the Governor said :—

"Your Highness the Thakor Sahib of Bhavnagar,—I shall immediately, with very great pleasure, perform the task you have requested me to perform, and in doing so I desire to congratulate Your Highness upon so worthily following in the footsteps and the example of your illustrious predecessor, whose demise we all so much regret. Your Highness, and Chiefs, ladies and gentlemen, we are met here to-day to commemorate the memories of two gentlemen, whose names will always be associated with the Rajkumar College, two men brought up in their youth in two very different countries, and amidst totally different associations and traditions. One was born to rule over a large State, the other to make his way in the world by his own exertions and his own character. You, Mr. Waddington, referred first to the late Mr. Chester Macnaghten, and I shall follow your example in a few words; but you have fully dealt with the subject, while at the same time you have not said a word too much. I also remember that I am speaking in the presence of an assembly the great majority of whom, at any rate, knew intimately the late Mr. Chester Macnaghten, and some of whom were connected with his work, and it is far better therefore that you should have paid a tribute of praise to his memory than that I should attempt to do so. In your speech, Mr. Waddington, you remarked that the task undertaken by Mr. Macnaghten was an almost superhuman one. I myself, having observed for about three years the native institutions of this country, can see that it must have indeed required all the character and all the courage possessed by him to carry through to completion a scheme of education such as belongs to this College. He had to overcome a great deal of tradition and custom, and no doubt a great deal of suspicion, but such was the man that these were successfully overcome, and from a small beginning of sixteen boys in the first term, you have now, I believe, all your College rooms full. Now, after what you have said, Mr. Waddington, the question that arises in my mind is, 'How did Chester Macnaghten acquire that power with the persons with whom he had to deal?' Wherein lay his magic giving that indescribable power to form character? As you all know, he was not possessed of that commanding stature which commands admiration, and which suggests to some minds that a man may be a leader. He was frail of figure and mild of face, but within that frail frame there was an unquenchable spirit. That he had great talents, none deny; but they are not everything. But it was not only owing to that spirit that he accomplished what he did; it was owing, I think, to his gentleness of manner and unbounded sympathy, which created affection in the hearts of those with whom he was brought in contact, and with affection and confidence more than half the battle is won. I have often observed, and so must you, that, in speaking to a very deaf man, he himself speaks in a very low voice. He appears to implore you by that action not to shout at him, but rather clearly to enunciate the words you wish him to understand. Now you are aware that the native character is extremely responsive and amenable to gentleness and persuasion, and far more is to be gained by demeanour of that description than by hectoring and bullying where gentleness would best succeed. Let me also remark that because a man is gentle it is no sign that he is weak, any more than roughness should be mistaken for strength and men are judged by what they effect and by the manner in which they exercise their influence.

"Mr. Waddington, in that hall which I have already had an opportunity of inspecting, and which I think is admirably adapted for the purposes for which it is intended, you have the pictures of many men of noble character who have been Political Agents or employed in various ways in the Province; but there is one picture which attracts me more than any other in connection with this College, and that is the picture of Chester Macnaghten. If I were Principal of this Institution I should lead each new boy to that picture, show him the kindness expressed on the face of the gentle Englishman, and explain to him the characteristics which prompted a feeling of friendship

THE CRICKET PAVILION, RAJKUMAR COLLEGE.

(*See page* 111.)

and confidence in the breasts of all who knew him: and further than that, all those who may at any time be appointed to become the tutors of young Chiefs cannot do better than take a leaf out of his book. Now, Your Highness and Chiefs, Mr. Waddington next referred to His Highness the late Maharajah of Bhavnagar, and also well said that the name of Bhavnagar was synonymous with loyalty to the Queen-Empress. It is a touching remembrance that the first boy in this College never forgot and never ceased to love the tutor whom he came under in Mr. Chester Macnaghten. You have referred, Thakor Sahib, to the happy days you spent here. His late Highness fully recognised the great benefits that were to be reaped from studying here, not only in books, but also in the training of character, and as I told you before I began these remarks, I am glad to see that Your Highness equally recognises their value. The list of benefactions of His Highness the late Maharajah is indeed a long one, and whilst his Highness did so much for the actual College, it is interesting to note that he recognised the value of sports and pastimes by erecting a cricket pavilion for the College, and it would have rejoiced him, no doubt, to see his son performing his feats of horsemanship and taking part in all those recreations which we consider go to make the character of the man as well as book-learning. I should only like to say one or two words more in regard to this College. To this College there is no competitor, and I should like to see the sons of all the Chiefs who are eligible sent here for education. There are fifteen Chiefs now ruling belonging to Kathiawar who have been educated here, and several who rule States, outside Kathiawar, and there are no fewer than thirteen, I think, who are ruling or have ruled, and whose sons now occupy the College. The College opened its term with sixteen boys only, but now a hundred and ninety have passed through its portals. Your Highness and Chiefs, in declaring the Bhavsingji Hall open, and in also unveiling the statue and bust of His Highness the late Maharajah, I have but to add that it is, I think, very fitting indeed that the two memorials should be unveiled on the same day, to master and pupil, to the one who by his character practically created the Rajkumar College, and to the other who, with his son, in disposing of his wealth, has done so much to make it magnificent and complete."

CHAPTER VIII.

FIRST FURLOUGH HOME AND RETURN.

In 1871 I obtained my first leave of six months. Thirteen years had passed since I left home, and I was very glad of the opportunity of seeing the old country and people again. The more so because my eldest girl had for some time been ailing, and a change was advised for her.

Mr. Walter B. Blaikie, C.E., son of the late Professor Blaikie, of Edinburgh, who had lately been appointed State Engineer for Junaghud, acted for me during my absence.

It was early in June when we left Rajkote, and we had a trying journey of 150 miles to Ahmedabad before we would reach the railway line. My wife and one child occupied one covered shigram made up as a bed, the ayah and the other two the second, whilst I rode, and a couple of bullock carts with our kit and food, etc., accompanied us. The heat was intense, no rain having yet fallen. It occupied a week to reach Ahmedabad, where we stayed a couple of days with Mr. and Mrs. Beatty, of the Irish Presbyterian Mission. We proceeded to Bombay by the night train, where we met my brother and put up at Pallonjee's Hotel till the departure of the P. and O. steamer.

Our voyage home was an experience which I took care to avoid in future. There were 95 children on board, and about double that number of adult passengers. The boats were not so large and convenient as they are now, and we had not made ourselves so comfortable in the way of deck chairs as was necessary. For some days the general sea-sickness and everlasting noise from so many children were almost unbearable. My wife was down for nearly a week, unable to move, and I, with the assistance of one Hindoo boy had the care of the three children until on arrival at Suez, I, fortunately, got the chance of engaging a Cingalese Ayah returning to India. The heat in the Red Sea was appalling, but after we reached Suez, and got over the very uncomfortable railway journey on to Alexandria, our troubles were ended.

Alexandria has been appropriately called the centre of the earth, and certainly it is a meeting place for all nationalities. In those days, too, it was not a very safe place for Europeans to wander about in alone, especially after nightfall; the place was a den of rascality, and law or police protection no more than a name.

I recollect I had occasion to go into the city while the steamer waited, and hired a boat for the purpose, taking with me a dragoman or guide. On arrival at the landing place, I was assailed by a crowd of donkey men, each one insisting that I should engage his animal. I tried to force my way through them in vain. I was pushed here and there until, getting out of temper, I raised my umbrella and hit one of them over the head. Instantly some 50 of them surrounded me in a very threatening manner, and had not my dragoman arrived on the scene and succeeded in appeasing them, I would doubtless have been injured or killed.

The voyage up the Mediterranean was delightful. We called at Malta, and had some six hours in which to visit the town, lunch on strawberries, and buy curiosities. Three days after, we were off Gibraltar, where again we had some hours on shore, while coaling proceeded. From thence to Southampton occupied five days, and we had lovely weather till nearing England, when for a whole day we lay by in a dense fog, with the fog horns continually blowing, and others in the distance were occasionally heard. When the pilot boat arrived, it was not seen till nearly run down by the steamer and somewhat injured. I have rarely heard better swearing than proceeded from that pilot boat.

We arrived at Southampton early in the morning, and took ourselves and possessions to an hotel. It would have been simpler to have gone direct to London and taken the Holyhead train from thence, but we ignorantly decided to go from Southampton by some other route, by doing which we had to leave our heavy baggage to come on by goods, and we were obliged to change trains many times before we arrived the following evening, very tired and exhausted, at Holyhead, and found it necessary to stay at a small hotel near the docks for two days; this was, however, very pleasant to all of us. On the third evening we crossed to Kingstown, and soon reached my mother's house in Dublin. Since my father's death, and the breaking up of the old home, she had taken a house in Dublin, near which she had engaged rooms for us. I went to visit my relations the Rowleys, at Sylvan Park, near my old home, which was not much changed, except that it was occupied by strangers. The old country folk and labourers whom I had known as a boy thirteen years before were mostly to the fore. I visited them all, and received a hearty welcome everywhere, and hearty kisses from the old women—all were delighted to see Master Bob once more. At the park I had excellent shooting, and much riding, and gaiety. We had altogether a very fine holiday, and although I was glad to return to my work, I was sorry to leave so much that was pleasant and enjoyable. I had some other matters also to attend to in England. I wished to utilise my time at home in visiting some of the principal jails, asylums, and other institutions, as I might have occasion for the knowledge of their construction and management in Kathiawar, and I had obtained introductions to members of the India Office to enable me to visit some of the best. For this purpose I spent about one month in England.

My wife decided to remain with the children, so early in December I left them all in Edinburgh, but I had run my time so close that I was obliged to travel with the mails across the Continent and join the steamer at Brindisi. This was not so easy in those days (especially for any person new to the journey like me) as it is now, and to make matters worse, it was during the Franco-Prussian War, when the ordinary mail route was altered. Having got my ticket, I left by the night mail from Charing Cross, reaching Dover about midnight. Seizing my handbag and rugs, I proceeded to the steamer, and was on board when I discovered that I had lost my satchel, which I carried on a strap round my shoulder, and in which was my money and ticket. In a state of alarm, I rushed to the captain, and told him. He bid me run full speed back to the train, and he would delay starting for five minutes. I went like a madman, and half-way up the platform ran into the arms of a porter, who was also running in my direction with my satchel in his hand. A moment explained matters. He found the satchel in the carriage and was running to the ship, knowing it belonged to some passenger. I was too pleased and grateful to speak; but I gave him a good reward, and ran for the boat, where I found the captain anxiously waiting and the men ready to draw up the gangway.

We arrived at Calais after a windy passage, and got on board the mail-train. At 4 a.m. we reached Brussels, and had to wait there nearly half the day. It was a miserable experience. I was cold and hungry, and could find neither fire nor food. After walking up and down the deserted station for a couple of hours to warm my limbs, I discovered, sitting disconsolately on a trunk, another passenger, the only other English passenger, it turned out. He was Lieut. Montgomery of the 2nd Queen's, also bound for Bombay. We were strangers, but very speedily became friends, and very pleased we were, indeed, to stumble across each other. He had been out foraging, he told me, for food, but every place was closed. After a while we made another attempt in company, and were fortunate in obtaining in a café down a side street some very execrable coffee and coarse bread; but anything was welcome. We bought some rolls of bread and a bottle of cognac, so called, to support us in the train, not knowing when and where we would find any food again. I recollect that most of the journey, till we reached Munich anyhow, was terribly cold, and that for two days and nights we had no food but our rolls and the cognac. Much of the country was covered with snow, and the carriages were so heated with hot-water pipes that inside we were melted, and if we put our heads out of the window they would be frozen.

We here made the acquaintance of a Mr. Drinkwater, who I believe spoke every language on the Continent. He was a good companion, and full of entertainment. On stopping for an hour at Cologne, he took us to see the Cathedral, which has been 800 years in building, and now only the front towers were under construction. The snow lay heavy on the ground, with much mud and wet, and the cold was bitter. On reaching Munich he got us an excellent dinner, and a supply to carry us on to Bologna, where we arrived at midnight. Here we found we would be detained till nine the following morning, and were preparing to roost in the carriage, when the officer in charge of mails (an Irishman, by the way) discovered us and took us to his shanty at the station, a room about 10 ft. by 6 ft., with two wooden benches, a table, and a small fire. Here we three ate what we had, and sat by the fire all night—sleep of course was out of the question. The run next day from Bologna to Brindisi was pleasant enough. We were soon on board the P. and O. steamer, and bound for Alexandria.

The remainder of the journey does not need writing about. It was terribly hot in the desert and on the Red Sea, but that is usually so, and with a good boat one does not mind. On arriving at Bombay I took Montgomery to Tom's bungalow at Malabar Hill. And the following night I left for Ahmedabad, and he for Poona.

During my absence another Political Officer joined the Agency staff as Judicial Assistant to the P.A.; this was Mr. Henry Aston, I.C.S. He was now living with Macnaghten, in his college residence, the former being still a bachelor. It was very pleasant to return to the old scenes in rude health, and to all my friends, who, like myself, were little more than commencing life's works, and had everything to look forward to.

While I had been away the construction of the north wing of the College had been put in hand, and the work was far advanced under Blaikie's supervision.

CHAPTER IX.

FERRY OVER THE BHADUR RIVER—SOME OF THE FIRST LARGE BRIDGES IN KATHIAWAR.

I have furnished a general statement of road construction up to 1878, but I must return to 1872 to give a few details concerning some of the large bridges constructed for road purposes since the latter date.

The first of these was the Anderson Bridge, over the Bhadur River at Jetpur.

The Bhadur is the principal river in Kathiawar, having a drainage area of about 4,000 square miles. It takes its rise in the great watershed of the Choteela and Anandpore hills, running in a south-westerly direction till it empties itself into the Indian Ocean at Nowee Bunder. For two-thirds of its length from the source it is well defined between rocky, or otherwise solid, banks, which it rarely overflows, but on its lower section it annually floods the country for many miles. To these inundations, after heavy rainfalls, is due the exceeding richness of the plains for some forty miles from the mouth. The land is so flat and the fall so gentle that no injury from scour occurs, and the deposit of black soil laid by the inundations is of great depth and richness, and grows marvellous crops of cotton and grain, needing little or no artificial irrigation. On these plains the villages are built on artificially raised mounds at distances of a few miles apart. I have sometimes seen as much as 200 square miles of this country submerged, with the villages appearing like so many little islands over the surface.

At the Kathi town of Jetpur, about the centre of the province, the Bhadur had been from all time a serious obstacle to traffic. During the monsoon a traveller arriving at the river was fortunate in finding it fordable. If not he might be delayed for days, and have to retrace his steps to a neighbouring village for shelter.

There was no boat, and indeed during a flood no boat could live, but when the water had partially subsided, foot passengers were occasionally taken across by parties of expert swimmers, four in number, who supported on their shoulders or heads a light cot on which the passenger sat high and dry. We sometimes crossed the Bhadur in this manner.

In the latter end of 1872 Captain Wodehouse, the Assistant P.A., Sorath, induced the Kathi Chiefs to grant Rs. 1,000 for the construction of a ferry, and the work was handed over to me to carry out.

The ferry, which I had made in the Rajkote School of Industry, was 22 feet long by 12 feet wide, and was intended to convey across the river a laden dray and bullocks. It consisted of a platform of timber supported on a pair of pontoons and connected by two central pins, by which the pontoons could be made to revolve so as to place them in a position diagonal to the stream alternately as the ferry moved either way and thus be to a certain extent self-acting. It was guided and worked by a strong cable passing through pulleys on the parapet rails, the ends being secured to stout mooring posts at either bank. The river having a wide sandy and rocky bed, with ill-defined banks, was not well suited for the working of a ferry, and it was doubtful if sufficient arrangement for its security could be made during heavy floods.

It was completed and set to work in January, 1873, and during the following fair season worked satisfactorily, but early in June an exceptionally violent flood passed suddenly down the river, and the Jetpur people not having time to moor the ferry so as to give it free play to rise with the flood, it broke loose, and was carried twelve miles down stream, where it was almost entirely smashed on the rocks.

It was then that the necessity for bridging the river was so strongly urged, and the States of Junaghud, Gondal, and Jetpur, being those who would be most benefited, were asked to subscribe the necessary funds.

Gondal was then under Agency management, and the Political Officer in charge, Captain A. M. Phillips, immediately came forward with an offer on the part of that State to pay one-third of the cost of the bridge if the two other States would defray the remainder, which they decided to do.

A site for the bridge was selected three-quarters of a mile below the town, where a favourable rock foundation was obtainable. It was to consist of twelve spans of 50 feet, and eight of 20 feet, besides twelve of 20 feet over side bifurcations; the piers were 35 feet above low-water level, with rise of arches 14 feet, making a total height to roadway of 55 feet.

THE BHADUR BRIDGE.

(*See page* 119.)

No public works having yet been carried out at Jetpur, the first business was to find suitable building stone, lime, etc., which were fortunately discovered within a reasonable distance. Work was put in hand after the rains of 1873, and by the following June the piers were three-fourths finished, and all the arch stones were cut and ready on the quarry. On the bridge works, quarries, etc., I had from 500 to 700 labourers and artisans employed, and a permanent camp pitched on the south bank.

As the erection and part backing of the twelve arches would necessarily be the work of one fair season, of something under eight months, and as any delay or accident which would lengthen the time of their construction beyond that period might result in the loss of the entire work, very complete arrangements for their uninterrupted and speedy erection had to be made. During 1873-74 most of the arch-stones, which each measured 6 cubic feet and 850 pounds in weight, were prepared and carried to the site. and three centres had been laid ready. Work was got under weigh at the end of September, and by the 25th of May the last arch was in progress. It was an anxious time, for if a violent flood had come before this arch had been completed, keyed, and backed up, the loss of the entire bridge would probably follow; but all was completed in good time. The last centres were removed on the 11th of June, and the same evening a flood, rising only 10 feet, passed down harmlessly.

The Jetpur folk had up to this time been doubtful that the bridge would stand against the fury of a monsoon flood, and many went so far as to say that the god of their sacred river would surely circumvent its destruction. But an opportunity for showing how far reliance could be placed on the supposed intentions of the god of the Bhadur occurred on the 15th of July, when the highest flood on record for many years swept down the river, rising in less than an hour to 33 feet, and running with immense velocity. But the god was powerless, and the bridge stood.

Shortly before the completion of this bridge I had one morning an unexpected visit from H.E. Sir Richard Temple, Governor of Bombay. H.E. was very fond of paying sudden visits, which not infrequently caused inconvenience to officials in the districts. I had a note the previous night from Mr. Peile that the Governor was to arrive the next morning at Verawal, from thence drive to Junaghud, sixty miles, and early the next day would come to Jetpur to see the bridge works. Fortunately, I was at Jetpur at the time, and I had to receive the Governor and the P.A., with a member of the staff, show them over the works, and give them breakfast. The Governor was much interested, and complimentary. After breakfast, in the T. Bungalow, it was arranged that he would receive the eighteen Kathi chiefs of Jetpur and I improvised for the occasion a durbar room with my easy chair at the head as a throne. H.E. seated himself in the chair for his smoke while awaiting the Chiefs, and, being somewhat tired after his hard morning's exercise, he fell asleep. The Chiefs arrived, and were seated in the verandah to await the Governor's awakening, but it was in vain ; H.E. slept on, and nobody liked to rouse him. Time was up. The Chiefs could not wait, and as the party had to start for Dhorajee at 2 p.m., the Political Agent was obliged to excuse H.E. from seeing them at all.

By June the following year, 1877, the bridge, with approaches, etc., were all completed, and were opened for traffic on the 17th by the Political Agent, Mr. (late Sir) J. B. Peile.

EXTRACT FROM OFFICIAL STATEMENT.

"Early on the morning of the 17th of June a great assembly of people collected at the bridge. The Karbarrie of Junaghud was present on behalf of H.H. the Nawab and the Talukdars of Jetpur attended in large numbers. Mr. Peile, with Mrs. Peile and Major Phillips, First Assistant Political Agent, arrived at the bridge punctually at 8 a.m., and were received by the Engineer, Mr. R. B. Booth. When the centre of the bridge was reached Mr. Peile first addressed in Guzerattee the representatives of the States there assembled. He expressed his satisfaction at meeting on that spot and that occasion those who had supplied the funds for this great work. It was no ordinary work, and it had been completed at no ordinary cost and labour. They knew the temper of the Bhadur and what trouble the river often gave to the traveller. Great honour therefore was due to those who had joined to effect the construction of a work of such general benefit.

"Mr. Peile then turned to Mr. Booth, and congratulated him on the completion of so important a work. The bridge would rank as a great work anywhere, and it was the greatest of the works they had before them when in 1873 they had taken up the task of giving bridges and metalled high roads to the province.

"A salute was then fired from the guns of H.H. the Nawab, and the assemblage crossed the bridge to the north side and returned to the south side, whence it dispersed. This bridge is a most important work, as it connects northern and southern Kathiawar, hitherto separated by a rocky stream liable to sudden and violent floods."

On the construction, a few years later, of the metre-gauge railway, it was permitted to run over this bridge, which till now has remained a combined road and railway bridge.

During a part of the three seasons I had my camp pitched at Jetpur I was a grass widower, my wife being at home, but my loneliness was compensated to a great extent by visits of friends, who pitched alongside. One of these was the late Colonel A. Pullen, chief of the trigonometrical survey. He was one of the best amateur landscape painters in the Presidency, and under his guidance I first learned an accomplishment which has ever since been a source of amusement and interest. Another was Mr. Thornton, of the Telegraph Department, for whom I entertained a great liking. Also Colonel Warden, on special boundary duty, and on at least one occasion Mr. and Mrs. Macnaghten, spent the College holidays with me, when part of the programme was an expedition to the Girnar Mountain. Mornings and evenings fishing and shooting, when work permitted, and a pleasant dinner to finish up with. Happy days they were, and pleasant to live over again in remembrance.

In February 1877 funds were obtained for building a bridge over the Bhogava river at Wudhwan Civil Station, to be called the Keatinge Bridge. Owing to the great depth of the quartz sand forming this bed and the difficulty of pumping to obtain foundations, I decided to make the main portion, 500 ft. of iron girders on screw piles with two 45 masonry spans at either end, what is called a composite bridge. The ironwork was made by the Darlaston Company under direction of Mr. J. R. Manning, M.I.C.E., and it was erected by our own men. The entire bridge, with approaches, were completed by the monsoon of 1878, but time was lost owing to cholera visiting the station in April, when all hands fled from the locality for two months. For over twenty years this bridge has carried the Morvi railway in addition to carriage traffic.

In March 1875 the second great masonry bridge over the Bhadur river was commenced by Mr. Gunesh Govind, State Engineer of Gondal, my former assistant, and carried to completion in June 1879. It consisted of 11 spans of 60 feet eliptical, rising 60 feet to roadway. It reflected the highest credit on its designer and builder, and he received a handsome honorarium and well-merited encomiums on the occasion of the opening by Major W. Scott, A.P.A. in charge Gondal. It is called the Peile Bridge.

Another fine bridge built by Mr. Gunesh Govind, and opened by H.S. Sir Phillip Wodehouse in 1875, was the Gondal bridge over the Gondali. It consists of seven spans of 40 ft., and two of 30.

The Kaisar-i-Hind bridge over the Adji river at Rajkote, the cost of which was presented by H.H. the Maharajah of Bhavnagar in honour of the Delhi proclamation on January 1st, 1877, was commenced at the close of that year, and was opened by the P.A., Colonel Barton, in August, 1879. It consists of 14 segmental arches of 45 ft., with total height of 36 ft. The bridge is decorated at either end with a pair of lions sculptured in stone, modelled in the Rajkote school of art by Mr. Sykes, superintendent.

On the occasion of the ceremonial opening of this bridge, together with that of the south wing of the Rajkumar College, the funds for which were also provided by H.H. the Maharajah, and which will be referred to in its proper place.

The following extract is from the speech of the Political Agent on the occasion :—

"I have now the pleasure, ladies and gentlemen, to draw your attention to another act of munificence on the part of his Highness. I allude to the Kaisar-i-Hind bridge, which we are to open formally to-day. When His Highness went to Delhi to attend the ceremonies there at the proclamation of Her Most Gracious Majesty as Empress of India, he expressed a wish to commemorate the auspicious event by the erection of some suitable memorial in his native province, and the happy thought occurred to him of bridging the Aji river, which flows past this town and cantonment. It is, I believe, the fashion, at all events it was so until very lately, to abuse the roads in Kathiawar. Well, ladies and gentlemen, I can remember the time when there was not a mile of made road in this Province of 22,000 square miles, and many difficulties had to be over-

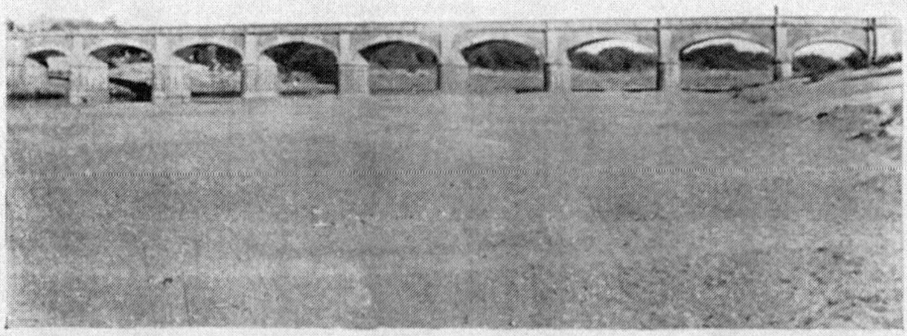

The Peile Bridge over the Bhadur, Gondal State.

Lalpuri Bridge.
(*See page* 122.)

KAISAR-I-HIND BRIDGE, RAJKOTE.

THE " KEATINGE BRIDGE," WUDHWAN.

(*See page* 122.)

come before a system of united action and co-operation on the parts of the Chiefs of Kathiawar could be devised. Such a system was, however, at last matured, thanks principally to the energy and perseverance of my predecessor, Mr. Peile, and it was resolved that two trunk roads, traversing the entire peninsula from east to west and from north to south, be constructed at the expense of the Chiefs of this Province. It is unnecessary to trouble you with details, but I may say, generally, that Chiefs of the first and second class agreed to construct the portions passing through their several territories, while all, down to the fourth class, were to give fixed subscriptions, according to their means, for a period of ten years, for the construction of the portions passing through the estates of the smaller Chiefs. Government also aided us with a subscription of one per cent., from the tribute levied from the Chiefs. Well, this system enabled us to construct a good proportion of the roads, and we hope that by the end of the ten years the trunk roads as described above will be in good working order, and here I may parenthetically remark that the Bhavnagar administration has completed all its portion of the trunk road falling within its territory, and that all its communications are in excellent order—thanks to the talented state engineer, Mr. Proctor-Sims, whom I am happy to see here to-day. But there was another difficulty to be faced. The roads are intersected by large, broad, and at times unfordable rivers, and the amounts subscribed were not sufficient for the purpose of bridging these rivers (bridges, ladies and gentlemen, are expensive luxuries, as Mr. Booth and His Highness the Thakor Sahib will tell you). In this matter the Chiefs of Kathiawar again came forward in aid of the Province. Through the liberality of the States of Gondal, Junaghud, and Jetpur, a noble bridge was raised across the Bhadur at an expense of Rs.2,06,600. Another across the same river was erected at the sole expense of the Gondal State, and was opened for traffic in June last. This bridge cost the State Rs. 2,35,400. A third was erected across the Bhogava river near Wudhwan, at a cost of Rs.1,32,740. The State of Wudhwan most liberally gave Rs.82,740 towards the construction of this bridge. All these are situated on the line of the trunk roads, but these roads all concentrate at Rajkote, and there was still the formidable gap of the Adji river, which had to be spanned before they could be connected. It is true that there existed a causeway over the Adji, which was built at the expense of the Rajkote State, and which has been a great convenience; but this causeway is liable to be rendered impassable by heavy floods, and mails and traffic were often impeded during the rainy season. I repeat, therefore, that it was a happy thought which inspired His Highness the Thakor Sahib of Bhavnagar to devote Rs.1,10,000 for the erection of the splendid bridge that it is our good fortune to open to-day for public traffic.

Ladies and gentlemen, the Chiefs of Kathiawar are an eminently conservative body. Twenty years ago the Potentates of this Peninsula were not alive to the responsibility of devoting their surplus revenues to the furtherance of public works, even in their own territories. None would have dreamt of spending money on works of public utility far away from their own territories, and yet so rapid has been the change of opinion in such matters, that we find his Highness the Nawab of Junaghud spending a lac of rupees in the erection of a High School in the centre of the Province. We see the stately building of the Rajkumar College built entirely by the liberality of the Chiefs of this Province (and amongst the greatest benefactors we number my friend the Thakor Sahib of Bhavnagar), and finally we find that when this prince wishes to commemorate a most important political event in our Indian history, the assumption by her most Gracious Majesty of the title of Empress of this vast Empire, His Highness does not confine himself to his own territory, but adds the missing link to our system of trunk roads. Without his aid this system would have remained incomplete. With it we may hope that the intercommunications of the Province will be placed on a firm basis, and that its trade will be greatly developed. But you must not suppose, ladies and gentlemen, that His Highness, in devoting these munificent sums to the adornment of our principal civil station has in any way neglected the claims of his own subjects. Some of us have been at Bhavnagar, and have seen the vast improvements that have been effected in the city and district during the last few years. The new suburbs cover a larger area than the old town, and are adorned by such noble edifices as the High School and Courts of Justice. A dock has been built for the accommodation of the shipping, and before long the railway now in progress will be carrying down the produce of the interior for shipment to the west. Roads have been constructed in every direction through the principality, and districts hitherto inaccessible have been put in direct communication with the capital by a steam ferry. His Highness's attention was directed, immediately after his accession to power, to the medical wants of his subjects, and he is now further adorning his capital by the erection of a spacious hospital which will contain all the latest improvements of modern science for the alleviation of suffering, and will be lighted with gas. Ladies and gentlemen, it is a pleasure to me to see some of the College companions of His Highness, who are now ruling their States in conformity with the principles which were instilled into them during their College career, present on this occasion. We have the Thakor Sahib of Rajkote, who would, I am sure, have been only too happy, had circumstances permitted him, to build the bridge at his own expense; we have the Thakor Sahib of Morvi, who has now projected a splendid bridge to connect his capital with the railway; we have the Thakor Sahib of Limbdi, who has visited England, and with whom you are doubtless acquainted from his predilection for manly sports. They were all schoolfellows of his Highness the Thakor Sahib, and they all, I know, regard with kindly feeling the Institution to which they owe their education, and the worthy Principal who led them with kindly hand along the thorny path of knowledge.

CHAPTER X.

VISIT TO THE GIRNAR MOUNTAIN. FANATACISM. THE SHETRUNJI HILL.

It was during the cold weather of 1873, after my wife had returned from home, that we made our first visit to the famous Girnar, in company with Major and Mrs. Phillips, Miss Creed, their niece, and Walter Blakie, who was again living at Junaghud. I met the Phillips at Dhorajee, where I had work in connection with the ginning factory. Phillips was now in charge of the Gondal State in succession to Captain Lloyd.

The Girnar Mountain forms the highest and most central position of the Girnar group, which is about 30 miles in circumference, and is approached from the city of Junaghud. The entire group is of volcanic origin, apparently thrown up out of the huge crater, long extinct, lying to the north of the great peaks. The highest peak is 3,600 feet above mean sea level, and is composed of granite, sienite, and trap. The summits are crowned with temples sacred to devout Hindus, and they are approached by a steep pathway mostly built in steps now, but at the time to which I refer three-fourths of the approach from Junaghud to the first summit, some five miles, was a rude pathway either paved with rough granite boulders or made on the natural surface anyhow, without regard to gradients; and a very precipitous and hard three to four hours' climb it was. On the first summit are some hundreds of temples, many of them of great antiquity, perhaps thousands of years, and all of them contain shrines which are visited continuously by pilgrims from all parts of India. Indeed, a Hindu who has not at least once made a pilgrimage to the Girnar is not held to have performed his duty here below in a manner to give him a claim to a place in Paradise hereafter.

Some of the principal temples of modern construction are of great size, covering some acres and comprising large courts and vestibules. No persons other than Hindus are permitted to enter the precincts of a temple or approach the Holy of Holies where reside the idols, unless under guard, and after they have removed their shoes or boots, and either walk without, or in slippers provided by the attendants. The idols in some of these temples are of great

GIRNAR GROUP.
(*See page* 126.)

size, made of polished marble or granite, and are decorated with jewels of much value. On the first summit, on which the great mass of temples stand, there is a small building set apart as a rest house for Europeans or any others than Hindus visiting the Hill. There are two small rooms on a terrace, and a small court with old cells or cloisters around. In these servants may prepare food, but no animal must be killed. No life can be taken on this sacred ground; the entire mountain is holy, base to summit, and strictly guarded. Above this summit the pathway, made of cut stone, ascends to the first peak called "Amba Mater," and many shrines and temples are passed on the way. Before reaching Amba Mater another pathway leads for about a quarter of a mile to a point called "Bairav Jāp"—the Leap of Death. Here is a singular vertical rock of great size, like a huge pillar standing on the extreme verge of a precipice two thousand feet in sheer depth. Near it is a rude hut, in which resides the Bawa or priest in charge, whose duty in ancient times was a gruesome one. It was the custom for devotees to this shrine to try to balance themselves on a cocoanut placed on the outermost edge of the rock. If they succeeded well and good, they were permitted to return to this life; if not, they were precipitated over the precipice and smashed to pieces. But it was a leap into Paradise!

From this point a narrow and tortuous pathway descends into what was once the crater, a basin or valley of immense extent, all thickly covered with the densest jungle, in which bamboo predominates. This path bifurcates again and again, traversing for miles the great basin in every direction to hermitages and shrines, where are found ascetics who have renounced the world and buried themselves in caves or mud huts. These creatures are sometimes of unearthly appearance, almost or entirely naked, covered with ashes, emaciated, or with self-mutilated limbs. They are considered to be absolutely holy, and are worshipped by pilgrims. I visited many ot them (not as a worshipper). and took sketches of them and their surroundings. One whom I rather fancied was not a bad fellow at all. He was of great height, about 6 feet 4 inches, clothed only in ashes, and was barely more than a skeleton. I don't suppose he would have weighed three stone. His fancy was to live in a hole, into which he could just crawl, and was only large enough to take in his body coiled up into a knot. He possessed no means of existence beyond what occasional pilgrims brought him, and a few nimboos (lime trees), some of the fruit of which he very kindly presented to me, and for which I gave him a rupee, which perchance would purchase some food from a passing pilgrim. He could scarcely speak, but I understood from him that he had occupied that hole for eighteen years, during which time he had never been further from it than a few yards to tend his nimboo trees. These ascetics as a rule are absolutely ignorant, and can neither read nor write. Some of the Bawas, however, are intelligent and educated. I was once passing through these jungles by a short cut from Junaghud to Bhilka, on the other extremity of the Girnar group. The distance was 14 miles, seven of which I was enabled to ride, as far as a large temple on a bit of flat ground, where I was given to understand I could leave my horse with the presiding Bawa until my return. On arriving at the temple I met the Bawa in his garden. He was a fine-looking man, naked except for a loin cloth, but well fed and prosperous. I spoke to him in Hindustani, saying, I understood that he was the "Great Bawa." "Nay, Sahib," he replied, "It is true I am a Bawa, but the Great Bawa lives above," pointing upwards. I felt rebuked. He talked with me a little while very interestingly about the mountains, gave me directions for my seven-mile walk through the jungle, then took charge of my horse and led him to a stable. On my return the following evening I found the horse well fed and groomed, and the Bawa offered me chowpatties (bread) and milk, and would accept no remuneration.

Now to return to the summit after this digression. From the Amba Mater there is a short descent to the foot of the great peak called Gurocknath. This peak is approached by a very steep, narrow pathway, and is about 300 feet higher. On the topmost point is an ancient little temple with shrines, and the residence of attendant priests. The place is very holy. From this point, 3,200 feet above the plains, can be seen on a fine moist day an immense panorama. The sea, which is sixty miles to the south, looks like a silver sheet at our feet. The distant hills of Junaghud, Chomardi, Palitana, Otium, and others, 40 to 60 miles off, seem to dot the plain below, while the great arteries of the Bhadur, Ojut, Shetrunji, and other rivers can be traced from source to mouth.

The next highest peak, Datathria, which is two-pointed, and also crowned with temples, is no more than a rifle shot distant, but it takes a long and hard day's climb to reach it, as to do so it is necessary first to descend about 1,000 feet, and then climb the same distance, through almost impassable jungle and huge rocks, there being no pathway. The last and furthest peak is called the Kalika Ma (Mother of Death), and is very rarely visited by pilgrims, as it would take some days to accomplish the journey there and back. It is said to be haunted or inhabited by people called Aghôris, who live upon human flesh, and that those who venture on the journey rarely if ever return.

Blaikie, who, as I stated, was State Engineer at Junaghud, rode over to Dhoragee to arrange for our visit, and returned the following day. A Durbar carriage arrived in the evening for the ladies. Phillips and I rode. The distance to Junaghud was twenty miles across country by native cart tracks, no roads having yet been made, and the journey was a somewhat rough one for the heavy Durbar carriage, as the streams *en route* had to be forded; but a relay of horses were posted half-way. There was no bungalow or rest house at Junaghud for European visitors, and so our quarters were arranged over one of the city gateways. One large room, for sitting and dining, with a smaller one for the ladies, while Phillips, Blaikie, and I slept on the verandah, a portion of which had been curtained off. And there was a spacious terrace on which there were several easy chairs.

The Durbar, as is customary, made all arrangements for our ascent of the mountain. A number of coolies started with tiffin baskets and other necessaries at 4 a.m., and we all followed (except Mrs. Phillips), at 7 a.m. It was three miles to the foot of the mountain, and this distance we rode by a very beautiful pathway, passing for the first mile through the city and round the fortifications of the Upar-Khot, a great stronghold of ancient times. Then we entered the boundary of the sacred mountain, and followed a lovely paved pathway for about a quarter of a mile by a rushing and rocky stream. Here we stopped to inspect the famous Asoka stone covered with edicts of King Asoka (75 B.C.). It is a hugh granite boulder about 12 feet high and 30 feet in circumference, closely covered with inscriptions cut in the stone, all of which have been deciphered. They are all laws for the good governance of the country and people.

After leaving the Asoka Stone we proceeded across a very ancient stone bridge, and followed the pilgrims' track on the opposite side till we arrived at the Damodhar Kund;

where is a little village of temples on either side of the sacred stream, over which a bund is built forming a large basin of clear water. This is the great burning ghăt and bathing ground. Dead bodies are almost constantly being cremated here, after being bathed in the sacred tank. Those who can afford the expense bring their dying from immense distances for this double ceremony, believing in its efficacy for assuring the speedy entrance of the spirit of the dead into Paradise. From the Damodhar Kūnd it was nearly two miles to the foot of the ascent by a broad pathway through dense jungle, in which teak and bamboo and huge bhir trees form very varying and delightful scenery, enhanced by the mountains towering on either side and magnificent views of the Girnar itself. About half-way we stopped at the monkey grove, a great jungle of huge trees with temples beneath them, and here were hundreds of monkeys, huge fellows, who came bounding towards us in a very friendly way. Pilgrims always feed these monkeys, and can procure grain for the purpose from the Bawa, who lives on the spot. These animals, although apparently tame enough, will not permit strangers to touch them, and are inclined to become dangerous if over much meddled with.

Soon after the monkey grove was passed, we reached the foot of the ascent, where we found our servants and four dhoolies with bearers awaiting us. The dhooly is simply an ordinary chair with arms, to which are fastened a couple of stout poles. Two bearers called dhooly wallahs take hold of the poles in front and two behind, and the passenger sits on the chair. The dhooly wallahs each carry a long stick shod with iron in one hand, while the other is thrown over the pole which rests on his shoulder. The stick helps to support and balance them over rough or uneven ground. The ascent made in this way is, of course, very comfortable and easy for ladies, or those who are unable to climb on foot. Phillips and I, scorning such a mode of conveyance, started on foot, and commenced by making the common mistake of going too fast. We were very soon pumped and obliged to rest, and the dhoolies overtaking us, we got chaffed by the occupants. We had no intention, however, of being beaten, and now followed the example of the numerous pilgrims who were going up with us, and who we remarked took the business in a particularly easy and eisurely manner.

THE DAMODHUR KHUND.

(*See page* 130.)

The ascent occupied nearly three hours, and there were six or eight little rest houses *en route*. These are diminutive rooms with a stone seat outside. Phillips and I were young and strong, and I recollect that on reaching each rest house we lit pipes, and sometimes indulged in a drink, which a coolie carried for our delectation.

The views from the pathway increased in magnificence as we ascended, and the huge eagles soared high over the valleys, or were seen resting in their dark recesses in the great precipices above us. Some time before we reached the first summit the sun had risen around the eastern side of the mountain, and the heat was great where no shade was available. We were not sorry to reach our resting place, and to find that breakfast was waiting us in the cool cloisters.

After a hearty meal in picnic fashion, we proceeded to explore some of the temples, but there is a considerable monotony about them; we had to put our feet, with or without shoes, into slippers, and they being either too big or too little, our progression was neither graceful nor comfortable. The idol is usually seated with hands in lap, garlanded with flowers, and not infrequently decorated with jewels. No visitor can approach near enough to touch it. The Holy of Holies is railed off, and the presiding priest or Bawa alone goes inside. Chanting and bell ringing, or some mummering, is all that goes on. The devotees worship outside the railing, on their knees or flat on their faces. The ladies were too exhausted to ascend any further on this occasion, so we provided a place for them to lie down and rest, and Phillips and I went up to the Amba Mater and Bairau Jāp, already mentioned.

Then we had a picnic lunch, and about 3 p.m. left for our return, Phillips and I again on foot. It takes much less time naturally going down, but it is much harder on the legs, and ours ached for days after the unusual exercise. We reached Junaghud about 6 o'clock, and found Mrs. Phillips very glad to see us. She had been a good deal alarmed about the goings on of a pet monkey and a panther cub of Blaikie's, both of whom persisted in inviting her to take part in their gambols.

Religious fanaticism is very prevalent in the province, and I have noticed many queer instances of the extent to which it is carried—or rather was, for I believe it is not indulged in so much now that education and civilisation are spreading over the country.

By the roadways, or near towns and villages where the population is numerous, the religious fanatic may be daily seen. In one instance the devotee has taken a vow to lie nearly naked for so many hours each day on a bed of spikes. Another may be seen suspended by his feet to the branch of a tree while he sways backwards and forwards over a slow fire which his head almost touches each time. A third has taken a vow to stand on his feet for so many years, and is permitted no assistance beyond a rope tied between two posts on which he may lean. In front of him may be seen a stand on which is a vessel containing a plant, the sacred Tulsi, and the sacred fire. Attendants are near to minister to his bodily needs. I knew one of these fanatics when he commenced the observance of his vow—a fine healthy young fellow—I saw him eight years after, little more than a skeleton, still leaning on his rope, 'a miserable and emaciated spectacle, but in the eyes of his brotherhood and religionists in general, a saint ripe for Paradise. He had two years still to stand—his vow being for ten. Another vow taken is to stand on the head for a term of years. The devotee is fixed in an inverted position, out of which he cannot move. It must be a fearfully painful experience, especially in the beginning, but the man never shrinks. At Rosibunder, near Jamnugger, I saw one of these devotees who had just completed his fourteen years ordeal. He was a mere skeleton with a skin on, but the most remarkable thing about him was the enormous extent to which his hair had grown. When rolled up on his emaciated head it was in bulk larger than the wretched body, and when laid out measured fourteen feet in length. He was lying on a scented bed of silks with high caste attendants in waiting upon him, and was held in veneration as a saint of extreme holiness.

There are many other forms of self-mutilation or torture. One is to tie up an arm in a vertical position until it gets fixed, and gradually withers up. Nothing can be more hideous than the withered limb sticking straight up above the head.

Another horrible performance is passing a large iron hook through the loin, by which the body is suspended from the branch of a tree, while the admiring and faithful sit around in adoration of so holy a man.

The Shetrunji hill near Palitana is another of the famous places of pilgrimage. The mountain, which is an isolated one, stands about 2,000 feet high, and its summit is crowded with a city of temples sacred to the Jains.

APPROACH TO SHETRUNJI HILL, WITH PILGRIMS.

(*See page* 133.)

The City of Temples, Shetrunji Hill.

(*See page* 133.)

A Fakir on the Road to the Girnar.

Tomb of Mahomedan, Priest showing Child's Cots.

(*See page* 133.)

The summit is approached by a paved footpath about three miles in length, with occasional rest houses and tanks for the accommodation of pilgrims or visitors. The ascent is easy and open until within a quarter of a mile of the summit, when the path suddenly curves and winds along a precipice amidst luxuriant tropical vegetation, and the first view of the city of temples is very imposing.

The enclosure is entered through a small gateway in the enclosing wall to a large open court, from which the streets of temples diverge. A silent and solemn feeling pervades the place, all is apparently without life, and one feels shut out from the world. The temples, which are built for the most part close together, at the private cost of devout pilgrims, or Jain residents of Palitana or elsewhere, present a modern appearance, all being kept up and maintained at great expense. The gods are usually depicted seated cross-legged under their canopies, and many are of gigantic proportions. They are made of white marble, or cement plaster, and enamelled to represent white marble—and many of them are decorated with costly gems.

There is a considerable monotony about them, all being fashioned for the most part from the same model, but some of the structures are huge, with their towering pinnacles a hundred feet high.

Over the gateway is a small room with verandah, reserved for the use of visitors other than Hindus, where refreshment may be taken, but this must be carried with one, as no cooking of food is permitted on the hill—within the sacred enclosure.

Outside the enclosing wall a pathway runs, giving fine views of the country and plains, and this leads to (among others) an interesting tomb of a great Mahomedan priest, within an iron rail or enclosure. Here may be seen hundreds, or thousands rather, of diminutive children's cots, or swinging cradles. A current belief exists that if a childless wife performs a pilgrimage to this shrine, and presents a child's cot, she will forthwith bear a son.

The old Chief of Palitana was a good friend of ours, and we frequently enjoyed his hospitality in a fine garden bungalow he had erected specially for his European visitors. He was a racing man, and a well known breeder of horses. He died twenty years ago, and his two sons, also friends of ours, have followed him. The State is now under charge of the Political Agency.

CHAPTER XI.

NOTES FROM MY DIARY OF 1876.

During the latter part of 1875 I was again a grass widower, and obtained leave of absence for a few days to spend the Christmas holidays at Khangaum with my brother, sister, and her husband. Some years previously my brother had started a firm in Bombay, under the title of T. R. Booth and Co., with branches at Khangaum and Oomrawattee, and carried on business as cotton merchants.

My brother lived and attended to the head office at Bombay, whilst my brother-in-law, Kleinknecht, lived with his wife, my sister, at Khangaum, where they possessed a fine bungalow, and where Kleinknecht was the boss of the place. I had not yet been there, and was looking forward to a pleasant holiday. I left Rajkote on the 20th of December and stayed with my brother for a day and night at his bungalow on Malabar Hill. We met a number of old friends at the Apollo Bunder in the evening, and the following day we left by G.I.P. Railway, having with us as travelling companions Dr. Fraser, of Bandora, and Dickson, another old Bombay friend.

We arrived at Khangaum at noon on the 23rd, met Theodore and my youngest brother George at the station, and walked up to the bungalow, where my sister was waiting to receive us. The bungalow was very luxurious and comfortable, with its long wide verandah filled with easy chairs, large open rooms, nice gardens, yards, ponies for riding and driving, and withal, a regular home welcome, which was very enjoyable. After a late breakfast we visited the club in its fine gardens, all designed and carried out by Kleinknecht. Then to the presses, and about the station. In the evening we played tennis, badminton, and billiards at the club, and met all the other European residents, some of whom dined with us afterwards.

On Christmas Day we were a family party. The following six days were a round of walking, riding, and shooting excursions, sketching, etc., and one evening the whole camp dined at the Club, at a dinner given to Kleinkneckt, by the members, and we kept the fun rolling till well into the small hours.

On the 2nd January I left for Bombay, dined with Tom the following day at Byculla Club. On the 4th, dined again at the Club with Tom, Sedgwick and Macnaghten, and left on the 5th, for Kathiawar, after a most pleasant holiday. Arrived at Wudhwan on the 6th, and dined with Hancock and Humphrey at the refreshment room. Got letter from the wife, all well. Colonel Wodehouse was now A.P.A. at Wudhwan, and I had work going on there, and at surrounding localities—Boika, Limri, Drangadra, etc., and I was building a bridged road between Wudhwan City and Limri. Another old friend, Robert Beadle, was a permanent resident at Wudhwan, as representative of Gaddum and Co., of Bombay, in the cotton business, and I saw much of him on my frequent visits to the neighbourhood at this period.

A proposal was made at this time to build a bridge over the Bogava at Wudhwan civil station, and I had a gang of men employed making trial borings in the sandy bed. On the 18th of January this work was finished, with the result that I was obliged to recommend an iron screw pile bridge, as pumping water through 18 feet of saturated and loose sand, which would be necessary to obtain a foundation for masonry, would be tedious and very expensive.

On the 20th, I left for Muli and Choteela. Met Colonel Baird taking levels along the road line. Stayed at Dholia the night, and on to Choteela on the 21st. Met Phillips with his squadron from Rajkote. Found the east pier of Sanganee bridge undermined, and had to make immediate arrangements for closing the road over it and having the contractor down for repairs. The bridging of the road on to Rajkote was under weigh, and during the following two days I was on inspection. I did a good deal of sketching in those days, principally pencil.

On the 24th I came into Rajkote and dined at the Macnaghtens, where I met the Le Fevres, Singletons, and Barrens, and next morning to the School of Industry with Colonel Law and Edward Candy, dined at Mess, and walked afterwards with Colonel Battye, C.O. My big brown horse, Bilkha, laid up again with cracked heels.

On the 29th, to Jetpur, driving Captain Candy's mules to Gondal, rode Bilkha to Virpur, and Piebald on to Jetpur. All works on bridge going on satisfactorily. Letters from P.A. (Mr. Peile) and Stace, latter coming here on the 4th.

The country is full of kullum; I knocked over six with one shot this morning.

5th.—Busy with Stace on town works and inspection, letters from wife; Thornton arrived, and left for Rajkote.

11th.—Finished two sketches in water colours, sent off design for Wudhwan bridge to Manning. Gorawalla and Hubbah very sick with bronchitis, had to send to Gondal for medicine; Nisson of the Gaekwar Sowars arrived, and stayed the day with me.

14th.—Left for Porebunder road works. Stopped at Opleeta in the old palace overhanging the river bed, and very nearly fell out. I was stepping back to view a sketch when I came against one of the arcade pillars, which saved me; six inches one side or the other would have sent me 50 feet on to the rocks. Rode on to Gunod, and slept in a small temple. Suckia, the butler, had all comfortably arranged.

18th.—On to Kuntiana, a Mahomedan town, where my camp was pitched and office at work. Letters from Peile, Hancock, Pullan, and Stace. Preparing plans for Captain Mayne's buildings at Amreli. Supply of vegetables, beer and soda water arrived. Busy surveying road line on to Porebunder.

21st.—On to Kundorna, laid out proposed bridge; 24th to Porebunder, put up in old bungalow infested with pigeons and dirt, walked on to the beach, which is a fine one.

22nd.—The Rana Sahib called, on his elephant, a fine old fellow and a real courtier (the Rana I mean) subsequently came Soucar Khamdass, full of complaints against the former, which, of course, did not concern me. Went for a sail on creek in the evening.

23rd.—Returned Rana's visit. Busy till 1st March locating road to Karee, and laying out the bridge over creek, sent office to Jetpur.

March 2nd.—Rode to Junaghud, 40 miles; very hot and tired. Next day I went on to Bilkha, and stayed there for night, on to Kotra inspecting road, stayed in a routi at Kotra, and got turned out at night by black ants in my bed. Shot two snake birds. 5th, to Maneckwarra and dined with the Maynes.

On the 6th, rode to Bogusra, 8 miles, and met Warden. Both of us dined at Maynes that evening. On the 7th, rode to Jetpur, 24 miles. Bridge works progressing well.

Major Warden and Thornton joined my camp on the 10th, and we had many morning shoots, the country abounding with game. I also had our Rajkote boat brought up, and put on the Bhadur, where we had a mile of good boating ground.

(I used to shoot numbers of fine murrel along the weedy banks of the Bhadur. The fish would lie basking almost on the surface, and when approached within 10 or 15 yards, a simple charge of powder discharged at one would cause him to sink stunned to the bottom. An expert diver would then jump in and seize the murrel before he recovered consciousness. I have also frequently killed them with an express bullet or a charge of shot, but they should be very close to the surface for a shot to be successful.)

14th.—Captain and Mrs. Scott arrived from Gondal, dined with me, and we had a jolly evening. Warden had a touch of gout in the knee and Thornton was very shaky. He smokes too many cigarettes.

16th.—Warden and I to shoot to Petereo, 5 hares and 14 brace partridge; Warden's knee better. He rode the Piebald, I Bilkha.

18th.—Warden to Maneckwarra. Hancock arrived.

19th.—Hancock and I to shoot, got a good bag. Home letters.

20th.—Again to shoot round Jetpur gardens; a big bag of hares and partridge. Left in bullock dumney after dinner for Rajkote, arrived at 8 a.m. 21st.

On 30th. left for round of work at Choteela and Wudhwan, stayed for six days at Choteela, busy at Sangani bridge, had much difficulty in making good the scamped work. Macnaghten arrived very tired *en route* to Wudhwan—very sorry they are going away for a time. Leggatt arrived. Going into Rakjote with him to-morrow in mule-cart, met the Singletons, going to Matharan.

10th.—Rajkote. Busy around Civil buildings, and in office, dined at Mess with Dr. Morton, a sort of cousin of mine.

11th.—Busy all day, dined at Mess and left in covered cart for Kuarwa. Rode Bilkha to Bamanbore early morning. For the following ten days I was kept swinging between Wudhwan, Choteela, and Rajkote. On 22nd, I slept through to Gondal at night in a bullock cart, 25 miles, having sent on two horses to ride from thence to Jetpur, where I arrived at 9 a.m. All satisfactory. 11th arch going up.

27th.—To Rajkote, cholera in camp, dined with Ketchens, and went the grand round with him.

May 12th, discovered scamped work on the Beti bridge. Jutha Pancha overseer must be discharged at once. It is a terrible thought that the men I trust to see honest work done in my absence prove such villains.

15th.—Came to Wudhwan yesterday with Morton, and to-day my brother George arrived from Khangaum. He experienced a railway accident near Surat. An engine wheel came off, and nearly upset the train, several passengers injured. Weather fearfully hot. Dined with Beadle.

The following day I drove to Bhoika and back, 60 miles tonga, with three relays of horses, and took George. It was a terrible day of heat, dust and bad tracks, but we had a good supply of nourishment with us, skins of water, etc. Cholera prevalent in most villages.

18th.—George and I to Muli. Shot some black buck en route. 19th.—To Dholia. 20th.—to Choteela. Plan for Wudhwan Bridge. Sangani and Beti bridges now right.

21st.—To Bamonbore, Cholera very bad, 5 deaths this morning.

23rd.—To Rajkote. Dined at Mess.

25th.—Busy at office and station work. Asked the young Nawab of Surat to dinner.

26th.—Letters from the wife. All well, she takes the two girls to the country, leaving boy at a boarding school. Got George to go in for Hindustani under Laljee's tuition. Stayed in Rajkote till 4th, and to Jetpur on June 5th.

7th.—Scott and Humphrey came to Jetpur; dined with us. Arranged for shoot on Monday.

8th.—All four of us for a shoot to Petereo for partridge. Shot 12 brace. Humphrey and I rode, Scott and George rode camel. Caught a lot of fish in the evening.

9th.—Scott and Humphrey to Gondal.

12th.—To Rajkote. Heavy rain clouds, very monsoonish, a few drops of rain fell. Went to an evening entertainment at the Palace. Fine supper and much champagne.

14th.—Bought a bullock shigram to assist me about local works and to travel in at night, and got a fine pair of trotting bhails (bullocks). Left for Palri on inspection. Dined at Mess.

15th.—To Bamonbore. Heavy storm and rain.

16th.—To Choteela. Heavy downpour, rollers at work. Home letters.

19th.—Returned to Bamonbore. Cool after the storm.

20th.—Returned to Rajkote, and met the rain. Had to put self and horse into tapal hut for an hour.

22nd.—Reports of heavy floods in Bhadur and Beti rivers. First day of Gymkhana, rifle and pigeon shooting.

24th.—Got my new pony from Humphrey; very good one. Badminton at Kothie. Busy. Dined at Mess with Morton. Sore boil on knee.

* * * * *

July 1st.—To Bamonbore. Home letters. Fishing.

2nd.—Simpson and Thornton came from Rajkote.

3rd.—Cholera broken out in Choteela. Much want of rain. Farming suspended.

4th.—News from Bhavnagar. Mr. Wait, Assistant Engineer, committed suicide. Rain threatening, high wind, hot and muggy.

July 6th.—Muli. Went, in evening, to visit great Jain temple. Busy all morning road inspection and office.

7th.—To Wudhwan. Dined with Warden at T.B. Tom wired "Coming on Sunday."

8th.—Walked to Wudhwan with Warden; got soaked. Beadle and Thornton joined us at dinner.

10th.—Tom arrived. Warden drove us to Wudhwan.

11th.—Gleig arrived, tiffed with us, all dined with Crawford, A.P.A. Heavy rain.

12th.—Sent off kit early morning, rode to Muli afternoon. Tom on Bilkha, George on the pony, and I on Piebald. Gleig with us, in his cart. He snored much at night.

13th.—All came to Dholia and Gleig on to Choteela. Had a good shoot in afternoon, and dug out some porcupines from the river bank.

15th.—To Choteela. Tom shot a fine bustard on the way. Home letters.

16th.—Bamonbore, good fishing in the evening.

19th.—Last two days at Bamonbore. Got much shooting To Rajkote to-day, heavy rain.

20th.—Gymkhana. Shooting, and camel races. Took Tom to see the lions of Rajkote. Friends to dinner. Tom bought Wait's tonga and ponies to present to me, after using it here.

22nd.—All to Kotaria for quail shoot, killed 53 brace, and some hares and partridges.

27th.—Been in bed with bad boil on leg. Blomfield lanced it yesterday. Tom and George dissipating.

28th.—Heavy flood in Badur, 33 feet. New bridge all right. Another boil on finger. Tom and George shooting, got five florican.

31st.—Round station with Peile, P.A. Settled for a house to be built for me.

August 2nd.—To Jetpur. Tom and I had breakfast at Gondal with the Scotts. Carriage dak all through. Met Staces.

4th.—Tom shooting. I had to go inspecting and am very busy at bridge works. Had fishing in morning.

7th.—To Rajkote. Races. Dined at Mess.

12th.—Tom, Anderson, and I to Rajas Bhid to shoot.

14th.—A large party to Kalifat to shoot, but had bad sport.

Every day, now, is a round of dissipation, being the Parliament week.

19th.—For the past week we had shooting, and dining and fishing, and general dissipation. Tom leaves to-day *en route* for Bombay. To Bamonbore for breakfast, where we met Peile and Percival.

21st.—Yesterday stayed at Bamonbore for shoot. To-day to Choteela.

22nd.—Tom and George to shoot; got two neilghai (blue bull).

23rd.—All to Tonga Hill, two neilghai.

24th.—To Dholia. News by Mr. Harridas that the puggie of karkana was killed, and safe broken open and looted. Must go to Rajkote.

25th.—Arrived Rajkote night.

26th.—Saw Mr. Peile, and did all that I could. The case was this: Some Rs. 7,000 were received from the Treasury on Saturday evening for labourers' wages, but having been sent out too late could not be distributed till Monday morning. The head accountant, instead of returning the money to the Treasury, as he should have done, placed it in the office-safe not a very secure one.

On the next morning—Sunday—at 7 o'clock, Mr. Candy being out for a walk past the School of Industry, saw a man lying against the wall near the gate, the latter open, and a broken iron safe, was on the roadway under the arched entrance, while a number of rupees were scattered about. On inspection he found that the man was the office puggie or watchman, and he was dead, with his skull smashed in. The safe, which was intended to be built into a wall, had its back made only of sheet iron, in which a hole had been broken for the extraction of the money.

The police were called in, and rewards offered for information, with the result that four men were arrested at the instigation of a woman. One was a jeweller and the other three were in his employ. In his confession the jeweller stated that he had information of the money having been put in the safe from one of the office employees. They went to the office at 3 o'clock in the morning, and on the puggie refusing to give up the keys, they killed him with a pickaxe, took the keys from his person, opened the entrance gate and office, dragged the safe to the entrance so as to command a view of the road in case of surprise, and broke it with a pick. As the hole made was not large, and they feared to make more noise; they succeeded only in extracting about half the money.

The jeweller and his men were tried, the former got 10 years, and the latter 7 years with hard labour. They should have been hanged, but the law is full of loopholes. It was agreed that as they went with the intent to steal only, not to murder, they were not guilty of the latter, although they deliberately murdered a Government servant in the discharge of his duty, and defending his charge.

The money was almost all recovered.

28th.—To Muli. Met Macnaghten and Leggatt.

31st.—Two days at Wudhwan. Shooting and feasting for Tom among his friends.

1st September.—Tom and George left for Bombay, George probably for home, as he does not appear to take to business very well. Warden here, and Morton, and Colonel Sturt, the former stays with me.

6th.—Busy at office and work, but get out sometimes with the others, for shooting. Had much ortolan and quail shooting.

7th.—Colonel Baigrie arrived, and lunched with us. Then we all went fishing or rather spearing fine fish in the Bogava, which come up from the Nall at this season. We speared 29, average 3 to 4 lbs. each.

8th.—Baigrie and Morton to Rajkote, I to Boika, put up in a routi, no sheep, took one by force, and had a row.

9th.—To Dhundooka, good bungalow, but dirty town. House and stables full of bugs and ticks.

11th.—Came to Burwalla. Government road to Bhavnagar; all good, barring where there are broken-down bridges.

12th.—To Wullah, nice clean bungalow.

14th.—Spent two days at Wullah with the Thakor, ancient place, and some curiosities. Drove and rode direct to Bhavnagar. Arrived 9 a.m., put up in fine new traveller's bungalow. After breakfast, to call on Sims, Nutt, and Percival, the administrator, who asked us to dinner.

15th.—All about Bhavnagar with Sims. Some fine works and improvements going on. Sims is a good man for this place. Dined at the Nutts. (Major Nutt is tutor to the young Maharajah.) After to Percivals. Rain all evening.

16th.—Badminton at Moti-Bagh. To lunch with Sims. At 2 to billiards with Percival, and dinner at Nutt's.

20th.—Songhudh. Been here three days with the Hunters. Went to shoot this morning, got 20 brace quail, and two florican. On our return had kubber of a panther at Shehore. Went off there after food. Also Nutt, who had just come. Not successful. Sims arrived afternoon, had a smash, pony fell, broke his knees, and he hurt his head.

27th.—Sims came to Chawand with me, then on to Koondla. I to Babra, then to Maneckwarra, and Amreilie. Stayed with Staces. Called on Mayne. Visit works; very busy.

28th.—Busy on works about station with Stace and Mayne; on to Bilkha in the morning, returned 29th; busy all day at office.

30th.—To Jetpur, where I shall make a stay.

2nd October.—Laid out south approach to Bridge; find matters in office very much in arrears; pitched into Surujlall. Grey horse came in from Rajkote looking well; I have five on my hands now. Want to sell tonga and Piebald. Heavy expenses last three months.

4th.—Got the bungalow fitted up with punkahs and furniture, as I will make it a residence on and off till bridge works are over. Rode Grey. Easy action, but shows signs of vicious temper.

5th.—Grey girth-galled again. Letter from Colonel Parr; nice and kind as usual. Approach curve incorrect owing to Lilas's stupidity; must do it over again. Nettle has a sore foot, always in trouble that dog.

15th.—Nelly, favourite dog, got mad to-day, and I had to shoot her.

30th.—Went to Rajkote. Got home letters, all well.

6th November.—Jetpur. Laljee now gives a statement about key of safe, making all Surujlall said false, latter denies. Wrote to Laljee for explanation.

9th.—Letter from Hempchand conveying news of Laljee's death yesterday; very sorry. He was a good lad; I was often strict with him, but it was for his good. Have my doubts about Surujlall, looks like his having given false evidence.

14th.—To Maneckwarra. Met Grant and Mayhew.

15th.—Mayhew and I to Bhilka. Shot a number of green pigeons, fine birds they are.

16th.—Jetpur to-day. M. left this evening.

23rd.—Till now busy at Jetpur. On to Gondal this evening.

24th.—To Rajkote, dined at Macnaghten's.

25th.—Round college with Macnaghten. Dined at Mess. Visited all Civil buildings.

26th.—Met Dr. Bühler.

29th.—Left for Choteela and Wudhwan districts. Foot very painful; Guinea worm forming. It takes a year to develope.

December 10th.—To Broach to see the new Nerbudda Bridge. Put up with Bailey and Hargrave.

12th.—Returned.

13th.—Sims arrived and I invited all the station to meet him.

14th.—Took him to see Wudwhan and the Kari bridges, which he liked much.

18th.—Left with Sims for Rajkote, by easy stages arrived 19th.

20th.—After two days at Rajkote left for Bhavnagar *via* Sirdhar; first day made Sirdhar, 18 miles driving. Following day arrived at Babra, driving and riding. Sims and Grant left in bullock shigram for Bhavnagar after dinner.

The Hunters, who are camped eight miles away, invited me to spend Christmas. Accepted, had a good day's shoot on 26th, and started for Jetpur, 60 miles, arriving following day. Home letters. Howls from Maneckwarra, must go there soon.

31st.—Sunday, the Scott's came and stayed the day, he is not well. Going home, Reeves, to act for him.

January 1st.—Went to Junaghud to Pullan and stayed four days with him, sketching on the mountains, etc., etc.

CHAPTER XII.

OUTLAWRY — DEATH OF CAPTAINS HEBBERT AND LA TOUCHE—LIEUT. GORDON—RAJKOTE JAIL.

I referred under the head of "History of the Rajkumar College to the untoward deaths of Captains Hebbert and La Touche, when engaged in action against the Waghhēr outlaws. This event occurred during the Christmas week in 1867. A large band of outlaws from the State of Oakamundel, under the Baroda Mahals, were at large, and committing various crimes, including murder. For years these outlaws had evaded the police, chiefly no doubt through friends who sheltered them from interest or from fear. Two brothers called Manik were the leaders, and heavy sums were on their heads, dead or alive. Just before Christmas 1867 it was reported to Colonel Anderson that the outlaws had been tracked to a district in the Jamnugger State, and he at once took action to follow them up. Hebbert and La Touche had both left Rajkote with their young wives for the Christmas holidays, and both were immediately recalled. A company of native infantry under Major Bains, another of cavalry under Major Harris, with Captains Hebbert and La Touche, Jemmadar Syed Ulvi, and a party of police formed the force taken by Colonel Anderson. On reaching the locality it was reported that the outlaws had moved to and taken possession of an isolated conical hill called Toba Hill, ten miles further west, and a forced march was ordered, which enabled the pursuers to reach the place a short time before sunset. A hurried disposition was made, as to delay action till darkness set in would enable the outlaws to evacuate. The cavalry were ordered to surround the hill and cut off any trying to escape, Hebbert, La Touche, Bains, and Syed Ulvi, each with a party ot Sepoys, were to scale the hill from different points. This was immediately put into effect. The hill was thickly strewn in parts with large boulders, especially near and on the summit, behind which the bulk of the outlaws had concealed themselves. As the attacking force mounted, Hebbert and La Touche being within view of each other, the latter noticed an outlaw emerge from a boulder behind Captain Hebbert and shoot

Toba Hill,
With Monument recording fight with outlaws, Christmas, 1867, and Cemetery enclosing graves of Captains Hebbert and La Touche and five sepoys.

(*See page* 144.)

him through the back. La Touche rushed to avenge him, fired at and wounded the outlaw, who ran down the hill trying to escape. La Touche, seizing a horse, with sword in hand galloped after the outlaw, who, falling wounded to the ground, waited till LaTouche was close to him and shot him dead. In the meantime the fight was raging on the hill-top, Major Bains got a scalp wound; five Sepoys had been shot down and several of the outlaws killed. The remainder were not all taken. Moola Manik, with three or four others, strangely succeeded in escaping, notwithstanding the exertions of the cavalry. Nine I believe were taken. But the success was dearly bought by the lives of two young and promising officers and five Sepoys. It was a melancholy and sorrowful camp at the village that night. La Touche had been killed instantly, but Hebbert lived till midnight. They were laid together in a rough coffin made of planks found in the native village, and the following morning were buried in a plot of ground temporarily fenced off. Friends in life and comrades in death, only a few hours before full of youth and hopefulness, with their young wives waiting for them at home, and the world before them, they were laid at rest together in that wild and lonely district. Near by, a common grave enclosed the remains of the five Sepoys who fell with them. The prisoner outlaws were hanged the same morning upon the bough of a banyan tree a mile distant. A monumental obelisk was erected on Toba Hill, and tombs placed over the graves, which were duly enclosed.

MIANI OUTLAWS. RAJKOTE JAIL. DEATH OF LIEUT. GORDON.

On December 17th, 1892, the sad death of Lieutenant Gordon, with three Agency Police sowars, occurred at Mararia. A band of Miani outlaws had been committing depredations for several years in the Northern part of the province, and as yet the local authorities had not been able to capture them. Several expeditions had been ordered from Rajkote, formed of cavalry and police with military and civil officers in charge, but without result. These dacoits had so many native friends and supporters and had established such a name of terror amongst the villagers that it was almost impossible to obtain information of their whereabouts, while their movements were so secret and quick that when trustworthy information was received, the nest was usually found empty when the intending captors approached.

Indeed, the terror these bandits inspired was such that when a capture was made of any of the gang, although it was well known that he was a murderer and thief, no witness had the courage to appear against him while any others of the gang were at large, and so the most notorious criminals escaped punishment.

The gang of Mianis above referred to, were one of the worst, and local measures had so completely failed to rid the province of them that Government deputed a special officer for the purpose of hunting them down. With a selected number of sowars from the agency police and durbars, Lieut. Gordon went to work on a system of his own, and in due time he obtained reliable information of their whereabouts. After committing some assaults on villages in the neighbourhood, they had removed themselves to a wild district on the border of the ran some ten miles north of Miani, and Lieutenant Gordon decided that the only way to succeed with them was to hunt them down in the open. It was a risky business, as these men were armed with modern rifles, were well supplied with ammunition, were all good shots, and would fight to the death.

Gordon knew this, but in an interview with the Political Agent before starting, he expressed his determination to run them in, and fight them in the open, as being, in his opinion, the only possible way of ending the trouble.

Captain O'Donnell, Political Assistant at Wudhwan, was directed to concert with Lieut. Gordon, and moved his camp to Miani for the purpose.

Gordon had with him only about twelve mounted sowars, when he heard that the outlaws had encamped on the border of the ran, and he started at once for the locality intimated. It was a wild deserted country, not a vestige of vegetation beyond short grass, but there were abundant places, such as dry watercourses and small hills, which would afford cover for the outlaws, and it was a fearsome work for this small band of Gordon's men hunting for the outlaws, whom they knew were concealed near about, and might fire on them at any moment. At length they noticed, in the midst of a small open plain, a black flag hoisted on a pole about 8 feet high. This appeared to be at the distance of about a mile. No shelter near it, but Gordon felt confident that the outlaws were concealed where that flag was, and although he could not see any sign of them he decided to charge. It was well arranged on the part of the outlaws, as they could only be approached from the open, and would have their enemies exposed to their fire while they lay concealed, and Gordon knew that in charging down on their standard, certain death awaited at any rate a portion of his little force; but he was nothing daunted, and gave the order to charge, himself leading, and in his uniform a conspicuous mark. When within 50 yards of the black flag they were met by a volley of rifle bullets, Gordon himself was shot in three places, one bullet through his forehead must have instantly killed him, while two of the sowars fell mortally wounded. The remaining sowars discharged their carbines on the outlaws before the latter had time to reload, and in a few moments the entire band was destroyed, not one escaping.

Gordon's body was taken to Morvi, and forwarded to Rajkote the following day, where all the residents and crowds of natives awaited its arrival at the little railway station. Sir Charles Ollivant accompanied the procession. On arrival the coffin was first taken to the West Hospital, where it was opened, and Sir Charles cut a lock of hair from the head to be forwarded to his mother. Then after we all took a last look at the face of the brave young fellow we had seen only a few days before in life and strength, the coffin was refastened and the procession moved to the cemetery. There being no chaplain at Rajkote, the service was read by the Political Agent, and the following day, Sunday, a special service and sermon was given by the Rev. R. Scott in the Mission Church, where all attended.

These are sad functions, especially when they occur in a lonely up-country station, and where there are no relatives of the deceased to accompany him to his last resting place.

Subsequently a handsome trophy, in commemoration of Lieut. Gordon and the sepoys who lost their lives on the occasion, was erected in the Memorial Institute Library. This comprised a bust in white marble of Lieut. Gordon surmounting a bas-relief of the engagement and flanked by two figures of Agency sowars, all executed in marble.

Over the tablet and bust was a fine trophy of the arms taken from the outlaws.

A notorious outlaw named Sawani, also of Mallia, was at large for many years, and had successfully evaded the police. He was said to have committed more than one murder, besides many other atrocities, but, although the villagers around dreaded him, they were terrorised into affording him shelter and protection, and it was for long impossible to obtain trustworthy khubber of his whereabouts. Agents employed by the police would send secret information that Sawani was in a certain locality, when it turned out that he was pursuing his vocations in some other part of the province.

On one occasion I had the honour of joining in an amuinsg hunt after this outlaw. Mr. Percy Fitzgerald, son of the late Sir Seymour Fitzgerald, Governor of Bombay, was then Assistant P.A. at Rajkote. He received one Sunday evening secret information that Sawani was in hiding in the Hullenda Bhid, a large tract of grass country 24 miles from Rajkote, and he immediately organised an expedition to the place under cover of the night. As I was well acquainted with the Bhid he asked me to accompany him and Mr. Warden, the Chief of Police: and he arranged with the officer commanding at Rajkote to assist him with 50 men of the cavalry, with a native officer in command. Our horses were despatched after nightfall, with the cavalry to Sirdhar, six miles from the scene of operations, and we followed at midnight in a horse carriage. We stayed at the old Rest House at Sirdhar till dawn, then mounted and started, fully armed. On arrival at the Bhid, the cavalry stretched out in line, 100 yards between each Sowar, and up to midday every corner of that Bhid was searched in vain. We returned to camp chagrined and tired, to learn from another report that the outlaw was seen the previous day 60 miles away in another direction. Some years subsequently Sawani was captured by Mr. F. Soutar, who had lately been appointed chief in command of the Agency Police.

At this time I was engaged on the building of the large district jail at Keatinge Pura. The old jail, as I before mentioned, had been handed over to the military authorities with certain land adjoining, in exchange for the land on which the Memorial Institute had been built, and it had been proposed to construct the new district jail on a piece of ground originally occupied by the Gaekwari lines. Sir Charles Ollivant decided to erect the jail where it now stands near the new Agency Police lines. The site of the Gaekwari lines was in future to be used for Horse Shows and such like.

The then Inspector-General of Prisons, the late Mr. Macartney Filgate, paid annual visits to Rajkote, and I had many consultations with him. He desired the new district jail to be designed and built on the most approved modern lines, and took the keenest interest in examining and conferring with me on the plans, before their submission to Government. The military authorities had also a good deal to say in this special matter, as it was directed that the jail should be designed so that it could be used as a place of refuge and defence for the station inhabitants in the event of trouble, such as mutiny, etc. The outer boundary walls were to be built of massive masonry with rows of loop holes, and at each corner of the square towers were to be erected and fitted for carrying guns to command each side of the enclosure. The jail was designed on the circular and radiating principle. I recollect meeting the Commanders-in-chief, Sir George Greaves and Sir George White, in inspection of the defences when they visited Rajkote. Subsequently when the Jamnugger Railway was projected, and laid out to run within a short distance of the jail, there was an outcry from the military authorities of the Station, which led to further visits and much correspondence and eventual removal of the proposed railway embankment some hundred yards further away. Well, in time all was settled satisfactorily, and the jail was built and occupied, and approved by the Inspector-General and Government, and a water supply from the Randerda was laid on to it and the Police lines in 1898.

CHAPTER XIII.

VISIT TO THE HARBOURS OF THE WEST AND SOUTH COASTS, 1884.

I think it was during the cold season of '84 my duty led me to visit the different harbours of the province. These are for the most part open roadsteads for all boats—other than small pattiamas or cotton boats, which trade with Bombay and Karachi, Zanzibar, etc., and are from 50 to 200 tons burthen.

The most northern port on the Gulf of Kutch is Joria, a considerable trading centre with a regular ferry over the Gulf (which is here narrow) to Kutch. No large seagoing boats can approach Joria. Next is the harbour of Rosi, belonging to Jamnugger, where a weekly steamer of 500 tons register called, but she lay eight miles from the port proper (Bori Bunder) of Jamnugger, which is a pretty large trading centre, with a well-made pier and landing stage, almost dry however at low water, and to which only 80 to 100 ton pattiamas can approach.

My friends the McClellands lived near Bori Bunder, and I stayed with them while waiting for the arrival of the s.s. *Arrow*, Captain Baker, as it was my intention to go to one or two of the south ports, especially Porebunder and Mangrol, to consult with him about lighthouses, etc.

I joined the *Arrow* by means of a small steam launch at midnight, and at dawn we left Rosibunder, as owing to the sand banks which it was necessary to thread our way through, daylight was needed. By mid-day we anchored off Mangrol, on the Kutch coast, where an iron pier and breakwater had been long under construction by the Rao Sahib of Kutch, and was under charge of Mr. McClelland. Here a south-west wind blew, and the little steamer rolled and pitched so horribly that I felt ill all day. The boat, too, was crowded with pilgrims on their way to Dwarka and the discomfort was indescribable. To go down to the stifling cabin was impossible, so I was obliged to make the best of a very nasty

LIGHTHOUSE AT POREBUNDER, BUILT 1886.
(*See page* 151.)

business. The Captain came on board at evening. He was a big, brawny half-caste, a very good fellow, and he shared his little deck cabin with me. After starting we experienced some improvement, as it was cooler; but the pilgrims and their wives and children were either eating or ill, and they were all jabbering and howling. Early the following morning we lay off Dwarka for two hours while the pilgrims were mostly sent ashore in boats. There is a very famous temple here which is annually visited by thousands of devout Hindus, but we were not able to land owing to the rough sea, and started onward to Porebunder, which we reached at midnight. This is, or used to be, one of the largest of the south ports, and five-hundred-ton boats could berth in fair weather within a quarter of a mile of the town, but owing to the want of a good lighthouse in a proper position, it was always dangerous of navigation. The old harbour of Porebunder lay inside a creek divided from the open sea by a sand spit about half a mile in length, but the creek was rock-bound at its mouth, so that even small coasting vessels could enter it only at full tide.

The old lighthouse then existing was a makeshift sort of lantern fixed on an old tower on the city wall, but it was not visible at any great distance, and was useless as a guide to large boats entering the bay, in the central approach to which is a large submerged rock.

Here I remained two days with Captain Baker, and had many consultations with him. Having fixed the position of the rock we decided on the site for a new lighthouse, which when taken from seaward on a line with the southernmost end of the Burdah hills would command a safe entry into the bay at any state of the tide. This, with other suggestions I made regarding the removal of the old city wall on the sea face, and construction of a sea wall, and wide road in lieu of it, completed my work at Porebunder. My report to the Political Agency on all was approved, and the new lighthouse and all the improvements I suggested were carried out within the next two years at the Durbar expense—under the direction of Mr. (now Sir Francis) Lely, the newly appointed administrator at Porebunder.

Our next stop was off Verawul, belonging to the Nawab Sahib of Junaghud, the premier Chief of the Province. Here was a small masonry pier and lighthouse, for the use of the usual coasting craft, of which a very large number traded with Verawul during the fair season, but owing to the violence of the Monsoon and the hot season winds—the port was usually closed from May to September, and all boats moved to a place of safety.

In 1866, when the late General Keatinge was Political Agent of the Province, an engineer, Mr. Scott, was appointed with the view of making improvements to the so-called harbour.

Mr. Scott made various plans and proposals for extensive additions to the pier, with scouring channels, etc., but the proposals were not accepted, and since that date I do not think anything has been done; and it is questionable whether anything could be done which would pay for any great expense. Steamers lie off about two miles in the open, but they can only be approached during the fair season.

The next harbour visited was Mangrol. Here we lay off the little bunder, and went ashore to visit the young Chief, a Rajkumar boy.

The landing stage was simply a flat reef of limestone rock running out from the sandy shore. At full tide the reef was covered, so the loading and unloading of the pattiamas which came alongside had to be done between tides. It was a primitive little bunder, and the heavy monsoon seas were reducing its extent annually. The reef was cracked in many directions, and without tying it together or securing it in some form it was not likely to last many years. I recollect often visiting Mangrol and advising the Chief, but he was not a wealthy man, and did not see his way (no doubt rightly) to spend money on what was after all more or less a doubtful experiment.

At Mangrol I left the steamer, my horse and kit meeting me there, and proceeded to Jafferabad.

The town of Jafferabad is situated some miles up an estuary or creek navigable for small trading boats of 100 to 200 tons, and a considerable amount of trade is carried on. It is a safe harbour of refuge during the monsoon. From here I was anxious to visit the newly proposed harbour, to be called Port Albert Victor, 10 miles up a large navigable creek in the State of Bhavnagar. This was only on an invitation from my friend Proctor-Sims, as I had then no charge in that part of the province.

As there was no practicable road, and the country was covered with rugged limestone, rendering it very difficult to ride, much less to convey camp kit, I decided to make the journey to Albert Victor by sea, and engaged a pattiama sailing boat for the voyage. This boat was about 60 tons, and had nothing in her but some tons of stone ballast. She had a huge raking mast and mainsail, and looked a lively enough customer. I got provisions for a few days on board, and took with me Javerchand, my head draughtsman, a cook, butler, and puttywalla. We started at midnight by moonlight with a light wind, which soon carried us out of the creek, and in the open sea there was a steady wind, which carried us pretty rapidly, so that by midday we arrived off the island of Beyt, some five miles from the mouth of the estuary. Here we met with disappointment; the wind increased and blew directly from the land, so that we could not make the mouth, and we lay off in a choppy rolling sea all day, under a broiling sun. Things did not improve with nightfall, and the lascar in charge said it would be impossible under existing conditions to make the creek. As we could not tell how long it would be before the wind favoured us, and our provisions and water were running short, with no means of replenishing either on that wild coast, and no means of approaching the land anywhere, we decided to return to Jafferabad.

The return voyage, with a side land wind, was a very unpleasant experience. The huge empty boat under its powerful sail rolled tremendously; poor Javerchand and the cook prayed incessantly, and gave themselves up for lost. Indeed, I was not sorry to find ourselves, the following afternoon, inside the Jafferabad creek in safety and comfort.

One other harbour on the south coast—viz., Dieu—I had previously visited, having been sent there in connection with the settlement of a boundary dispute.

The Island of Dieu, eight miles by about two, is the only remaining possession of the Portuguese in Kathiawar, who formerly ruled over the entire province.

The Governor of Dieu is a Portuguese, direct from Portugal, but he was the only European there—except his private secretary.

His officers and police are all natives of India, and the population now is chiefly Hindu and some Mohammedan.

The fortress of Dieu was once one of the strongest in that part of India, and it was very interesting to visit. It stands immediately overhanging the sea, and on its other side is surrounded by a deep fosse or ditch cut out of the solid rock and spanned by drawbridges, now mouldering in decay. Above the fosse the battlements are of great strength, built of limestone, and innumerable old cannon with their carriages rotting are seen in every direction. I was taken over the arsenal, a very weird place, full of thousands of ancient Portuguese weapons, which took part in old days in many a bloody fight, huge piles of stone cannon balls, from 3 to 9 in. in diameter, occupied positions in the arsenal, and had evidently not been moved for near a century. The armour, swords, guns, flint locks, shields, etc., crowded the walls, in a state of rust and decay, but these are all kept as relics of the old days, and not one of them could be removed. I was presented with a couple of stone balls, but no weapons.

I camped on the mainland, and on the following day, being Sunday, a gaily appointed barge was sent to take me to the island to visit the Governor. On arrival I was escorted by his bodyguard to the Residency, a plain, comfortable house, and shown in to the sitting-room. Presently His Excellency came and spoke very cordially in French, to which I replied in English or Hindustani, I forget which. Then he tried Portuguese, equally in vain. Then we walked round the hall, saw the pictures, etc., until his private secretary arrived, who acted as interpreter, after which we got along very well, and I rather enjoyed my visit. He placed his fine barge at my disposal, and sent me a supply of fruit.

During my three or four days' duty here I visited every part of the island. It was formerly a place of great importance, and presented a somewhat European appearance, chiefly due to the number of old Roman Catholic chapels to be met with, most of them now used for other purposes than worship—one is a hospital, another, I think, a jail. The roads were well walled and laid out, and it was curious to see effigies of the Virgin Mary and some Hindu god side by side, with many crosses and decorations.

Dieu trades a good deal with Madagascar, and is famous for white and red wines, Tinto and Pinto, some of which I carried away with me.

The boundary dispute was surveyed and settled in a few days, and I have never visited old Dieu again. It possesses an excellent creek, well sheltered, and fairly large sailing craft can use it in all weathers.

CHAPTER XIV.

1878.—COMPLETION OF KEATINGE BRIDGE—CHOLERA AND FAMINE—FURLOUGH—VISIT ROME, NAPLES, AND PARIS EN ROUTE.

During the year 1878 cholera was very prevalent in the Province. I had a large number of workmen engaged in the construction of the Keatinge Bogava bridge, which was commenced early the preceding year, and I hoped to have it completed and be able to take my promised leave home in March. The epidemic was, however, so severe that the labourers ran away, and for two months the work was nearly at a standstill. However, by the end of April the bridge was completed and opened, and I obtained my leave, but instead of six months I got only four, and Mr. McClelland, who had just been appointed Engineer to the State of Jamnugger, acted for me.

On board the P. and O. steamer at Bombay I met two friends, Wyer and Bryce, who were also going home, and we settled to make the journey together, visiting Naples and Rome *en route*. The passage in the Indian Ocean was somewhat rough, being the monsoon season, and in the Red Sea it was grilling. Wyer possessed a magnificent voice, and he improvised concerts on deck nearly every evening. It was a great treat to listen to his songs, and many others took part. The journey overland from Suez to Alexandria was as usual dusty and hot, and we were glad to find ourselves on board a fresh steamer in the Mediterranean with cool breezes and fine weather before us. Three days took us to Brindisi, where we landed with a handbag each, and sent the heavy luggage on to Southampton by boat.

We left about midday by train for Naples, and arrived about ten o'clock that night. The passage through the mountains and on to Naples was delightful, and the country was looking its best in its summer clothing, with vineyards and olive groves, cascades and mountains, rivers and precipices, light, shade, colour, and everything needed to make a charming variety of pictures. Long before reaching Naples we passed the remains of some of the ancient aqueducts, and Vesuvius looked very grand. We could not hear the noise of the eruption then going on, but every few minutes a shaft of flame shot up, apparently some hundreds of feet from the crater, and we felt that we were fortunate in the time of our proposed visit.

On arrival at Naples we went to one of the large hotels opposite the gardens. Although it was not then the season there was a sprinkling of English and Americans. And the gardens which extended all along the sea front were a blaze of light, with numbers of people sitting out; while the band played and refreshments were served.

We were speedily sitting down to an excellent dinner in the hotel, which we ate to the strains of a musical trio who stationed themselves at the open window, and very delightful it all was, music and supper. After restoring the inner man, we adjourned to the gardens for coffee and cigars. The whole scene, as I recollect it, was like fairyland. The hanging lights and fanciful booths and tents; the trees and shrubs and gardens and pretty forms flitting and moving about; flower girls gracefully presenting their bouquets, and all enjoyed to the strains of music. It was fully 2 a.m. before the Neapolitans left the gardens, and we remained to the last.

At about six next morning I was up. The excitement of the journey and all we had passed through the previous day, with the brilliant light of the summer morning coming into my bedroom, drove sleep away. I got up, dressed, and went in search of someone to give me tea or coffee, but it was labour in vain. The hotel was open, and some attendants or waiters were asleep in the hall; but to rouse anybody at that hour was an impossibility, so I went out. I remember it struck me as very strange that anybody could remain in bed on such a glorious morning, but so it was. The town, the gardens, every place was completely destitute of life. I wandered about the empty streets for two hours without seeing a sign of life except two dogs.

My friends did not appear till breakfast at nine o'clock, and then, after a smoke, we hired a trap and went out sightseeing. I recollect visiting the shops, where an enormous collection of coral, red, white, and pink, was displayed for sale either in its native condition or worked into ornaments. Then there were curiosities in mosaic and marble and inlaid work. We visited the Museum, where we saw very wonderful things—models of Pompeii and the treasures found there, which were being constantly sent to Naples from the excavations then proceeding. But a great deal of our time was occupied in the picture galleries, where are innumerable works of the old masters, and where we sawmany artists copying them. There was a room devoted only to holding the copies, and we were pestered by artists of all sizes and ages. They even followed us in the evening to the hotel, and offered their paintings at such ridiculously small prices that both Bryce and I were induced to become purchasers. For a small sum I procured a Madonna and Child after Raphael and a Magdalene, both life half-portraits, a Cenci, and two other small pictures. The smallest of the lot would be deemed cheap in England for the money.

In the evening we went to the Opera. The following day was devoted to visiting the San Martini and various other famous places. After dinner and a little recreation in the gardens we started at 11 p.m. for Vesuvius. We fortunately had a covered carriage and four horses, for it rained steadily till dawn, when we arrived at the foot of the mountain, and transferred our persons from the carriage to the backs of ponies, which were to convey us over some three miles to the commencement of the cone. This distance lay over great beds ot lava, which looked like a huge wilderness of twisted tree-trunks, burnt and black. At the foot of the great cone of sand and ashes we dismounted, and found a number of guides collected to assist us in climbing to the summit. These men were each provided with a staff and a large iron hook with a handle. This implement we were supposed to hook on to a guide's belt, and, holding on to the handle, allow ourselves to be thus pulled up. However, we gave great offence by scorning any such assistance, and our ignorance of the language doubtless assisted us to keep our tempers, for from their demeanour, the remarks of the guides were evidently anything but courteous. We took one man with us to show us the path and carry our breakfast. Soon after sunrise we reached the edge of the great crater.

It is not easy to give a correct idea in writing of the scene from the edge of that crater. Imagine a great basin, say, 1,500 feet long by 500 feet wide, with vertical sides 25 to 30 feet deep. At one end of this was then the living crater, in the form of an inverted basin some hundreds of feet in diameter. The surface of the cone, which sloped up from the edge to the centre, was black cinders, with great radiating open cracks, showing the fire beneath, intersecting it from the edges to the centre, where was the mouth of a great pit or furnace of living fire, from which every few minutes, preceded by a rattle from the bowels of the earth like thousands of artillery, was vomited some 300 feet into the air hundreds of tons of red-hot lava and cinders, which fell on and rolled down the sides of the cone. The vertical sides of the great crater were smoking hot with sulphur and lava; everything around was hot and sulphurous.

We sat for a while on the upper edge, where we roasted eggs for our breakfast in the hot sand. Then I went down into the crater and up to the edge of the living cone, and gathered some specimens to take away as mementoes of the most awesome and singular sight I ever experienced.

Our return was a very speedy journey compared with our coming up. We simply precipitated ourselves down the side of the huge cone of ashes and sand, every leap sending us 30 or 40 feet. After the descent we proceeded at once to Pompeii, which we reached about 2 p.m.

This is another place which must be seen to be understood. The excavations of this buried city are now very much more advanced than they were in those days, but there was sufficient then for all intents and purposes. A small fee had to be paid for permission to enter. Near the entrance was a room used to contain any treasures pending their conveyance to the Naples Museum. Here, as in Naples, we saw models of some of the bodies which were discovered. These are obtained as follows: When, in excavating, the workmen come across a cavity which appears to have once contained a human form, the space is carefully filled in with a preparation of liquid lime, which is allowed to harden before the surrounding material is taken away. By this means very perfect models are obtained. The Museum is rich with beautiful specimens of the pottery and metal vases and utensils which have been recovered—some of them scarcely injured after being buried under ashes for 1,400 years.

The streets of Pompeii are usually very narrow, and those I saw were paved with stone, while along the centre were more or less deep ruts formed by the passage of wheeled vehicles. The ruins of the great amphitheatre for games were in very complete preservation, and on the walls of many public and private buildings frescoes were still decipherable. The frescoes, however, which are best worth retaining are sent to the Naples Museum. They were doubtless originally beautiful works of art, as were also their house decorations, mosaics, etc. On the pavement in front of one of the residences is the picture of a dog with "Cave Canem" beautifully worked in mosaic.

It was late in the afternoon when we completed our inspections of these wonderful remains, and again the rain came down in torrents. It was fortunate that we saved a little of our breakfast, for there was no refreshment to be had, and it would be two hours till a train left for Naples; this time we passed in a very poorly furnished waiting-room. We eventually arrived at Naples for a late dinner, very pleased with our excursion and all we saw, but very hungry and very tired.

The following day we left for Rome, arriving there early in the afternoon. At the station at Rome an annoying, although somewhat amusing, incident occurred. Along with our small amount of luggage, I had forwarded in the van a wooden case containing my specimens and curios, lava, marble, sulphur, etc., which I had collected at Naples.

Wyer was proceeding direct to London, and Bryce went to see him off, leaving me to get the luggage cleared. I passed into the large shed reserved for such purposes, but found considerable suspicion exercised over my wooden case, so much so that the railway officials present would not permit me or it to leave the premises, and I was locked up with my luggage after the other passengers had left. After some delay the officer returned with an interpreter in uniform. I assured him that the case contained nothing dangerous or illegal, but all in vain. He stormed and gesticulated, and ordered his men to break open the box, which was securely nailed down and corded. This was a job none of them appeared eager to do; evidently they suspected it to contain infernal machines. Seeing their hesitation, and unwilling to be delayed longer, I commenced to open the box myself, and then the interpreter assisted me. When the cover was at length removed the first thing visible was a soiled flannel shirt, under which appeared a quantity of stones and lumps of sulphur, etc. The disgust and chagrin expressed on the countenances of the officials was, to say the least, remarkable. With a very bad grace they helped me to patch up the box, and made a hurried departure.

Bryce was a collector of carpets, curios, and pictures, while Wyer cared very little for any of the three. In comparison, I liked them all in a more or less moderate degree, and was glad to have Bryce's company alone for a few days at Rome. That evening we visited the gardens and took life easily. But the following day we were up betimes, and made a day of seeing the churches. Indeed, there is not much of the ancient architecture of Rome left. A few churches, the Forum, some triumphal arches, the baths in partial ruin, the Colosseum, the pagan tombs, and the catacombs and aqueducts, all of which we saw.

Of course, the first church we visited was St. Peter's, the great dome of which is sixty feet higher than St. Paul's in London, and is somewhat dwarfed by the great flight of steps leading to the Grecian pedimental entrance, and thereby something of its grandeur is lost. This is a great and wonderful structure, but it would occupy too much space in these reminiscences to attempt any lengthy description, even if at this space of time I could attempt it. Besides, people must see Rome to appreciate it. It will be sufficient to give just a few figures. It is the largest church in the world, and perhaps the most imposing and beautiful in its interior. It covers 3½ acres of ground, being twice the area of St. Paul's in London, and 1½ times as large as the Milan Cathedral. The height ot the dome from the ground to the summit of the cross is 435 feet, and its width 138 feet. The total length of the structure is 700 feet, and width of transept 450 feet.

Under the centre of the dome stands a magnificent bronze canopy, supported on four gilt spiral columns, and 95 feet high. Under this canopy is the high altar where the Pope only reads Mass on high festivals. The canopy stands over the tomb of St. Peter. Near is a bronze statute of St. Peter, standing on a pedestal about 5 feet high. One toe, which projects from the top of the pedestal, is kissed by each person entering the chapel, and as it usually gets a wipe of the sleeve before operating with the lips, it is brilliantly polished.

The interior of the dome is covered with marble mosaic, and around it are carved galleries, which possess peculiar acoustic affects. On the upper part of the dome are seen figures worked in mosaic of the twelve Apostles. Viewed from the floor of the church these look the size of ordinary men, and very beautiful paintings. But, to give some idea of their actual size, the pen which St. Peter holds in his hand is over 12 feet in length. We ascended the dome to the copper ball, which is large enough to hold half a dozen people. The interior of the church is viewed from here, but the view from the dome externally is not remarkable.

We next visited the Vatican Palace, also the largest in the world, as well as the most magnificent. The statuary, frescoes, paintings, and mosaics are amongst the finest ever produced.

Another church I recollect we visited was the Santo Stefano Rotundo, the largest circular church in existence, and called the Church of the Martyrs. The interior walls are covered with life-size paintings representing the most horrible scenes of martyrdom.

We spent three very delightful days at Rome; it was far too short, but we were both tied to time and wanted to get home.

From Rome we travelled direct to Paris *via* Bâle. I think the journey occupied two days and a night. We engaged a coupée, and were most comfortable. I recollect drawing up to a pretty station just as we felt a good breakfast would be welcome, and seeing a number of tables covered with white cloths and attended by smartly dressed girls, with trays of smoking hot beefsteaks and other eatables, yards of bread, and flasks of wine. Having secured a plentiful supply for a few francs, we took the viands into our carriage and then enjoyed one of the best breakfasts I ever ate. We arrived at Paris in the evening, and put up at the Hotel d'Albion. It was the year of the Paris Exhibition, and the city was very full. I forget how we passed our first evening, or night rather, but I think we did no more than take a ramble through the brilliantly lighted streets and cafés. The following day we spent some hours in the Exhibition, visited the Louvre and some other famous galleries, took a trip down the river, saw the Notre Dame and some other churches, visited the Morgue, etc., and in the evening went to the Opera.

The next day we left early for Calais, and arrived in London about 7 p.m.

I had a few hours business to attend to in London, which detained me till the following evening, when I left by the Scotch express, and arrived at Bridge-of-Allan about 10 a.m. the next day, where I found the wife and the three bairns waiting for me on the station platform.

They had taken a nice house for a month's change in that bracing and delightful locality, and we all thoroughly enjoyed our stay, making visits to the Scotch lakes and surrounding interesting places. It was a great treat to me, the fishing and wandering all together in the woods and the delightful weather we enjoyed all the month we stayed at Bridge-of-Allan.

On the completion of our stay there, we returned to Edinburgh, where we had taken temporary rooms, as it was our intention to leave Dick at Dr. Bryce's school, and the two girls with Mrs. Hill, at her school in Chalmers Street. This was all arranged principally through the good offices of my wife's old friend, Miss Robertson, of the Grange, of whom we saw a good deal. I also here met Dr. Duff, of Calcutta fame, and several other old acquaintances of my wife's when she was a child.

We parted from the children one night early in November, and took train to London, embarking thence in the s.s. *Hibernia*, on board of which we found several Indian friends, amongst them the Rev. Dr. and Mrs. Beattie, of the Irish Presbyterian Mission at Ahmedabad.

We had an excellent passage, except crossing the Bay of Biscay, where a storm had just been, and the ship rolled tremendously in the heavy seas. I did a good deal of sketching on my way out, to add to my collection, which we now find on our retirement to be so great a pleasure to have about us.

ALA KACHAR CHELA, C.S.I., CHIEF OF JUSDAN.

(*See page* 16.)

Picnic Bungalow, Randerda.

(*See page* 163.)

CHAPTER XV.

WATER STORAGE, 1867 to 1891—JUSDAN AND VICTORIA JUBILEE WATERWORKS.

The first Chief who personally took an interest in water storage was the late Chief of Jusdan, the head of the Kathie Clan of that part of the province. I was invited by him, in 1867, to visit Jusdan and give my opinion on some projects he was considering. He sent a four-wheeled bullock shigram for me to Rajkote, in which my bed was made, while another cart carried my kit and servants. We travelled through at night, reaching Jusdan early in the morning, and found a comfortable tent ready for my occupation. After exchanging visits and riding round the city with the Chief, we left in the afternoon on horseback for Hingulghudh, his hill fortress, some 20 miles distant, near which, in the valley, we halted at a fine garden of fruit trees and flowers, in the centre of which stood a handsome summer residence, fully furnished in a luxurious manner. Here I found my servants and belongings and dinner awaiting me. The Chief with his mounted escort proceeded to the fortress, about a mile distant. Having bathed and dined I took a stroll round my new residence. The garden was a square block of land containing about 10 acres, laid out in a series of parallel walks with others radiating from the centre. Every part of the garden was planted in evergreens and many kinds of fruit trees, such as mangoes, oranges, peaches, plantains, figs, etc., while the rich foliage of the bhir tree with its aerial roots hanging from its wide extending branches provided great masses of shade. Cocoa-nut and several other palms waved their graceful fan-like leaves, making a rustling music with the slightest wind. Along the borders of the walks were thousands of roses, the old pink "Edward" predominating. The garden-house stood in the exact centre of the quadrangle, and immediately around the building were masonry tanks filled with running water supplied from wells. The house was small, consisting of one large room, with four small corner rooms on the lower floor and two upper rooms, all subtended by wide verandahs; it was a quiet, dreamy place, conducive to rest and ease and sleep. The only movement or sound being the whispering of the wind through the foliage, and the monotonous creaking and singing of the koss as it drew water from the well near by. The air, too, was fragrant with the heavy scent of the mango and orange blossoms, roses, etc.

Early in the morning a fine Kathie horse, with attendant sowars, was awaiting me in front of the house, and I was speedily cantering to Hingulghudh. The fortress, which in old Kathie fighting days was doubtless a formidable one, occupied the summit of a conical hill, about 300 ft. above the plain, or rather undulating ground, upon which the village was built. The only approach to it was on foot, by a circuitous and in some parts very steep pathway. The walls were very thick, and every angle was protected by bastioned towers, loopholed. The entrance was through a small archway of great thickness, and a powerful door of teak, studded with steel spikes.

Inside was a considerable courtyard, around which stood the Durbar buildings and living apartments. These were extensive; several thousand men could be accommodated, and no doubt often had been in times of trouble, and there was storage room for a large force. Every part of this hill and valley was commanded from the battlements which were of unusual strength, and were maintained in perfect repair. Although, indeed, it was not at all likely that the fortress would ever again be used for warlike purposes, it was evident that the Chief and head of the Kachar Clan and representative of a long line of fighting ancestors took a very natural pride in maintaining it as of old.

A principal object of my visit to Hingulghudh was for consultation as to the best means of providing a supply of water for this fortress. Hitherto it had to be carried by hand from the valley and kept in cisterns; a work of great labour and expense, rendered all the more difficult owing to the fact of water in the immediate neighbourhood being very scarce, except during the rainy season. Wells had been sunk, but they were not satisfactory nearer than the gardens, a mile distant, and to pump water from such a distance, and to such a height, would mean a heavy recurring expense.

The Chief's idea was to dam a small valley near the foot of the hill, so as to retain the monsoon flood water, and after examination it was decided to do this and to establish force pumps worked by animal or manual labour to send the water to the top of the hill. Owing to the limited gathering ground and porous nature of the valley (being all stratified limestone) the project was not a very great success for all the year round, but I am particular in referring to it, as it was the first water supply scheme I was connected with, and it was the forerunner of many to follow. The Chief Alakachar was the head of the great Kachar Clan, and at the time was one of the most intelligent and go-ahead rulers in the province. His State was a pattern of good management and sound, pure government, and the Bombay Government on more than one occasion recognised his value by conferring on him much coveted honours.

He could not speak English, and my acquaintance with the vernacular was at that time very slight, but with the aid of an interpreter we contrived to get along. He was keen to obtain knowledge of every kind. He accompanied me regularly when taking levels and sections, and learned to use the instrument himself. When I went out sketching he would ask for paper, pencil, and colours, and work away too, and after a time he got to be fairly expert. During all my residence of thirty-three years in Kathiawar, Alakachar remained one of our best friends.

Two lakes which I designed for him were the first irrigational works in the province, and have proved to this day remunerative and successful. The first lake was in a rocky valley, formed by damming a mountain stream, and the water was conveyed by means of an open aqueduct nearly three miles to the fields to be irrigated. Although the fair weather supply was little more than sufficient to make up for natural evaporation and percolation, the water impounded during the rains proved sufficient to irrigate some 200 acres of cereal crops during the cold season, and paid a good return on the outlay. Since those days the Chief of Jusdan has carried out several other projects for irrigation and town supply.

VICTORIA JUBILEE WATER WORKS, 1887–91.

Up to 1887, however, practically little else was done in the way of storing water supply, notwithstanding various attempts made from time to time in that direction. It was in 1875, I think, that, in conjunction with the late Chief Karbarrie of Rajkote, I surveyed and put forward a proposal for bunding the Randerda Valley, as an irrigation scheme for the Rajkote State, and the then Thakor Sahib Bawajee was favourably inclined to it. But, owing to the advice he received from certain officers, whose opinions he asked for, the project was shelved. This scheme I estimated to cost Rs. 40,000, and I did my utmost, as also did Mr. Motichand, the State Karbarrie, to get it sanctioned, feeling confident that it would be not only a paying concern for the State, but a valuable standby in event of a bad rainfall or famine year. But we were powerless. Government would not interfere or give encouragement, and the Durbar without political support feared to undertake so great an outlay. So we saw no option but to bide our time and hope for some other chance of again putting the scheme forward. This happily occurred in the year of Her Majesty's Jubilee of 1887.

To commemorate this event the Chiefs of Kathiawar, with their usual loyalty and public spiritedness, decided to vote a sum of money to commemorate the Jubilee, and various suggestions were put forward as to the best means of carrying it out.

The then Political Agent, Colonel W. Watson, and I were both at home on furlough. And during our absence the Acting Political Agent, Colonel Wodehouse, proposed and got approved the erection of a public museum and hall at Rajkote, to be called the Victoria Jubilee Hall and Museum, and he commissioned Mr. Chisholm, a well-known Bombay architect, to prepare designs for the building. On my return at the end of 1887 I found his design approved, a site selected, and arrangements made for a foundation stone ceremony, which actually took place, and the work was handed over to me to be carried out. The design originally supplied by Mr. Chisholm would no doubt have answered the purpose well enough, but as the estimate was much above the funds at disposal he was called upon to reduce it, and in doing so the design was made entirely unsuitable, and the estimate still exceeded the funds available. On my representing this to Colonel Wodehouse, operations were ordered to be discontinued pending further consideration. Very fortunately at this juncture Colonel Watson returned from furlough, and took over charge of the Agency, and I had then the opportunity I awaited to put forward my proposal for a water supply. In this I was happily assisted by the fact that the season was an exceptionally bad one, the previous year's rainfall having been below the average. Many wells had run dry, and the water prospects for the approaching dry weather had become alarming. No man knew Kathiawar and its necessities better than Colonel

RANDERDA DAM, LOWER FACE.

(*See page* 167.)

Watson, and he was a safe man to guide the ship in a contingency such as this. The State Karbarries also had been at heart adverse to the hall and museum project, and were far better pleased to back up that for a water supply to Rajkote if such promised to be a sound scheme.

The project I had to put forward, and which I had carefully resurveyed, was the original scheme for bunding the Randerda Valley, and I found that a lake there would provide a sufficient head for supplying the entire military cantonment and the Civil Station.

Colonel Watson applied to the Bombay Government to send an expert water engineer to examine and report on my plans and proposals, and in due course this officer, Mr. Doig, M.I.C.E., arrived, and after an exhaustive examination he reported the project to be a sound and suitable one. The chief engineer, Mr. T. D. Little, confirmed Mr. Doig's report, and so the matter was settled.

It was not, however, until November, 1889 that the works were commenced, owing to delay caused by awaiting sanction of the Bombay Government and the submission of elaborate plans and estimates called for by the P.W.D. Also it was found that the money subscribed would not be sufficient, and Government was asked to supplement it from local funds. The Civil Station of Rajkote further contributed Rs. 50,000 towards the project, so the entire amount provided amounted to about two lacs, £20,000.

It was during the operations connected with the furtherance of this project that the sad death of Colonel Watson occurred. He had been in ill-health since his return from England, and of late had lived to some extent in retirement, except so far as his official duties were concerned. On the morning of March 25th, 1889, when his servant went to call him he found he was dead in his bed.

Mr. (now Sir) F. S. P. Lely, C.S., was now appointed Acting Political Agent, and to his endeavours was due the obtaining of Government sanction for the water works project, which arrived in November, 1889. Two months after the commencement of the works, Lord Reay, Governor of Bombay, visited Kathiawar and met me at Randerda, when I explained all the proposals to him.

The works were completed in 1891, and much rejoicings were in the camp when the first water supply was laid on. The formal opening, however, did not take place until August 2nd, 1892, of which the following is the official account :—

OPENING OF THE VICTORIA JUBILEE WATER WORKS, RAJKOTE.

Sir Charles Ollivant, I.C.S., K.C.I.E., the Political Agent in Kathiawar, performed yesterday the opening ceremony of the Victoria Jubilee Water Works, Rajkote, in presence of a large and distinguished assemblage. Some of the Chiefs, representatives of Chiefs, and officials had specially come down for the purpose. On an extensive piece of ground on the border of the lake four shamianas were pitched for the accommodation of those assembled, and the locality was splendidly decorated, the letters V.I.R., with a fountain playing close by, giving it additional effect. Sir Charles arrived at 5.30 and was received by the members of the water committee headed by the chairman, Rao Bahadur Kesharao Bhaskerjee. After all had taken their seats the Rao Bahadur stepped forward and thus addressed those assembled :—

> "Sir Charles Ollivant, Your Highness, Chiefs, and Representatives, Ladies and Gentlemen.—In thanking you heartily for kindly responding to the invitation of the Victoria Jubilee Water Works Committee to witness the interesting opening ceremony of this day I deem it proper on behalf of the members of the Committee, to give a short history of the origin of this most useful and philanthropic scheme, and to lay before you some of the main points in connection with the Randerda lake, upon the resources of which the success of the scheme depends. Within the recollection of all those who have honoured this assemblage with their presence the celebration of the Jubilee of the happy and eventful reign of Her Most Gracious Majesty our benign Queen of England and Empress of India must be quite fresh. To perpetuate that memorable epoch the Princes and Chiefs of this ancient and historic Peninsula in 1887, resolved to erect a building at Rajkote to be styled the Victoria Jubilee Hall and Museum, and in furtherance of that aim they, with their usual liberality, subscribed to a fund which amounted to the handsome figure of Rs. 1,60,000. The foundations of the institute were laid soon after. Circumstances since then changed. The rainfall in 1888 was not as it should have been, and the water supply for the requirements of the first British Station in Kathiawar began to fail, threatening serious consequences. The attention of the Station

authorities was drawn to organising plans to avert a dire calamity. The then Political Agent, the late lamented Colonel J. W. Watson, with his usual foresight, lost no time in bringing this important subject of water supply to the notice of the Princes and Chiefs of the Province, and suggested that a considerable portion of the funds already raised by them should be appropriated for the laudable and philanthropic object of saving the population and cattle of the Station from a water famine. To the great credit of the Princes and Chiefs the hint thrown out was at once accepted by them. It was not strange that this should be so, since in every native State, from time immemorial, the charitable and religious acts of the reigning chiefs and charitably disposed private individuals consisted principally in making ample provision for drinkable water for wayfarers, pilgrims, cattle, etc., by sinking wells, constructing tanks and water troughs, along roadsides and at places much frequented by such persons and cattle. The Station water supply was one of such acts. They were fully aware that Her Most Gracious Majesty the Queen-Empress took a keen interest in all works of charity and public utility, and that their diverting a portion of their funds from the object for which it was originally intended to the water supply project would meet with unqualified approval. In November, 1888, they unanimously consented to make an allotment of the large sum of Rs. 1,60,000. This sum, however, was not deemed sufficient successfully to carry out the water scheme, so in August 1889, at the suggestion of the Political Agent, the Princes and Chiefs supplemented the grant by a further allotment of Rs. 50,000. The sum of Rs. 1,36,000 so liberally voted by the Princes and Chiefs was also found insufficient, so the Civil Station Committee came forward, under the advice of the then Acting Political Agent, Mr. Lely, to give its helping hand, as the scheme was of an immense value to the station, and voted the sum of Rs. 50,000 from the surplus balance of the funds which Government placed at their disposal. The total capital devoted to these works amounted to Rs.1,86,000, which has enabled our experienced Agency Engineer, Mr. Booth, with the full concurrence of Government, to undertake the work and bring it to its present state of completion. The station has thus had conferred upon it the boon of a copious supply of excellent fresh water at the very doors of its numerous inhabitants. Although the Princes and Chiefs have, with their characteristic good sense and liberality, allotted the magnificent sum of Rs. 1,36,000 out of Rs. 1,60,000 collected for the construction of a Hall and Museum to an object of vital importance they have not lost sight of the usefulness of having a Hall and Museum at Rajkote. The site selected for storage of water for the waterworks is the fine lake we now see before us. The valley which is now turned into a lake has been kept in sight by Mr. Booth for some years, and he has been but waiting a favourable opportunity to give effect to his project. The Jubilee of the reign of Our August Sovereign Lady has furnished the golden opportunity at last, and the valley is now a beautiful lake. The following few details relating to the lake will no doubt be found interesting. The bed of the lake is the same level as the highest point of the Rajkote Civil Station. The catchment area is about 7 square miles in extent. There are three dams which have impounded the valley water: (*a*) The main dam is about 1,600 ft. long, and 37 ft. at its greatest height; (*b*) the middle dam, which is also a weir dam, is about 400 ft. long and 35½ ft. high; (*c*) the weir dam is about 350 ft. long and 35 ft. high. The maximum height of the water in the lake, therefore, will be 35 ft. The area of the lake at 35 ft. is about 1,867,700 sq. yds. or something less than a square mile. The capacity of the lake when water is 25 ft. above the lowest inlet pipe which is 10 ft. above the bed, is about 4,340,000 cub. yds. or 117,180,000 cub. ft. or 732,375,000 gallons. The daily supply to Rajkote is about 250,000 gallons. The decrease by evaporation and other natural causes will be about 7½ ft. in the year. The average rainfall at Rajkote for 25 years is 26½ in. The average rainfall on the Randerda gathering ground last year was 18 in. The cost of the lake is Rs. 1,26,000. The cost of pipe service is Rs. 60,000. The length of the pipes laid is 7 miles. These are the works which, in Rajkote, will commemorate Her Majesty's Jubilee, and which we beg that your Highness, on behalf of the contributors, will invite the Political Agent to inaugurate this day."

This done, H.H. the Thakor Sahib of Morvi expressed, on behalf of his brother chiefs who contributed to the Victoria Jubilee Water Works, the pleasure and satisfaction

Main Dam, Randerda Lake, Rajkote, 1890.

(See page 170.)

they all felt in learning that the works were completed, and, to show their gratification, called for three cheers for Her Most Gracious Majesty the Queen-Empress. The cheers were vigorously responded to by all respectfully standing. The Thakor Sahib then requested Sir Charles to declare the works open.

Sir Charles, in addressing their Highnesses, Talukdars, Representatives, Ladies, and Gentlemen, observed that it was with many feelings of misgiving that he first learned that it was their intention to ask him to take a leading part in the ceremony; and he trusted that no deficiency of speech would lead them to the wrong conclusion that he undervalued the importance of the occasion or their kindness in asking him to open the works. Notwithstanding those misgivings, upon further consideration he could not but feel that there was something appropriate in asking him to take a leading part in the ceremony, because in his official capacity he was an humble representative of His Excellency the Governor of Bombay; and therefore it seemed that there was no other fitting person than him in Rajkote to acknowledge their kindness in thus bringing to a close a beneficient work which happily commemorated a beneficient reign. (Loud and prolonged cheers.) There were two other reasons which gave him gratification to accept their invitation. One he would immediately allude to, and the other he asked to be allowed to defer until in accordance with their request he had formally opened the work. The first of these was, it afforded him intense gratification to have been the means of expressing to the Chiefs of Kathiawar the appreciation of the Rajkote Civil Station for giving them this magnificent work. It was not this alone, Sir Charles observed, that deserved to be remembered on the present occasion. In running over some notes he found that during the last twenty years the Chiefs of Kathiawar gave something like half a lac a year in connection with the Civil Station of Rajkote. (Applause.) His Highness the Jam Sahib had given them the Clock Tower and the Utara, H.H. the Nawab of Junaghud had given them the Alfred High School, and only a year ago a reservoir in connection with this lake; H.H. the Maharajah of Bhavnagar, whose never-ending beneficence was well known, gave one wing of the Rajkumar College. He gave the Aji Bridge and many other things in Rajkote, which commemorated his generosity; H.H. the Raj Sahib of Dhrangadra gave the Dhurmsala. Besides those mentioned by him there was much which he could not enumerate in detail; but he must say that collectively the Chiefs, high and small, had given them a great many things not only in Rajkote, but throughout the length and breadth of Kathiawar.

Sir Charles then proceeded to turn the silver key. On declaring the work open amidst cheers, he returned to his seat, and observed that, as he had alluded to their graceful tribute of respect to Her Majesty and had expressed his recognition of the generosity of the Chiefs of Kathiawar, he wished to say a few words as to those who were engaged in the works. First of all, he, an utter stranger, should mention with admiration and respect the name of Colonel Watson, the historian of Kathiawar, to whom they owed the undertaking, and (feelingly observed Sir Charles) that it would have given him immense pleasure to have seen him present on the occasion to take the place he now occupied. How pleased he and his family would have been to see the magnificent work completed! He, however, begged all not to forget what was done by Colonel Watson; though the waterworks had been constructed to commemorate the reign of Her Majesty, the idea of a museum was not lost sight of. That museum would perpetuate Colonel Watson's name, for Colonel Watson was a profound antiquarian, and his researches were immense.

Sir Charles then referred to one who had taken a leading part in the waterworks from the day of their construction up to the day of their completion, the Agency Engineer, Mr. Booth. (Cheers.) Sir Charles, who had in a previous state of existence something to do with waterworks and other similar undertakings, said without hesitation that it was work which reflected credit upon any engineer. He spoke not only of the engineering ability in the construction of the works, but also of the firm courage which induced Mr. Booth to go on. He went on on the conviction that the works would prove successful, and they have fulfilled his most sanguine expectations. The works were a very fitting crowning to the twenty-six years' work which Mr. Booth had done in Kathiawar.

(FROM AN OCCASIONAL LADY CORRESPONDENT.)

The account given by our local newspaper and copied into the Bombay papers omits so many of the most interesting parts of our gala day on the 8th, that I think a short further description will not be out of place.

BAHADUR KHANJI RESERVOIR, RAJKOTE, 1890.

RANDERDA LAKE.
(*See page* 173.)

Fortunately the day was one of the most lovely of the season, calm, and cloudy enough, with just sufficient sunshine to make everything look its best. A wet or stormy day would have ruined all the decorations.

The ceremony at the Randerda Lake took place on a promontory, to reach which all had to leave their carriages and walk across the large bund, which is more than a quarter of a mile long, and has handsome parapets, and a little castellated tower, on which the Union Jack was hoisted.

On the promontory a large shamiana was pitched, and other tents for band and refreshments, etc. The shamiana was seated for about 400; at the upper end was a dais, and down the centre and up to the water's edge stretched a beautiful line of gardens, with concealed fountains, and at the end of all the letters "V.I.R.," six feet high, picked out with white pebbles on a sloping bank of grass surrounded with ferns, grasses, and shrubs. At the rear of the shamiana was a huge tower, all covered with greenery, and with castellated battlements, from which flew a large flag, with "Victoria Jubilee Waterworks" in white on a red ground, and on the various hills and crags which bound the lower end of the lake were placed other flags suitable to the different native castes, while half-way up the lake, on a promontory overhanging the water, our picnic bungalow stood out in fine relief, and the thousands of people who attended from the city and elsewhere in their many-coloured dresses gave additional brightness to the whole.

At half-past five the Political Agent, accompanied by some of the principal Chiefs, arrived, and took his seat on the dais. Then an address was read by a native gentleman on the part of the Water Works Committee, after which H.H. the Thakor Sahib of Morvi requested the Political Agent to open the Waterworks. Sir Charles Ollivant then made a very eloquent speech, thanking and congratulating the Chiefs for their magnificent present to the Station, and for all that they had done of a similar kind for the province. Then he turned the key, a bar of solid silver, with two handles, all beautifully chased, and immediately the fountains played, and water spouted in thousands of jets from the "V.I.R." Sir Charles then returned to the dais, and presented Mr. Booth with a gold cloth bag, containing a handsome present, accompanied by an illuminated paper, from the Chiefs of the Province, commemorating his twenty-six years of service.

After cheers were given for everyone, the ceremony closed, and the multitude wandered about the grounds for a little while; but as the dinner at the Residency was to be at 8 o'clock, we were soon on our way back to Rajkote.

The dinner table at the Residency (at which, owing to illness and absence of several, only about 30 guests sat down) was decorated in a novel and appropriate manner. Four fountains, placed down the centre, played into miniature lakes, with a running stream connecting them; within the lakes were grottos and islands, constructed of masses of agate spar and crystals, with ferns and palms growing among them. The beds of the lakes and river were sparkling white and coloured sand and shells, and the banks were of grass. The table was intended to be a surprise, and I think it was a very agreeable one; the supply of water and its egress were concealed, and everything was quite perfect, although at first sight it looked as if it might prove dangerous to the ladies dresses. At dessert the Chiefs of Morvi and Limri and some others joined us, and the first toast was "Her Imperial Majesty Queen Victoria," then the "Chiefs of Kathiwar," in proposing which Sir Charles made a most interesting speech. This was briefly responded to by the Thakor Sahib of Limri. Then the Political Agent proposed the health of Mr. Booth, and said many kind and humorous things about engineering in general, and referred to two other engineers present, Mr. Proctor-Sims and Mr. White, and others he had occasion to work with, and told us some amusing stories about their peculiarities, one of these in which I think he said Mr. Booth excelled was a partiality for elastic bands, in preference to red-tape! but he liked their profession best of all. He also thanked certain ladies for the assistance they had given him in the preparations.

Mr. Booth responded in a short speech, in which he thanked all for their kind congratulations, the Chiefs for their testimonial of his connection with Kathiawar, which he would always prize more than anything, and Sir Charles Ollivant for his kindness and the honour he had done him.

After dinner there was a reception, at which a large number of native gentlemen attended.

* * * * *

Although, as I said, nothing worth mention in the way of storage for irrigation was done previous to 1867, a fine lake had been formed at Bhavnagar, but it was chiefly for ornamental purposes. This lake was subsequently utilised by Mr. Proctor-Sims (who raised and strengthened the dam) for providing a supply of drinking water for the city.

During the 'eighties some water storage was undertaken in the Gondal State, but it was principally for securing a supply for cattle during the dry season.

A large proportion of Kathiawar does not lend itself by its natural conformation to the creation of large storage reservoirs. Towards the north it is too flat; and here for the most part the water supply must always depend on rivers and wells. And in other parts, where the conformation is more favourable, it is not often feasible to find a site for a storage reservoir where the gathering ground is not too restricted to provide a supply which will last during the hot season, when it is most needed, or where it would command a tract of land suitable for irrigation; and sometimes money which could be applied to a better purpose may be expended on storage works which cannot prove remunerative.

CHAPTER XVI

MONSOON—ITS BLESSING AND EVILS—PRODUCTS AND INDUSTRIES, ETC.

The monsoon is usually ushered in by more or less violent storms. The hot season commences about the 1st April and goes on increasing in intensity till the first fall of rain, which is due about the 20th of June. The nights during this period are a relief from the days, which from 9 a.m. to 6 p.m. are intensely hot, with a burning dry and piercing wind from the south-west. Bungalow windows and doors are closed by 9 o'clock, and punkahs and grass tatties employed. The latter are made of a scented grass, and are placed in a doorway on the windy side, and kept constantly watered. The hot wind passing through the tatties gives a very refreshing coolness to the interior, but a too near and constant use of them sometimes causes fever. During this season the country gets dried up, the grass withers to the roots, except where irrigation can be employed, and there is little green to be seen except trees, such as bhir and pepul, which, through some blessed dispensation of Providence, throw out their richest and greenest shade at this season, thereby affording shelter at least for the half-starved cattle. During this season also the sowing of the monsoon crops is put through, so that the seed is ready for the first and eagerly looked for rainfall, which, if it comes in proper time, causes a marvellous and instantaneous transformation—the grass shoots up so quickly that in a few hours the whole face of the earth is green. The young crops as if by magic are seen overground. The air becomes fresh, cool, and sweet, and all life is in motion, but there is too often another and sadder side to the picture, which means famine, loss, and desolation.

Once I recollect being at Wudhwan, on my way to headquarters, when I experienced one of the heaviest breaks of monsoon I have known. The day had been unusually sultry and hot, with a steely suffocating feeling in the air, and we knew that something unprecedented was on the way. I was staying in the travellers' bungalow, where, on the arrival of the Bombay train, I was joined by a Col. M., *en*

SANDSTORM AT WUDHWAN.

(*See page* 177.)

route to join his regiment at Rajkote. About 4 o'clock we were startled by an unusual sound towards the south-west—and on looking out noticed a tremendous sandstorm rapidly approaching. It was a literal bank of sand, some hundreds of feet high by apparently miles in length, tearing across the open plain and impelled by the strong south-west wind. Before it rolled, devils (so-called) composed of dry bordi, a thorny scrub used for hedging, and anything else picked up, with rubbish of every kind. It was black at its base, and cast a heavy shadow as it rolled along, sweeping and upsetting everything in its course. We rushed inside and secured the doors and windows, none too soon. In a few moments it was on us, and for the space of ten minutes we were in darkness. When the monstrous thing had passed, the scene of destruction outside was appalling—hedgerows and trees had been uprooted, carried away or spread piecemeal, many houses were roofless; but in the native bazaar the greatest loss occurred, where the shopfolk had their wares exposed in the open.

Very soon after this visitation the wind fell, and the rain came down in sheets for about one hour. We dined that night with the Assistant Political Agent and his wife, but the muggy heat was overpowering, even in the open.

Col. M. and I started in a couple of bullock shigrams at midnight, and reached Choteela, 35 miles, early the following morning. Here we rested for the forenoon, and started for Bamonbore on horseback in the afternoon. By the time half the distance was covered we saw that we were in for another bad break. The sky towards the south-west became black, and speedily worked up towards us, and we could already see the forked lightning shooting in zigzag streaks. All was deathly still. Not wishing to be caught in such a storm as we knew was approaching, we galloped all we knew, and just reached shelter in time. The Bamonbore bungalow occupied the summit of a small hill overlooking the village, and was entirely exposed. My servant had arrived earlier, and had food ready for us.

For the following hour I never experienced anything equal to the grandeur and violence of that storm. Before the rain began to fall we were in utter darkness, which was every instant brilliantly lit up by flashes of lighting. The forks of flame seemed to strike the ground close to us, and every flash was accompanied by an instantaneous roll of thunder which seemed to shake the very hills.

Col. M. was a nervous man, and called to me to follow his example, which was to sit in a chair and constantly carry it with him from place to place. I don't recollect whether I did it or not, but I was nervous enough too.

Towards the end of the pandemonium, a great succession of shouting and howling was heard on the road below, and on making enquiry we learnt that the villagers were carrying home some men who had been struck by lightning. On going to the village we were told that eight shepherds who were on their way home with their flocks when the storm came on took shelter under a Kakra tree: that seven of them were struck by lightning, and the one who had escaped rushed to the village for help. The seven men had now been brought in. Six of them had been killed instantly, and the seventh was unconscious—he died before morning.

Before we left the following day we went to the river bed to view the obsequies. The poor fellows were laid together on the shingle. Some were half sitting up, some had a leg or an arm raised, just as they had been when struck dead; there were no marks on the bodies. A number of men were collecting firewood to make a common pile, while two groups, one of women and one of men, the mourners, sat apart with their heads covered.

Another instance of an exceptionally severe break of the monsoon occurred at Virawal on the 1st May, 1892, although this, in fact, could scarcely be called a monsoon break; it was too early, but nevertheless very unusual on that account.

We were staying with some friends, who occupied the rest house near the shore, half a mile from the city. My two daughters were in tents, and another group of my office tents stood near by. The storm set in about 3 a.m., and until 10 o'clock it simply raged. The tents were levelled in a few minutes after the wind reached its height, and it was fortunate we had the bungalow for refuge, but the loss of boats on that occasion was very severe. Such a storm was not expected then, and the cotton boats had not been sent to their monsoon quarters. Many lay near the bunder, and many were anchored half a mile out; some empty and some laden with cotton going out, and some with sugar or other incoming goods. We watched several of these boats dragging their anchors, and presently they were driven on shore close to us, where they were smashed like matchwood. I do not recollect if any lives were lost, but I think not, as those men can swim like fish.

At the harbour at least a score of fine trading craft were thrown on the rocks, some with huge rents in their sides, while the rocks were strewn with wreckage and cotton, cargoes of rice, sugar, ghee, and other valuable property, which had been lost in the sea, and hundreds of men and women were at work for days salving what they could.

When the monsoon has set in properly the season is delightful, all nature starts into life. While in Europe it takes months for flower seeds to germinate and bloom, there it seems to be only days. The gardens are soon gorgeous with every kind of bloom, and one can stay in the open nearly all the day with comfort.

It is a country of marvellous changes. There is a set-off, however, against the delight of the monsoon climate in the form of the advent of insect life—flies, wasps, flying bugs, blister flies, midges, and mosquitoes now begin to abound. If you lie down during the day your head must needs have a muslin protection, or somebody must fan you to keep off the flies. At dinner, in the evening, the table is infested with flying bugs, which get into the soup and the gravy, or into one's hair or down one's back, and the act of removing one of the insects necessitates an immediate exit from the room. The Spanish fly will take its exercise on the tablecloth, or get under your clothes, where, in all probability you will discover a painful blister the next morning. The incessant and irritating buzz of the mosquitoes is always in evidence, and itchy yellow lumps are discovered on any exposed part of the body. Snakes are apt to come into the bungalows to escape the damp, which they dislike, and centipedes and scorpions turn up in unexpected places. But one gets accustomed to all this after a time.

Cotton is, of course, the standard crop, and the Kathiawar cotton is famous in all European markets, but the province is also a great grain-producing district. Wheat is grown to a large extent, especially in the great flats adjoining the large rivers where irrigation can be dispensed with nearly entirely, but on the higher lands irrigation from wells is indispensable.

Jowari and bajri are universally grown and need no watering, unless in a very dry season. They are splendid crops, growing 5 to 6 feet in height, with huge heads of grain. They form the staple food of the people.

Lucern grass is much grown under irrigation, also sugar cane and castor oil, rice in some districts, and numerous other cereals. Fifty years ago potatoes and cabbages were unknown, now hundreds of acres of them can be seen in every part of the province. Attached is an illustration of the ordinary primitive press used for crushing the juice from the sugar cane. When this is done it is boiled down, and the residue, the crude sugar, is cooled and packed for the market—and refiners.

The province is rich in many of the best varieties of building stones and clays.

Stratified Limestone.—A buff-coloured stone with a more or less mealy fracture, found in abundance over all the south and west of Kathiawar, forming deposits between five and thirty feet in depth.

The best samples are known by their fineness of texture and light colour. They will ring under the blow of a hammer.

It is quarried with a specially made axe, and worked at right angles to the stratification; when the cut has gone deep enough, the block is levered off.

Owing to its porosity it is necessary to protect walls of dwellings constructed of it, with verandahs or painting, against rain, otherwise the damp will pass through and injure plaster and decorations.

Sandstone.—A stratified rock found in a great variety of colour and texture over all the northern portions of Kathiawar, and an excellent building stone. It is found in all colours, from nearly pure white to grey, pink, speckled, marbled, green, yellow, and red. All the colouring is due to the presence of iron in one form or another.

Some samples of this stone contain a good percentage of iron ore, and in former days smelting was carried on at Than, Wankanir, etc., but the beds do not appear to have been rich or extensive enough to have paid for the working.

It is a porous stone, and the finest grained specimens of it, such as are obtained at Drangadra, are cut into bottles and jugs for filtering purposes.

In some few localities, principally adjacent to the Ran of Cutch, the stone has been found impregnated with salt, and great care is needed in testing it before employing it for building purposes, as such samples will corrode away when exposed to the atmosphere. The finest grained samples of this stone are extensively used for carvings and decorative purposes.

PRIMITIVE PRESS FOR CRUSHING SUGAR CANE.
(*See page* 180.)

RANI NAUDKUVERBA BANDSTAND, MEMORIAL INSTITUTE GROUNDS.
(*See page* 202.)

THAN POTTERS AT WORK.
(*See page* 181.)

A KATHIAWAR BULLOCK CART.
(*See page* 186.)

Trap in the various branches of its family underlies other formations. There are several forms of it, from the ordinary working trap of a dark blue-grey colour, easily worked with the chisel, to the hardest black basalt.

Basaltic Trap, not columnar, which is an admirable building stone, compact and impervious, of a dark grey colour, possessing great weight, hardness, and durability. It is difficult to work, but for structures where great strength and durability are needed it is invaluable. It breaks up under the blast into sharp angular blocks, of any size, peculiarly suitable for the rubble masonry of hydraulic structures.

Granite is found in the Girnar, Burdahs, Chomardi, and Otium Hills, but only a few samples of it are true granite. It is principally sienite, deorite, elaeolite (sienite intermixed with black garnets), micro-granite, etc. All varieties are so hard that it is only on rare or very special occasions that the stone has been employed for building purposes. It is a magnificent stone varying from light to dark grey and red, and takes a fine polish, as will be seen from the specimens worked into ornaments, or those occasionally employed in the building of the Girnar Temples. No doubt there is a future before it, and the supply is unlimited.

Laterite is found in some of the south districts, but it is not plentiful.

Clays.—Very excellent clays are found in the centre and north of the province, and many of them are suitable for the making of bricks and tiles, as well as for pottery. A fine class of pottery clay is found in the Than districts in a form of blue marl lying in the bed of the shallow tanks, and the villages here are famous for their pottery. Mutkas (water vessels), jars, kujas, and roofing tiles are turned out in large quantities, and exported or sent for sale to other parts of the province and Guzerat. Up to the date of this sketch machinery for pottery making was not introduced, except in one instance, when some hand-machines for the working and cutting and pressing of flooring and large roofing tiles were set up at Wankanir, and continued to work for a few years; but the industry needed skilled labour and direction, and was not then successful, whatever it may have since become.

Attached is an illustration of Than potters at work making Dutch roofing tiles and water vessels. The potter sits on the ground with a heavy wooden wheel in front. The attendant supplies a lump of kneaded clay which is placed in the centre of the wheel, which is then sent whirling round, and the pipe or vessel is formed by hand. They are then stacked in the sun to be dried before being burnt in open-air stacks covered with brushwood. These potters pursue their trade from father to son, and are very expert. They can turn out some really beautiful specimens of their craft.

From time to time some enthusiast has taken on himself the task of educating the Kathiawar kumbi (farmer) in the art of agriculture—introduced European ploughs, harrows, and winnowing machines, and held lectures where the value of draining and phosphates and scientific manuring, etc., were laid down for the benefit of the kumbis, who were invited to attend and learn.

Exhibitions were also got up where prizes would be awarded for the best agricultural products in the way of fruit, vegetables, grain, and every description of country-made articles in wood, leather, or iron, and very interesting and useful these exhibitions no doubt were; but to endeavour to teach the Kathi kumbi how to cultivate his land on European ideas, and with European implements, was useless. No English plough could work Kathiawar land and no European agriculturist could hope to compete with his Kathi brother on his own ground. There are no neater or better farmers anywhere than the Kathiawar kumbis. No doubt in time science and machinery will assist and develop existing methods, but the Kathi farmer needs no teaching how to get the best out of his land, and many a European farmer might take a leaf out of the Kathi's book in the way to keep his land healthy, presentable, and productive. The Kathiawar kumbi is a born agriculturist; his sons all follow their father's calling, and their sons after them.

It is the same with all the other callings; no young man ever thought of taking up any other trade than that of his forebears. Although I believe, of late years, the spread of education has led some here and there to try to enter the service of the Sircar, with the ambition of improving their position! This is one of the evils of education, but it can't be helped.

I recollect an amusing incident which took place at an agricultural exhibition held at Wudhwan, under the auspices of the late Colonel H. L. Nutt, A.P.A. A prize was to be awarded to the kumbi who would do the best and largest amount of ploughing on a strip of virgin grass land in a specified time—I think half an hour. There were many entries. Khumbis came with their teams from long distances, and the result of the contest was awaited by a large assemblage with great interest.

The teams, each comprising man, native plough, and a pair of oxen, were placed in line about 30 yards apart, and made a fine appearance. The bhails (oxen) were magnificent animals, mostly pure white, and standing seventeen hands in height—with their painted horns and shell necklaces. We (I was one of the judges) arranged that the signal for the start would be the firing of a small cannon, which we fixed on a mound at the rear.

When all was ready the signal was given, and the cannon roared. In another instant the bhails had started, not to plough, but for their villages, some with plough attached, and some without. They made bee-lines in many directions, tails on end, and in a few moments only one steady old pair (who no doubt had had previous experience of salutes), remained on the ground. I cannot recollect whether they were awarded the prize, but I think they were.

The soutars (carpenters) and küdias (masons) of Kathiawar cannot be beaten at their trade by any people in the world. The ancient architecture, much now in ruins, bears witness to what they could accomplish in olden times, and they have not lost any of their art—as modern works can show—they are quick, intelligent, and resourceful, as I can well testify after 33 years working with them.

Another industry for which Kathiawar is justly famed is that of the workers in gold and silver. They turn out beautifully made ornaments, as well as elaborately chased articles in the form of vases, boxes, and vessels of various designs. They are especially clever at working from drawings supplied to them, and their accuracy and taste are marvellous, considering their very rough and primitive tools and workshops, often occupying no more than a corner of their living room a few feet square, with a hole in the floor into which the workman inserts his legs, while the floor around forms his work bench.

I have had very beautiful designs carried out by them—caskets for holding addresses, implements for laying of foundation stones, enclosed in elaborate silver and ivory-bound ebony boxes, sporting designs, and equestrian figures for presentation on public functions. For the primary modelling blocks of lead are employed, in which the design is cut. The liquid silver is poured in and subsequently chased by hand. 50 to 75 per cent. is usually charged on the weight for workmanship.

Wood carving is, of course, a speciality.

Hand weaving of silk is extensively carried on, notably in Poribunder and Jamnugger.

It is interesting to watch the operation of drawing out the gold thread employed in the manufacture of the gorgeous kingcob and other materials. A stick of silver, about as large as a lead pencil, is covered with a layer of gold. It is then drawn through a bevelled hole in a steel plate, which increases the length and reduces the thickness, and the operation is repeated until the final thread obtained may be hundreds of yards long, every part of which is as accurately covered with gold as was the original pencil. When it is about the thickness of a hair it is hammered flat, after which it passes to the women of the family, who twist it by hand round a fine silk thread. It is now ready to be woven in the beautiful cloth of gold for which the province is so famous. The industry is confined to certain families, who only teach it to their sons and daughters-in-law.

TIMBER.

In the Bombay presidency there is little indigenous timber suitable for building purposes. There are abundant teak jungles in Guzerat and Kathiawar, but the timber seldom exceeds six to eight inches diameter, and so can be employed only in petty structures, where round framing is used. Most, however, of the round teak poles and rafters are imported.

Babul is plentiful in the northern part of the presidency, especially Guzerat and Kathiawar. It is a most useful wood, although rarely employed for building purposes. Its use is confined to the making of cart and carriage wheels, ploughs and other implements of husbandry, and for sugar and oil mills, etc. It is hard, tough, and of a dark brown colour. A well-grown trunk of babul, a foot to 15 inches in diameter, is worth a rupee per running foot, and the roots and branches cut up into the best fire-wood, worth 4 annas a maund.

The seed, sown broadcast over any fairly good soil or swampy land, will shoot up plentifully, and needs no watering or care beyond the pruning of side shoots from the time the young tree is 3 to 8 or 10 ft. high. The pruning is essential when the tree is quite young to ensure a clean, straight stem.

It is customary to sow it along the sides of country roads, where the young trees can be easily attended to, and they prove a fairly good shade.

Sajur, like teak. attains to only a small size and almost all of it used is imported.

Bamboo grows in profusion in the Gir jungles, and in the Burdahs and other hilly tracts in Guzerat, etc. It is employed for rafters for inferior dwellings, for trellising, and scaffolding, etc. It does not grow to any great size.

The timbers which are used and imported for building purposes are:—teak, sajur, kucha teak (Singapore cedar), eloss, pen, deodar, etc.

Teak from the Malabar Coast is pre-eminently the best of all woods, and its price is necessarily greater than the others. For building purposes its value is enhanced because it is the only timber that is almost immune from the ravages of white ants, and will not decay in almost any situation. Where strength and durability are required, it should always be employed. Besides constructive purposes it is extensively used for furniture, and carriage building, except for wheels and shafts, and it takes a fine polish.

Sajur is a heavy dark brown wood, tough and fairly hard, and it is used considerably for house building. It is a durable timber if protected from white ants. It is not suitable for joinery.

Pen is a jungle wood imported from Malabar, etc., in large quantities. The dark, reddish or heart portion of it makes a serviceable building timber, and it is fine-grained, and has a good appearance, but the outer ring of sappy light-coloured wood is liable to be affected by worms, which speedily destroy it unless they are checked in time. The timber is specially liable to attack if it is used in an unseasoned state, or placed in a badly ventilated and damp locality.

The presence of worms is detected by fine holes, from which will emanate a dry, yellow powder. When this is discovered, the infected part, if not too deep, may be chipped off, and the surface well saturated with a solution of carbolic acid or of very weak sulphuric acid.

The worms are produced from eggs laid by a flying beetle; they are soft, fleshy insects, with powerful boring mandibles, but are quickly destroyed by the above means.

Singapore Cedar (called Kacha sag) is often mistaken for teak, which it resembles in colour and grain. Next to teak, it is the best building-wood imported, and can be employed in fine carpentry. It is, however, subject to attacks of white ants, and should only be used in situations where it will be dry, and protected from the weather.

Eloss is a heavy dark, reddish wood, with a fine grain. The same remarks apply to it as to Kacha sag.

Mathia is a yellow wood very similar in texture to eloss, but it cannot be recommended for durability.

Deodar or Pine is now extensively employed for flooring and roofing boards. It is cheap, and in situations where it is protected from attacks of white ants is a serviceable and durable timber. It is imported from Norway.

White Ants are most secret and insidious in their attacks. They will make their way behind plaster or through the interstices of a wall, or up a staircase, or tree, or concealed behind door frames or wainscoting, till they reach the object of their desire, and will devour an entire ceiling or roof-framing before detection, unless special care be taken to watch for their approach. When once disturbed, however, they will not generally resume operations at the same place.

The country carts are beautifully built, principally of teak and babul—bound with worked iron and brass. A really good one is very valuable, and they are looked upon as heir-looms. They have no axle (*vide* side crutches and bars for keeping the wheels in position). This is necessary to enable the car to run in the deep ruts, which have been worn by years of traffic.

Sir Juswutsingji Fattisingji, K.C.I.E.,
Thakor Sahib of Limri.

Durbar Hall, Limri, Built 1885.

(See page 187.)

CHAPTER XVII.

1885—LIMRI DURBAR—FURLOUGH.

When Colonel Barton was Political Agent he gave me official permission at the request of the States to undertake such designing and works for them as would not interfere with my Agency duties.

The Chief of Limri was one of the first to seek my assistance, and during all my subsequent service in Kathiawar I did a good deal of work for him, and was frequently a visitor at his Durbar. He was one of the first pupils of the Rajkumar College, and a favourite of Macnaghten's. He had visited England and was now desirous of improving his State which lay on the east of the province, skirting the Run of Cambay and the Nall. One of the most important works I carried out for him was the formation of channels for straightening the Bogava river bed, and so preventing flooding and scouring of his cotton and wheat lands.

This had been proceeding, as funds permitted, for some years, and proved of value. Another was the designing and construction of his Durbar buildings at Limri.

The old palace occupied the centre of the town, and was in a very dilapidated condition and entirely unsuited for the wants of the present enlightened Chief. One large hall, which he had erected in the quadrangle in honour of H.I.M.'s Jubilee, had been put up in such a hurry that before completion it showed signs of collapsing, and I was hastily summoned to advise in the matter. The only thing possible was to take it down, a by no means easy job, but by elaborate staying and propping up this was accomplished, fortunately without accident, and then the entire arrangement for new buildings was placed in my hands. I enlarged the quadrangle by nearly twice its original dimensions, then laid off the principal buildings containing Durbar hall below, with reception-rooms above to face the principal entrance, and designed the public offices, living apartments, etc., on the other three sides of the square, also extensive stabling.

The work was put into hand in 1874, and proceeded for some four years. In olden days in Kathiawar it was the custom to store grain in pits underground during a plentiful year to serve as a supply in possible years of scanty crops, and several of these old pits were discovered in opening foundations for the buildings. Also two large wells built-in with brick of great depth were unearthed. One of them went down some 50 feet, and in the bottom of it under a filling in of ashes were found two large copper vessels containing about 8,000 rupees in old Mahomedan coins.

The Durbar hall and reception rooms above were each 75 feet by 35 feet and 25 feet high, subtended front and rear by wide arcaded verandahs, all of cut sandstone. The furniture of both halls was procured from London. The pictures were painted by Horace Van Ruith, and were all Indian subjects of great size and merit. There were also several portraits, life-size, including one of Queen Victoria and one of the Thakor Sahib. And in the upper room were a number of fine bas-reliefs, 7 feet by 3½ feet, representing Indian life and customs, executed in fibrous plaster from drawings by Van Ruith.

The furnishing and decorations of the Durbar hall included a number of very fine plaster statues procured from London.

The Chief was an accomplished horseman and whip, and his collection of carriages and traps included everything of the kind made, from a four-in-hand drag to a pony cart.

He was a keen patron of all kinds of sport, and spoke English fluently. At college he was a brilliant cricketer and a racquet player, and when he succeeded to his Ghadi he had a ground laid out for cricket, on which he built a pavilion, and here it was his pleasure to repair and personally practise his teams, which he captained in various matches throughout the province and even in Bombay. Guests were invited to this ground to witness wrestling and other athletic sports.

The Chief was an excellent and entertaining companion, and a really good talker on most of the subjects of the day, as well as upon the religious customs and history of his country. And among the pleasantest recollections of my life in Kathiawar are the days and evenings I passed in his society. One fault he had which I am afraid sometimes cost him dear—namely, a deep-seated love of litigation. He would go to law on any pretext whatever, and enjoy it whether he won his case or not. He might have been a great man if he had not been a Chief. I recollect on one occasion he had a dispute with the Collector of Ahmedabad, on some drainage question, which had been running on a long time, and Government had ordered that the matter should be settled forthwith by arbitration. The Collector employed a Government surveyor, and the Chiet asked me to represent him, and handed me all the papers on the subject. He appeared to be quite sure that the verdict would be in his favour. On visiting the locality, however, and making careful surveys and enquiries, I found it impossible to do aught but coincide with the opposite party. The Chief had not a leg to stand on. The verdict did not put him out in the least; he would gladly, I believe, have begun the fight all over again.

Sir Juswutsingji (Her Imperial Majesty Queen Victoria conferred on him the honour of K.C.S.I. for the exemplary government of his State) was with the Chief of Morvi, H.H. Sir Waghji, K.C.I.E., selected to represent the Kathiawar reigning Chiefs in England on the occasion of her Majesty's Jubilee in 1897. He extended his visit to the Continent and to America, and on his passing through Ireland I had the pleasure of meeting him in Dublin, and taking him to a few of the principal places of interest. He was greatly taken with the Irish cars, and on our visit to Powerscourt insisted on driving one himself. After my retirement he frequently wrote to me, and the last letter I received was one written on June 8th, 1906, in which he described the disastrous fire which had occurred in his Durbar a few months earlier, in which the whole of the old wing containing the living apartments and zenana was destroyed, including a great amount of jewellery and furniture.

Very soon after this catastrophe I heard of his unexpected death after a short illness. He was a pattern Chief in many ways—religious, beloved of his subjects, and one of our valued friends.

FURLOUGH.

In the early part of 1886 Colonel Watson was appointed Political Agent, on the decease of Colonel West. The latter had been suffering from bad health for a long time, and, indeed, the severe duties of the Agency were too heavy for him. If he had been a less conscientious man he would, perhaps, have taken matters easier, but he was a slave to his work, and his constant endeavour was to be thoroughly just, and see into all difficulties himself. The consequence was that he was liked and respected by all, natives and Europeans, but the constant strain was more than his delicate constitution could long stand. After trying change of air in India he was ordered home in April of this year, but lived only to reach Naples, where he died on landing.

Colonel Watson was only waiting to be confirmed as Political Agent to go home on furlough. He decided to leave in June, and as I had now obtained my fourteen months' leave we arranged to travel together.

Colonel and Mrs. Watson were staying during May at Gopenath, on the south coast, and I was called there to meet him on business. I took Bhavnagar on my way, where I spent a couple of days with my old friend Proctor-Sims. And from Bhavnagar I journeyed by bullock shigram, about 50 miles over country tracks. A very unpleasant journey, I recollect, which took me two days and a night, and the heat was intense, 115° to 120° during the day with a searing wind, and dust everywhere. After that I had a pair-horse carriage, sent to meet me by the Political Agent, and arrived that evening at Gopenath. The bungalow was built as a residence for the Acting Political Agent of the Gohelwad Prant, and Colonel Watson had, in former days, taken a good deal of interest in improving the surroundings. It was built by the edge of a cliff overhanging the sea, and commanded a fine coast view. It was a very lonely and isolated locality, but the country was full of game. The following morning Watson and I went for a walk to see the surroundings, and unfortunately took no rifle with us, otherwise we might have bagged a very fine wolf. They are rare and very difficult to get in Kathiawar now. We passed him lying under a cactus bush within 60 yards, and he merely stared at us. Later in the day we had some shooting of buck and partridge, but the heat was too great to stay out long.

That night I met with a nasty accident. I was walking from the bungalow to my tent, in brilliant moonlight, when in the shadow of a small hedge, I struck my toe against a piece of jagged rock with which Watson used to outline the walks, and fell violently. My left shin came into contact with the rock, and received a very deep wound to the bone. With some difficulty I managed to stagger on to the tent, only a few yards distant, where my boy, Bica, helped me to get into my cot, and washed and bound my leg. In the morning I could not move, and fearing that surgical aid might be necessary, a bed was made up in a bullock shigram for me, and I started for Bhavnagar. Two days under medical care enabled me to proceed to Rajkote by rail, but I contrived to contract a chill which gave me a very horrible and continuous pain in my right shoulder. At Rajkote I was obliged to sit in a chair with my leg on a rest, and my shoulder in constant agony, for three weeks and doing office work as well, and each morning was obliged to go a round of works in a Durbar carriage.

It was arranged that Mr. Sandford, a friend of Proctor-Sims, should act for me, and he joined me a week before I left. By that time my leg was fairly well, but the shoulder continued to give me much pain, and the doctor was unable to relieve me. It was some inflammation, he said, under the shoulder blade, and only time with change would cure it.

Mrs. Watson had preceded her husband, and I met the latter in Bombay. We travelled by P. and O. to Brindisi, crossing by rail from Suez to Alexandria. At Brindisi we took the Mail Express *via* Turin, etc., and enjoyed the trip and the pace, which carried us to London in two and a half days. There Watson and I separated. I had previously arranged with my wife for all of them to come and meet me in London, so that we could have a pleasant holiday there as a start off, and I found them the night I arrived located in rooms near the Mannings at Forest Hill, and so I surprised the wife and three bairns at about 11 p.m., when they were all in bed. I found the children greatly grown and improved; indeed, they were pretty well grown up, and quite companions.

Norwood being too far from town we stayed only a couple of days, and then took a house nearer London, where I think we remained a fortnight, and spent our time visiting what we could of the wonders of the city. We were now undecided whether to return north or go to Brighton, near where our friends Colonel and Mrs. Phillips were living. (Our house at Edinburgh would not be vacated for another month.) At length the Phillips induced us to go to Rottingdean, and took rooms for us near them. Colonel Phillips met us at Brighton, and we all walked the five miles to Rottingdean, on a most glorious summer day. But I was struck with the unusual features of the country, so bare of vegetation, great bleak rolling downs, with only trees visible in the little valleys here and there. We stayed at Rottingdean for a month, and enjoyed it immensely, making various excursions into the neighbourhood and to Brighton, as well as to Ovingdean, the residence of Mr. Macnaghten, father of Chester Macnaghten, of Rajkote. He was then a very old man, and I recollect it was somewhat of a trial carrying on a conversation with him, he being very deaf, short tempered, and short of memory, but a dear old man all the same. Mrs. West, who had been staying with her sister and brother-in-law at Langholm, on the Scottish border, since her husband's death, now wrote inviting me to visit them on my way to Edinburgh and have some grouse shooting. This I very gladly accepted, and sending my wife and the young people on I branched off to Langholm, arriving there at 9 p.m., and was cordially received by Mr. and Mrs Connell and Mrs. West.

Early the following morning four of the neighbouring squires arrived to an 8 o'clock breakfast in preparation for the day's grouse shooting. Mr. Connell had the shooting of his father-in-law's (Mr. Maxwell) moor of Broomholme. The latter was in bad health, and had gone to reside on the Continent. We (six guns) started at 9 o'clock, and after a walk or rather a climb of an hour reached the first stand, and were posted at intervals along a low stone wall, while the drivers, some 12 or 15 in number, appeared half a mile beyond beating in line. Presently a call to look out, and a few tiny black specks were noticed in the direction of the drivers. These were the disturbed grouse, and they were coming towards us at a tremendous pace. Not being accustomed to this kind of shooting (it was my first experience of a grouse drive) I allowed the birds to come over and past me before I fired, and in consequence missed with both barrels. A driven grouse should be taken as he comes, firing well ahead, and meeting him in his flight; if not, the sportsman is almost sure to miss. I was more successful after my first failure. After the drive was over the birds found and counted, we were moved a little further, and while the men started for a new drive, we had a nip all round of "Mountain Dew," and lit pipes. The ground was in parts covered with patches of snow, while little pools here and there were frozen over, and icicles hung from the bracken. The air was clear and exhilarating, and we did not feel the least cold. The day was calm and bright.

Before stopping for an excellent lunch, which was prepared for us in a sheltered quarry hole, we had many drives and many nips and pipes, and had put together a pretty good bag. After lunch we shot again until dark and walked home very happy and content with a most delightful day. At Langholme that evening there was a dinner party, at which we met several of the county residents.

Adjoining Mr. Maxwell's moor, guns were going all day on the Duke of Buccleuch's moors, where the Duke himself was shooting; not long before his eldest son shot himself by accident in the same locality.

The following day I took a long country drive with Mrs. West, and on the third day left for Edinburgh. Here we settled down for the winter, varying the monotony with an occasional visit to my mother at Dublin.

In the early part of the following season, April and May I made some visits to Loch Leven, near Kinross, and had excellent sport. The two girls accompanied me on the lake, and we had other pleasant excursions in the neighbourhood. I also had some good days on the Leader, one day catching as many trout as Dick and I together could conveniently carry to the hotel, and during part of that day it snowed and hailed! I decided to stay at Lauder over the night, but the next day's fishing did not repay me.

About the middle of May I went to Ireland with my eldest daughter, leaving my wife with the other two to finish their terms at school and college. And after a few days with my mother we went to Kilskyre, where we arranged with my sister, Mrs. Maunsell, and her husband to join us for a month at Lough Sheelan for the green drake fishing.

We had very few good days, and but very poor sport, so far as the fishing went, but we had a delightful time all the same in other ways. We lived in the open air, boated, lunched, and rambled in the woods and drove about the country, also visited the tenants on the old family land of Corralislea.

We saw something of the working and poorer classes, who remembered old and gone members of my family. I shot rabbits and woodquests at Bellsgrove, where the old gatekeeper, Paddy Lynch, and his older sister told me many stories of the days when the Bell-Booths lived there. This old man had been a herd under my late uncle, and was an excellent example of the retainer of those days. He was also totally uneducated, could neither read nor write, but was greedy for information about the outer world. He used to come up to the cottage in the evening and engage me in talk, and asked continuous questions, not always easy to answer.

On one occasion, I recollect, when I was telling him about India he said, "I'm tould, sir, that in them hot countries the noise the sun makes in rising would terrify you?"

"Why so, Pat?" said I.

"Well, to be sure, because you'd be so near it," he replied.

What dense ignorance for an Irishman at the end of the nineteenth century! Pat's idea was that the sun rose up every morning out of a hole in the earth, and the nearer one got to that hole the greater would be the heat. India, in Pat's mind, was not only very near, but within hearing of the commotion made by the sun in coming to the surface.

This was the Queen's Jubilee year, and the two young Chiefs of Morvi and Limri were elected to represent the Chiefs of Kathiawar. Colonel Woodhouse accompanied them in political charge, and they were both to visit America before returning. Mr. White, the State engineer of Morvi, accompanied his own Chief, while Mr. Brackenbridge, of London, was appointed to accompany Limri.

The Limri Chief stayed a few days in Dublin, and I had the pleasure of taking him about and showing him a few of the sights of Dublin and neighbourhood.

We returned to Kilskyre at the end of the month, and often went to Sylvan Park, and had rabbit shooting. We also made more than one excursion to Lough Bawn. My brother Tom was at home, and we had some fishing on Carrick and the little river. It was like a bit of the old days when we were lads together.

My son had now entered for his medical degree at Edinburgh University, which he passed with full honours, and it was my intention he should go up to Netley and try for the Indian medical as soon as he had taken a fling after his hard work.

We stayed near my mother at Bray till Michaelmas, and on that evening we all dined with her, and left the following day. I never saw my mother again. My wife and eldest daughter returned with me to India, while my son and youngest girl remained to complete their studies.

CHAPTER XVIII.

THE MEMORIAL INSTITUTE—DEATH OF COLONEL SCOTT—SHOOTING AT THE NAL.

The want of such a building at Rajkote as would provide a sufficiently large public hall for Durbar or other assemblages was long felt. Up to a few years previous to this time the only place for such purposes was the banqueting room at the Kothie, but with the advancement of the province, this was now too small to accommodate even a third of the chiefs, officials, and retinues who attended important state functions.

Since the construction of the Alfred High School in 1873, Durbars were occasionally held in the examination hall of that building, but even it was too limited in accommodation, and it was felt to be scarcely in accord with the dignity of these stately functions to have no place specially set apart in which to hold them.

The money voted by the Chiefs in 1887 to commemorate the Jubilee year of H.I.M. Queen Victoria was to have been devoted to such a purpose, but had to be diverted for the carrying out of the then urgently needed Victoria Jubilee Water Works. In 1889 Colonel Watson died, and the State, desiring to do something to commemorate his name, voted funds for the building of a museum to be called after him, and the proposal coming before Sir Charles Ollivant, now Political Agent, he advised the Chiefs to supplement their grant by the proceeds of the sale of the old Lang Institute building, till then used as a small library and museum, and to subscribe a further sum sufficient in all to cover the cost of a building to comprise a Durbar hall, library, and museum to be named the Memorial Institute. The museum to be a memorial of Colonel Watson, the library and reading room to be called after Colonel Lang, and the Durbar hall to be the Connaught Hall, in honour of the several visits of H.R.H. the Duke of Connaught to Kathiawar in his official capacity as Commander-in-Chief of Bombay.

This was in due course agreed to by the State representatives, and I received official directions for the preparation of designs and estimates.

There was the usual difficulty experienced in the selection of a suitable site, but it was at length decided to take over the whole of the old station garden, about nine acres, which had some years since been transferred from civil to military jurisdiction, making over to the military authorities an equal area of civil station land in the vicinity of their lines in exchange for it. This was an excellent site, and would enable us to lay out sufficiently extensive grounds as well as provide space for future possible extensions.

The building designed to accommodate the three institutions covered about 25,000 square feet, and occupied a central position on the site. The Durbar hall was in the centre facing the west, with carriage drives from the north and south. The library and museum had separate entrances on the extreme ends. Around and facing the three entrances about six acres were laid out in ornamental landscape gardens, and was extensively planted with shrubs and flowers and otherwise decorated. The grounds adjoining the museum were intended to contain archæological remains from the ancient architecture—religious and otherwise—in which the province was rich, and some of these were brought in before the opening day. Owing to the kindness of H.H. the late Jam Sahib, I pitched camp on one occasion at Ghumli, the ancient and ruined city of the Jetwa Rajputs, at the Burdah Hills, and unearthed archæological treasures which had lain buried for eight centuries. These were conveyed into Rajkote and erected where they now stand in the Institute grounds. One of the most beautiful was a richly carved cantilever gateway, which was erected at the entrance of a large fernery. The gateway is 30 feet high and 20 feet wide.

Another was a flat-topped doorway, leading to the Holy of Holies of an ancient ruined temple, and was made to form the entrance to a grotto. Another, a pair of monoliths, twelve feet high, carved, which had formed part of the roof supports to a temple, and several others; but this was only a beginning which has since been, no doubt, considerably added to.

The rear or east section of the grounds, about three acres, were laid out partly as gardens and party as sites for an aviary, etc. The principal part of the design for the Connaught Hall was that it should contain a portrait gallery of the Chiefs from first to fourth class, in residence in that year, as well as portraits of H.I.M. Queen Victoria, the Duke of Clarence, and the Duke of Connaught, the Governor of Bombay, and the Political Agent of Kathiawar, and other officials, natives, and Europeans. For the purpose of painting the portraits an eminent artist, Mr. Frank Brooks, was invited from London the previous year, and very excellently he completed his work in time for all the portraits to be hung in the Durbar hall before the opening day.

As the paintings were completed they were photographed for the album designed for the history and illustrations of the Memorial Institute, a copy of which specially bound was presented to her Majesty the Queen Empress.

The Institute was completed in 1893, and opened in state by H.E. Lord Harris, Governor of Bombay, in November of that year, and to further commemorate the event it was decided to hold an exhibition in the grounds. So the rear portion of three acres was covered with a huge pavilion and tents, filled with arts, manufactures, and curiosities, from every State of the province, as well as from other parts of India.

The opening was a gala time, and combined with the novelty of an exhibition was sure to draw the population of the province. The following is the official description of the reception at the Residency and the opening ceremony of the institute :—

The reception held by the Political Agent at the Residency last night was attended by all the Chiefs present in Rajkote, and by all civil and military officers, ladies and native gentlemen. The grounds of the Residency were brilliantly illuminated, and as the Chiefs of the first and second Class drove up to the entrance they were received with a salute by the guard of honour of the 23rd Bombay Rifles, and a flourish on the bugle. The guests were received on alighting by Lieutenant J. F. Harrington, Assistant Political Agent, and Ressaldar Major Sandullah Khan, native A.D.C. to His Excellency the Governor.

His Excellency, who wore the Ribbon of the Order of the Indian Empire, shook hands with the Chiefs and Kumars of the Rajkumar College, who were introduced by the Political Agent and Mr. Waddington respectively, and then with the European military officers, after which the native officers of the 3rd (Q.O.) Bombay Light Infantry, and 23rd Bombay Rifles were presented by Colonel Stevens, commanding the cavalry, and Captain Scallon, D.S.O., commanding the Rifles. His Excellency then moved about the large room, which was densely crowded and presented a brilliant scene.

THE DURBAR.

His Excellency Lord Harris held a Durbar this morning in the hall of the Connaught Memorial Institute, which was formally opened by him.

The road from the Residency to the Memorial Institute was lined by the 3rd (Q.O.) Bombay Cavalry and the 23rd Bombay Rifles, while the 55th Field Battery R.A. was drawn up on the open ground in front, and fired the usual salutes on the arrival of each first and second class Chief. A guard of honour of one British officer, two native officers, and one hundred rank and file with band was drawn up in the Institute grounds. The first Chief to arrive was the Thakor Sahib of Wudhwan (7.40 a.m.), who was followed by the other second and first-class Chiefs at intervals of five minutes, H.H. the Nawab Sahib of Junaghud arriving last at 8.25 a.m.

On the daïs, on the right of his Excellency, were seated the Political Agent, the Military Secretary, Mr. F. C. O. Beaman, C.S., Major Fenton, Mr. E. V. Mackay, while at the back seat sat Mr. Waddington and the Kumars of the Rajkumar College. To the right of his Excellency on the daïs were Mr. S. W. Edgerley, C.S., Private Secretary, Captain Cox, A.D.C., and Captain Forbes, the seats behind them being occupied by ladies. General Nicolson, C.B.A., D.C., Major Stevenson, Mr. Booth, Mr. White, and others sat in the body of the hall to the left of his Excellency, behind them civil and military officers and other European gentlemen, while to the right of his Excellency were the Durbaris with their retinues.

His Excellency was escorted to the Institute by a detachment of cavalry, a salute of seventeen guns being fired on his arrival. The guard of honour presented arms on his Excellency's arrival, and the band played while his Excellency was received at the entrance by their Highnesses the Nawab of Junaghud, the Maharajah of Bhavnagar, and the Raj Sahib of Dhrangadra, who conducted his Excellency to his seat.

On his Excellency taking his seat the following address was read by Mr. Booth :—

"Your Excellency,—Before H.H. Sir Takhatsingji Maharajah of Bhavnagar asks Your Excellency on behalf of the Chiefs in Kathiawar to formally declare this building open, I am directed to give a short

The Connaught Hall, Memorial Institute, Rajkote.

(See page 199.)

Memorial Institute from the North.

(See page 199)

Col. L. L. Fenton.

Col. George E. Hancock, Acting Political Agent.

(*See page* 199.)

history of the Memorial Institute, which comprises three institutions as follows :—

THE CONNAUGHT DURBAR HALL.

In commemoration of the visit to Kathiawar of his Royal Highness the Duke of Connaught, late Commander-in-Chief of the Bombay Army. The hall is 125 feet by 50 feet and 30 feet high. The floor is laid with marble mosaic. At the upper end is a daïs approached by steps of white Sicilian marble. The ceiling is of timber, worked in geometrical and floral designs. On either side at 16 feet from the floor line are projecting balconies of ornamental iron, intended to be used by ladies on occasions of State functions.

"Over the daïs the central portion of the hall is occupied by a portrait of H.I.M. the Queen Empress, painted by Macbeth Raeburn after Angeli, in a massive gold frame with crown, and above is placed the Royal Arms of England with the Union Jack and Royal Standard grouped.

"To the right is a portrait of his Royal Highness the late Duke of Clarence and Avondale, by Mr. A. Soord, and on the left a portrait of his Royal Highness the Duke of Connaught by Mr. C. L. Burns. The cost of these three Royal portraits were defrayed by general subscriptions of the Chiefs.

"Along the sides of the hall, below the daïs, are hung twenty-eight portraits of the reigning Chiefs of Kathiawar placed in order of rank ; and at the lower end of the hall are portraits of his Excellency the Rt. Hon. Lord Harris, G.C.I.E., Governor of Bombay, Sir E. Charles K. Ollivant, K.C.I.E.C.S., Political Agent of Kathiawar, Colonel Hancock, Acting Political Agent, Colonel W. Scott, and others.

"All the Kathiawar portraits, including that of his Excellency the Governor, were painted by Mr. Frank Brooks, who was invited from London for the purpose. The upper portions of the walls are decorated with trophies of ancient Guzerat armour.

THE WATSON MUSEUM.

"To commemorate the late Colonel John W. Watson, formerly Political Agent of Kathiawar, and connected with the province for over a quarter of a century, a portrait of Colonel Watson is placed in the museum with the following inscription on a marble tablet beneath :—

The Watson Museum
Built out of funds subscribed
by the Chiefs of Kathiawar
and private friends
in memory of
Colonel John W. Watson,
Political Agent, 1886 to 1889.
and for 25 years
connected with this province
the love of which
combined with rare ability
and antiquarian research
well fitted him to be
the Historian of Kathiawar.

"The museum measures 80 feet by 60 feet inside, and has a gallery, at the height of 16 feet, measuring about half the space of ground floor. The gallery is executed in teak, supported by cut stone pillars. An arcaded verandah, 10 feet clear, subtends the whole.

"The museum at first was intended to be confined principally to exhibits of provincial manufactures and products, and the local flora and fauna, with antiquities. minerals, etc., found in the province, but some valuable contributions have already been received from Mr. Phipson of the Bombay Natural History Society, and from other friends, and the Natural History Section has here an able and enthusiastic worker in Major L. L. Fenton, who has made considerable collections, while Mr. Turkhud, Dr. Evans, geologist now at Junaghud, Rao Bahadur Kesharao Bhaskarji, Rao Bahadur Gopalji Surbhai, Mr. Dahyabhai, and others take a considerable interest in the geological, botanical, and antiquarian branches, and as the work proceeds, doubtless many others will foster and assist an institution calculated to be of so great interest and value to the province.

THE LANG LIBRARY.

"The library founded to commemorate the late Colonel W. Lang, Political Agent in Kathiawar, originally occupied a small and very unsuitable building near the Residency. At the suggestion of Sir Charles Ollivant,

THE LIONS AT ENTRANCE TO WATSON MUSEUM.

(*See page* 200.)

opportunity was taken to dispose of this building for Agency purposes, and provide funds for giving the library a home in the new Memorial Institute. In February last the old Station Library, which was also in a somewhat homeless condition, was amalgamated with the Lang Library, by general desire, and the combined institution, which is to be accommodated here, is now in a very prosperous condition. This building is also 80 feet by 60 feet, and has a spacious gallery at one end with staircase approaching the balcony of the Durbar hall. Teak glazed bookcases, 12 feet high, surround the walls, and the room is otherwise furnished with reading and writing tables, chairs, and all useful convenience for members.

"On the centre of the west wall is placed a portrait of the late Colonel W. Lang, with the following inscription beneath:—

This Library,
formerly established in the Residency
grounds, was founded by
the Chiefs of Kathiawar
in memory of
Colonel W. Lang,
who served for 28 years in this province,
in which he was Political Agent
from 1846 to 1859.
A kind friend and firm administrator,
he endeared himself to Chiefs and subjects
and to his private beneficence
was due
the first Girls' School in Kathiawar.

"The walls are further decorated with portraits of the late Colonel W. Walker, the first Political Resident in Kathiawar, who effected the settlement of the Gaekwar's tribute and executed treatises with all the Chiefs in 1807; the late Colonel S. C. Law, first President of the Rajasthanik Court, and connected with the province so far back as 1864. A tablet in commemoration of the late Lieutenant H. Gordon and the police sowars who fell with him in a fight with dacoits on December 19th, 1892, is also to be placed in a conspicuous position.

"The archways between the Durbar hall and the museum and library on either side are fitted in with elaborately carved screens in teak and blackwood, made by Mr. Kanji Govind of Rajkote.

"The grounds comprise in all nearly eleven acres, and are laid out for the greater part in landscape gardens with ornamental ponds and fountains, etc., supplied under pressure from the Randerda Lake.

"A section of the grounds is devoted to a home for ancient archæological remains, of which there are many of great value and interest in the province. Some have already been brought in, and some very old and valuable inscriptions on stone have been received, notably one from the Chief of Jusdan, over 1,800 years old.

"The original grant for the works has been considerably increased by private gifts from some of the chiefs and others —as follows: H.H. the Thakor of Gondal presented Rs.3,000 for the construction of a bandstand in the name of her Highness the Rani Naudkuverba, who was the first Rajput Princess to visit England with her husband. This is a reproduction of old temple architecture.

"The next response was from the Thakor Sahib of Limdi who presented Rs.3,000 to construct the conservatory.

"It was then found that a laboratory was required for receiving and arranging specimens for the Museum and the States of Wankaner and Dhrol contributed the funds for that building.

"Mr. Pitamber Vasta, of Rajkote, presented a handsome fountain and basin, and Mr. Abubakar Jamal, also a resident of Rajkote, the money for a pair of stone vases.

"His Highness the Nawab Sahib of Junaghud contributed Rs.3,500 for the making of a pair of Gir lions in stone to be placed at the entrance of the Museum, as also the cost of an aviary.

"The drawings from life of the lions were taken by Mr. Frank Brooks, who modelled the works and directed the sculpture.

"The total cost of the buildings, grounds, furniture, etc. including presentations has been Rs.1.63,500."

His Highness the Maharajah of Bhavnagar, on behalf of the assembled Chiefs, then invited his Excellency to declare the Institute and Exhibition open in the following terms:—

"YOUR EXCELLENCY,—

"On behalf of the Chiefs of Kathiawar, I beg you with your usual kindness and grace, will declare open the Connaught Durbar Hall, erected by us to perpetuate the kindly recollections we have of his Royal Highness, and in token of our loyalty to our Queen-Empress the Kaisar-i-

Hind. The memory of two distinguished English officers who have served amongst us is connected with the wings of the building, and these also your Excellency will kindly open for the public use."

His Excellency then rose and said :—

"PRINCES AND CHIEFS OF KATHIAWAR,—

"It has given me the greatest possible pleasure to accept your invitation to take part in this ceremony and declare this Hall open. The account which Mr. Booth has given us of the history of the undertaking, of the architectural details of the building, and of its commemorative attributes render anything but a very brief allusion to it by myself unnecessary. It will, I trust, be a very useful as well as ornamental addition to the other public works, which, thanks to the liberality of the Chiefs, have been raised in the Agency Headquarters. It will, I hope, be a sign, a substantial sign, of the capacity of the Chiefs of the provinces to co-operate together for all good and useful works: not only that, for just as the skilful brush of the painter, and especially that of Mr. Brooks (to whom I am sure you are all grateful for the ability and interest he has displayed in the pictorial decoration of this hall), has brought together the likenesses of the Queen-Empress, her gallant son the Duke of Connaught, and her lamented grandson the Duke of Clarence; of many of the Chiefs and Princes of Kathiawar; and of the Governor of Bombay and the Political Agent, so we may hope all the powers and duties which are wielded and performed by those authorities are united in the common object of strengthening the Empire by improving the condition and caring for the needs of the peoples under their administrative control.

"With the opening ceremony is coupled an Industrial Exhibition; which shows that the Chiefs are fully alive to the necessity of encouraging their subjects to take to other industries than that of agriculture. That is a problem which we are suggesting within British territory, and as Your Highnesses are fully aware, central schools and institutes have been opened in Poona and Bombay, and Ratnagiri, and also by the help of some of the Missions, at comparatively out-of-the-way places, where a technical education is given. If it is the desire of the Chiefs to follow up this Exhibition by a really practical effort at giving a higher technical education, I would strongly advise them to co-operate in this matter also and to concentrate their efforts, at any rate in the first instance.

"As you will acknowledge, I think, my friends, I have showed a confidence in your good intentions as regards education in your States, and have in certain cases given you a far greater freedom in your educational operations. But in doing so I have, of course, thrown an extra responsibility on you, which you must not, as I feel sure you will not, avoid. If one effect of the removal of restraint were to be to encourage you to co-operate for the institution of a system of technical education, I believe a great benefit would accrue to your subjects; but I confess I am not hopeful of success in this branch of education if the effort is split up into a number of separate atoms, instead of being concentrated in one place where skilled teachers and the plant, which is so necessary, but so expensive, can be obtained.

"Your Highnesses and Chiefs, while congratulating you on your public spirit in raising this Memorial Hall, I must also thank you for the sympathy in his death as for the admiration of his courage which you have evinced by placing on these walls a commemorative tablet of my poor friend Lieutenant Gordon, who, with his gallant comrades fell under the bullets of certain Kathiawar outlaws doing his duty on behalf of you, the Chiefs of Kathiawar, and your subjects who were suffering from the atrocities and the ravages of the gang.

"Mr. Gordon knew that if the depredations of this gang were to be put a stop to, the only chance was to catch the outlaws in the open; he knew that the surest way of overcoming them if caught in the open was to charge at once. He must also have known that to do so was certain death to a proportion of his little force; but he and his gallant comrades never hesitated; they charged home like good and true soldiers with the successful but lamentable result we know of; that perilous duty was undertaken for you, my friends, and your subjects, to free you from a lawless pest; how originated, whether from an innate love of the reckless life of the freebooter, or through some sudden fit of rage, or through oppression, this is not the moment to examine. But the province has been freed from the molestations of that gang and by the gallantry of Lieutenant Gordon and his men;

and I am grateful to the Chiefs of Kathiawar for recording their sympathy and appreciation as they have done. You have, I am glad to think, done something more—recognising that it was a slur on this fair province that it should be possible for such a state of things to exist, and for a band of outlaws to pass unchecked from State to State almost at their own free will. Certain States have, at the advice of the Bombay Government of India, accepted assistance in the reorganisation of their police. You will recognise the bounden duty of the paramount Power to offer this advice, and you have followed it, or are, I feel satisfied, about to follow it, recognising that it is sound advice, and certain to result in an improvement of the efficiency of your police force. Those Chiefs who are concerned in this matter will, I feel satisfied, not linger over this work of reform, but will push it on and see it securely established at as early a date as possible on a thoroughly secure foundation. In such matters it is far from the wish of the paramount Power to interfere with the authority of the Chiefs, and they, happily, render interference unnecessary by undertaking the reform and the reorganisation themselves.

"Your Highness and Chiefs, the contemplation of the products of this province by no very strained stretch of imagination leads thoughts to the highly important inquiry that has been instituted in this country by her Majesty's Government, on the subject of the cultivation of the poppy and the manufacture and sale of opium, and as you are aware the Government of Bombay has addressed you on the subject of giving evidence to the Commission. I trust, my friends, that you will find yourselves able to meet the suggestions of the Government of India and of the Bombay Government in this matter, and will resist a possible inclination to stand on the letter of your Treaties or Agreements, and to say that those having been passed, no combination can come behind them. My friends, I can quite realise your receiving the Commission with some astonishment, and possibly some alarm, lest the effect of its recommendations should in effect be the imposition of a sumptuary law opposed to the tastes of your race. I was able to realise the standpoint which a native friend of mine took when he remarked to me, 'How would England like it if some Oriental country having the power forced upon her an inquiry to consider whether the cultivation of barley and the manufacture of malt and the sale of beer were not attended with results inimical to the moral advancement of the British race; and whether the tax on beer and the licensing of houses to sell beer were not connections with an immoral traffic which a Christian Government should give up?' I was forced to confess that I thought England would probably be somewhat annoyed at any such slur being cast on the national beverage; and that I thought the Government would reply that its system of taxation and of licensing were not merely a means of raising a revenue but also a very necessary check on the sale of an intoxicant, to which my friend replied that checks were necessary also as regards the sale of opium, and he could not see the difference between India raising a revenue by these means on opium and England doing so on beer.

"But my friends, I venture to suggest that this is not the spirit in which you should accept the position at this moment. You—or some of you—may possibly regard a cup of kusumba very much as an Englishman regards his cup of tea; you have got certain Treaties or Agreements regarding the supply to your States of opium by the British Government, on condition that you gave up the cultivation of the poppy and the manufacture of opium, and you may possibly be inclined, feeling it no crime to moderately indulge in what you consider an agreeable and harmless restorative, and feeling secure with your Treaties or Agreements, to allow the Commission to pass your doors without giving any sign of your neighbourhood. I hope that it is not the attitude you will adopt. Believe me, that such inquiries as this Royal Commission are not to be treated with disregard; it is of the highest importance that the fullest information should be laid before the Commission, not only as regards the subjects of the Queen-Empress and their tastes and needs in the matter of opium, but also as regards the subjects of the native States; I know how great is the loyalty, and how fervent the affection you bear for her Majesty the Queen-Empress; you will remember that this is a Royal Commission, so you will, I am sure, on consideration, agree that a most excellent way of displaying your loyalty and devotion will be by assisting her Majesty's Commissioners to arrive at the truth, and so, through their report, put the people of England, who have taken considerable interest in the subject, in possession of correct information.

"Your Highness and Chiefs, I pass from that larger subject to one which concerns only Kathiawar. I refer to the provincial institution, the Rajasthanik Court, and being so deeply concerned and interested in its labours you are, of course, fully conversant with the history of its establishment. How, out of the anarchy that prevailed, previous to Colonel Walker's settlement, when might was right, and though the Girassia might be supreme within his villages he nevertheless had to submit to superior force and pay tribute to anyone, Chief or not, stronger than he, —out of Colonel Walker's settlement came the practice of political advice to the Agency in cases of dispute between the Chiefs and the Girassias. That went on until the mass of work rendered some change necessary. That change took the shape of the Rajasthanik Court; and you will remember that it was at the wish of the Chiefs that that form of inquiry was adopted. It is a court paid for by the Chiefs of Kathiawar, but it is an impartial Court trying to do justice between the Chiefs and their Girassias on land questions. Now, my friends, that being the history of the institution of the Court, you have now and again to consider whether or not its existence shall be extended, and recently a large majority of the States decided to continue the Court for a period of two years. There were some dissentient States, and what I request those States to consider now and all the States to consider two years hence is what arrangements would you propose for the settlement of those boundary disputes between yourselves and your Bhayats? It is possible that some one not very conversant with the history of Kathiawar and forgetful of the ancient custom of an aggrieved suitor going out into Barvattia, might suggest that the State Courts are fully competent to try and settle these cases. My friends, as an absolutely impartial looker-on, I assure you that I think you will find on analysis that an independent as well as an impartial Court is not only a desideratum, but is a positive essential, for these disputes if the peace of Kathiawar is to be preserved.

"The subject has been brought into consideration in a perhaps somewhat convenient form, for the Court will doubtless continue for the next two years, at any rate as far as the cases of the consenting Chiefs are concerned, while the question of what is to be done if this Court be not continued has been directly raised by the dissenting States, and that question must, of course, be referred to the highest authority.

"Your Highness and Chiefs, I need detain you no longer on this point, but I commend to your earnest attention the consideration of this question as being one that concentrates within itself most of the elements that go to preserve the peace, the orderliness, the prosperity, and the independence of Kathiawar."

After congratulating the Chiefs who contributed so much to the cost of the Institute, his Excellency conveyed to Mr. Booth their joint congratulations on the success which had attended his efforts in the design and execution of the work.

His Excellency then formally declared the building and grounds open, and proceeded with the Chiefs to inspect the Museum, Library, and Industrial Exhibition.

One very sad event happened five months before the opening of the Institute, which cast a gloom over the whole province. This was the very sudden death of the acting Political Agent, Col. W. Scott. Sir Charles Ollivant having been transferred temporarily in June, 1893, Colonel Scott was appointed to act during his absence. He was then administrator of the Gondal State and had served many years in the Political Department in Kathiawar. He had been only a few weeks at Rajkote when he took ill—and passed away after two days. It was a sad blow and grief to all his friends, and poor Mrs. Scott, who was alone with him. The funeral took place the same afternoon. Col. George Hancock was now appointed Political Agent, and remained so until the return of Sir Charles Ollivant.

A few days after the funeral, Mrs. Scott's son, who was in the Lancers, arrived, and then they both came to stay with us until affairs were settled. But more trouble was in store for her. Her son Woodward got suddenly ill with an attack of typhoid fever, and after ten days he was ordered to be removed to Bombay. He was carried in a bed to the railway, accompanied by Mrs. Scott, a nurse, and a doctor, and arrived the following morning at Bombay. For a time his life was despaired of, but after two months of the best care and treatment, his youth and strength pulled him through. As soon as he was convalescent Mrs. Scott left for England, and he came on a lengthened visit to us to recruit, staying over the Christmas week, which we spent on the Nal Bauli duck and snipe shooting.

CHAPTER XIX.

EPIDEMICS—FAMINE—FLOODS—DISEASES—SNAKES, ETC.

I have casually remarked on the general climate and rainfall, and on sudden attacks of fevers, cholera, and other epidemics, and how much they are aggravated or allayed by weather conditions.

When these are favourable, when the rains come in sufficient quantity, and at the expected time for the growth of the crops and grass for man and beast, and the genial monsoon is followed by a plentiful harvest—all is well; but after a long hot season, when the ground is parched and the grass burnt to the roots, when the young crops, which have appeared above ground, are withering, and the unfortunate farmers who have sown their land with seed supplied by the soucar (moneylender) at an exorbitant interest look on in despair, praying and hoping against hope for the blessed shower that may mean for them and their families food for the coming year *versus* starvation, when the cattle, impoverished and emaciated after a long drought and partial starvation, begin to die off for need of the bare food sufficient to sustain life, then the case is very different, and it is a condition of things by no means uncommon.

It is, of course, partly with the object of averting or alleviating, so far as possible, such loss and misery that communications by road, rail, and canal, water storages, conservancy, etc., are projected, and the late great Indian famines have so shown their need, and so much has been done during the past forty years towards facilitating the carriage of food stores to famine-stricken districts, that such terrible famine results as have taken place can scarcely occur again in such intensity. Nevertheless, the danger is always there, and even a partial rain failure is sure to bring distress in a greater or less degree. After a food famine the poor, who are weakened by insufficient nourishment, contract fevers and die. Cholera visitations, however, do not appear to depend mainly if at all on weather or famine conditions. It is always and under all circumstances to be dreaded, and its appearance is frequent when no sufficient cause for any kind of illness is known.

I believe its vagaries are still a puzzle to the medical authorities, and it has never been proved whether the disease is infectious or otherwise, or by what means the germs are disseminated.

During my residence in India I had close experience of many cholera epidemics, and I have frequently noticed it at its worst in apparently the most healthy situations at the same time that filthy localities near by remained unaffected. I have known two villages, situated a short mile apart, where one was decimated by cholera, while the other remained immune. The latter village in this instance was surrounded by a belt of evergreen trees, while the former was entirely exposed. It was said, I recollect, that the immune village was protected by the trees.

I have known one side of a village street attacked throughout by cholera, while the other was not affected.

It was during the fair season of 1876–78 that many parts of the province were visited by an exceptionally serious epidemic, and that was after a good monsoon and a plentiful harvest. At the bridge works at Jetpur we were greatly harassed, and frequently four or five people succumbed each day, while the deaths in the town, a mile away, were often less in proportion; and this was while the bridge camp was in an open and pure locality, well looked after, and the town was especially impure and uncleanly.

On the bridge works the labourers, who mustered about four hundred, lived in grass huts or in caves excavated in the banks of the river, and it was often my daily and nightly duty to attend urgent calls to visit and physic people suddenly attacked. Those who came daily from adjacent villages would sometimes throw up their work and run away, but as a rule they stayed, the villages around being more or less infected. I kept a supply of cholera mixture (there was no doctor), but it was not often effective. The low caste native very soon caves in, and does not seem to mind much. Although cholera visitations were more or less frequent throughout the province in those days, the epidemic of that year was the most deadly of any I remember. Its work was swift and sure. Near the village of Thorala —three miles from Rajkote—I had road works in progress, on which about two hundred coolies were employed. When I was at tiffin one afternoon an overseer galloped up to report that the camp was just attacked by cholera. I jumped into my tonga, and sped over to the civil surgeon, Dr.

McDougall, who supplied me with a hospital assistant and medicine, and we started for the camp. On the way we met several victims being carried home by their relations, swung in a dhoti (loin cloth). One of these died while we administered a dose. Our object was to prevent those attacked being taken to villages. for fear of spreading the infection, and to send them instead to the Cholera Hospital at Rajkote, a structure improvised for the emergency, and under the charge of the Agency doctors.

A woman we met was carrying her sick child on her back. We gave it medicine, and sent her on to the hospital. On our return we again passed the woman, and found the child dead.

We succeeded in getting in all fifteen cases to the hospital, but all died during the night. On making a round with Dr. McDougall at 10 p.m., we found a mother squatting beside her sick son. whom she refused to leave. Early the following morning the son was dead and the mother dying.

Before we arrived at the camp the previous day all had left for adjacent villages, carrying away their sick with them. Several died on the way, or at their houses, but it was impossible to gather much information.

The attack on the camp was very sudden. All the coolies were well during the forenoon. At 12 o'clock they stopped work for dinner, and it was during that meal that the cholera attacked them. If they had all been eating food from one place one might have suspected that there was something wrong with the food, but the persons attacked had come from different villages, bringing their food with them.

One day, arriving at Bamonbore, I was met by some of the villagers begging me to see two men who were suddenly taken with cholera. I had no medicine, but as I was bound to try something, I got my butler to fetch a bottle of whiskey. The men were in a bad way—turned a yellow pasty colour—and were in a state of collapse. I poured a plentiful supply of neat whiskey down their throats, and got them well rubbed with whiskey externally. Both these men recovered!

Fevers, remittent and intermittent, are at all seasons common, although some conditions of the season are more favourable to them than others. The intermittent or malarial fever, although not so fatal as the other, is very persistent and weakening, and I was at one time a great sufferer from it. The attack begins usually a few hours after sunrise, with a shivering fit, when (although the temperature may be 100°) one's teeth chatter, and no amount of covering will keep one warm. After one or two hours of this the hot stage sets in, during which it is as impossible to get cool, and the skin is dry, parched, and burning. This, after about a similar period, is succeeded by the final stage, one of intense perspiration, at the close of which the sufferer is so weak he can scarcely walk across the room; but if he is a fairly strong subject he will soon recover, and on the following day may be quite fit. On the third day, however, he has probably to undergo the experience all over again, and with the usual one-day intervals the attack may continue for weeks, and if especially severe, a change of climate may become necessary. The best remedy, or rather preventive is sulphate of quinine, but if taken during an attack it is only effective in very large doses—ten to twenty grains.

The condition of a country during a famine-stricken period is heartrending. It is impossible to carry relief to more than a small section of those who need it, and who die daily in hundreds from want and fever.

It is the custom during severe conditions to construct at various central points, where medical supervision is available, camps formed of streets of huts made of matting and thatched with grass, and also large open sheds covered in a similar way.

All those in need were invited to these camps, where they were fed, and employment was found for any who were in a condition to work, but in most cases those who came in were not in such condition—and many came only to die. Even the lowest caste native is not keen to accept such aid, except in great extremity. Some would prefer to wander into the jungle alone, and frequently I have come across skeletons in some retired spot where victims of famine had hidden themselves to die, and where their wretched bodies had been torn up and devoured by jackals and pariah dogs.

After the famine of 1876-77, I recollect visiting Porebunder with Colonel Barton, Political Agent. Here the deaths from famine, fever, and cholera had been very severe.

The poor died in such numbers that there was no time or means to burn the bodies, so they were thrown into shallow holes scooped out of the sand near the beach. From these holes the jackals, pariahs, and hyænas dragged the bodies, and consumed them, scattering the bones around. We had to see that labour was employed to collect the bones and bury them in pits. The inhabitants did not see the necessity!

A. T. Whittle, C.I.E.

Mrs. Whittle.

(See page 213.)

A year rarely passes in which it does not become necessary to make provision for temporary want.

One of the severest famines on record in Kathiawar and Guzerat occurred in the latter part of 1899, due to an unprecedented and general failure of the monsoon. During this famine the evergreen trees and hedges even were cut down to try to find something to keep the cattle alive, but they died in hundreds; and so with the poorer inhabitants, although owing to increased facilities of carriage, food supplies could be brought into the province in large quantities, and works of every conceivable kind were started to find employment.

Among the chief workers who led the van during that terrible season were Mr. and Mrs. A. T. Whittle, who constructed a camp at Wudhwan, and maintained thousands of famine-stricken people for many months at their own unaided expense.

In acknowledgement of this special service, added to others of a like nature, Mr. Whittle was honoured by Government with the decoration of C.I.E.

Mr. Whittle was (and still is) connected with the cotton trade of Kathiawar since 1865, and did more than any man to foster and develop that important industry. He established the first large press and ginning factories at Veramgam, Wudhwan, and Dhollera.

Unexpected floods are another cause of sickness, loss, and famine. Although such are, as a rule, partial and fortunately not very frequent, occurring, as they usually do, after a long and severe hot season, when grazing cattle and other domestic animals are at their lowest state of vitality, they are very destructive to life.

Cattle, donkeys, sheep, etc., which are too weak to make much effort for safety, are swept into the rivers and washed away. I have frequently seen numbers of dead buffaloes and cows washed up along the river banks, while the native Dheds skinned them and fed on the putrid flesh, and the stench was overpowering.

Kathiawar is famous for a breed of large white donkeys. They are employed for carriage of grain, which is slung in little sacks over their backs, one on each side, and droves, numbering many hundred, may be met with travelling along, feeding as they go, to distant places in the province, or to other parts of India. I have often employed the animals for the carrying of stone or sand, etc. They are permitted to feed free at all times, and in all places.

During an unprecedented flood in the Oond river, I think in 1887, most of the country between Pardhari and Dhrole, fourteen miles, was under water, and as I rode over that district a few days after the flood had passed away, I was assailed by a horrible stench, and found numerous bits of rising ground more or less covered with the dead carcases of white donkeys. The animals had rushed for protection to these places, and being weak and emaciated after the long drought, had perished in hundreds from exposure to the rain and storm, which lasted nearly twenty hours.

The loss of buffaloes and other cattle by this flood was also very great, and many weeks passed before the district could be cleared of the rotting carcases.

Bubonic plague first visited Bombay in 1896, but it did not spread to any extent to Kathiawar for some years, and has never been very prevalent, I believe—strict precautions being employed to keep it out. Leprosy has always been common. It was nothing unusual to see lepers living free in any village. As early as 1865 a hospital was erected at Rajkote for the reception of lepers, but it was not freely attended, and it was not compulsory to send persons so affected there except in very extreme cases.

Recently H.H. the Nawab Sahib of Junaghud built, near his capital, an extensive leper asylum, open for the entire province, and the patients then in the Rajkote hospital were transferred thither.

Guinea worm is a disease peculiarly prevalent in Kathiawar at least, and is supposed to be caught directly from stagnant water in old wells and tanks, or from water carried from such for domestic purposes. The worm takes twelve months to mature, and its first appearance is when a little pimple forms, from which in a day or two the head of the worm appears. If this be in a fleshy part of the body, such as the thigh or calf, the worm, so far as it comes out day by day, is twisted carefully round a bit of stick or paper, and fastened down with strips of sticking plaster. With care, it may then be wound out in a week or two, but if by any chance the worm be broken, it all dies in the limb, and becomes putrid, and the patient may be laid up for a long time, or perchance lose a leg or foot. The worm is about as thick as fine whipcord, and varies from 2 to 3 ft. in length.

I had an attack soon after going to Kathiawar. The worm made its appearance on my instep, and could be distinctly traced all over my foot, and ankle, twisted in all directions.

It was a very bad place, as the boot would interfere with the operation of winding it out. I cut away the front part of the boot, and was succeeding in winding very slowly when it got broken, and immediately my foot swelled and broke into a horrible sore. The civil surgeon had had no experience of such cases, and after a few days' treatment he feared I would lose my foot. At this juncture a native doctor named Pitamber assured me he would cure me. He took charge and applied poultices, etc., which he prepared from herbs, and he proved as good as his word. In a month I was able to walk, but my foot did not assume its normal proportions for over twelve months. From that time I discontinued bathing in rivers, and had water for drinking filtered and for bathing boiled.

It is a common mistake to think, as I have noticed so many do, that a bite from every snake is deadly; as a matter of fact, only a very small percentage of snakes are harmful, although most of them will bite under provocation.

The cobras are, of course, the most to be dreaded, and they are common enough, as well as the most domesticated. During the period in which they annually shed their skins they will take shelter in any dry place—in the house, in closets, in waste-paper baskets, wardrobes, and such like. They are partial to fowls, and will conceal themselves in the roofs of fowl houses or in trellis work, where they can catch birds. A full-grown cobra will be four to five feet in length, and possesses a beautifully coloured head, which, when excited, spreads out like a fan, on which large spectacle-looking markings are seen. When surprised it will stand at bay, raising about a third of its length perpendicularly, while the remainder lies flat on the ground. If any person happens to approach within striking area, say two feet, it will strike, and if it strikes the flesh, the end of that person is very near. Recovery is almost unknown, but it is rare that a bite is effective through clothing, unless it be very thin. The poison is contained in a gland at the back of the teeth or fangs from which it is injected into the wound, but when clothes intervene the poison is generally absorbed in the latter.

The natives who go about barefooted and barelegged, such as coolies and grass cutters, naturally are the greatest sufferers, and the annual deaths from snake bite or its effects are according to statistics very large, although it may not be that all those who die from such effects have been bitten by a poisonous snake.

I have known several instances of this. One was a case in which my own gardener died. I was not in the district at the time, but I heard the full facts from the civil surgeon. The gardener, when at work cleaning dry leaves from a pipe drain, was bitten on the finger. The snake was killed and the man and snake taken to the civil hospital. The doctor found that the snake belonged to a harmless species, and tried to assure the patient of the fact, but it was of no avail. He believed he would die, and he did die, that same evening, after sending me his salaams and thanks for merbhan (kindness) and handing over his garden knives and other things for delivery to me.

Another instance was that of a grass-cutter girl, who was bitten while collecting grass. Nothing would induce her to believe that the snake which bit her was harmless. She had all her relations around her, and without any of the symptoms which usually accompany snake poison she died.

There is a very deadly and very beautiful green snake, about four feet long, and very thin. This reptile is found in the jungles, especially in Bombay districts. It will lie suspended among the branches of evergreen trees and bushes, and lives on birds and insects. Its bite is certain death. Another found in most parts is a small and beautifully marked specimen. It will lie coiled up on the ground resembling a stone—a very nasty handful to pick up inadvertently. A sad snake accident occurred once, in which my butler's brother was shot. I was away from home at the time. A large cobra was discovered in the roof of the fowl-house, and none of the servants present were able to get at him to kill or dislodge him. The cook, who was a Portuguese, suggested shooting him, and undertook to perform the operation if he was favoured with the loan of the Sahib's gun. This was supplied with cartridges, and the cook gallantly proceeded to the encounter, but by some mismanagement I could not get properly explained, the butler's brother, a lad of 18, received the first discharge in his head, and was killed instantly.

The cobra was subsequently dug out of a hole in the earthen floor which he, in company with his wife, had apparently occupied for a considerable time, and accounted for the disappearance of many fowls.

The cobra is held to be sacred among high caste Hindus, and is not therefore often killed by them. Bombay suburbs used to be in old days infested with them, and it was never safe to walk out after dark without a light, and a man going ahead with a bell stick to frighten them off the path.

Scorpions are plentiful everywhere, and like snakes, prefer dry quarters. During the rains they will secrete themselves on the highest ground under stones, etc., and are frequently found in the houses. The male scorpion is from four to five inches long, and entirely black, while the female is a dirty yellow colour, and much smaller.

The bite or sting of the male scorpion is sufficient to cause the death of a child, and sometimes even of an adult.

There are strange superstitions among the uneducated and ignorant natives regarding the power of incantations or invocations to prevent death from those bitten by scorpions. I recollect one evening, when dining, a servant rushed in to say that the butler had just been bitten by a scorpion, and was in a bad way. We immediately went to see what could be done. We found the man sitting on the floor of the verandah in front of his room with his back against the wall, while several persons were gathered around him. He had been bitten on the thigh, and the limb was laid bare.

At his side squatted a bhengi (sweeper) the lowest caste of Hindu, who was busily chewing a piece of dirty rag, while another bhengi chanted. The chewed rag was laid on the limb above the bite, and one of the men proceeded to massage the leg below it. After a few minutes the patient was asked where the pain was now, and he indicated a point a bit lower down. Another chewed rag was applied over this point, and the massaging and chanting continued. By these means, in the course of twenty minutes, the pain was steadily driven down to the sole of the foot, when the bhenji at once jumped up, finally screwed the rag into the spot, and ran away with it, taking the pain with him, and the butler rose and resumed his work, perfectly cured!

CHAPTER XX

THREE MONTHS' TRIP TO KASHMIR AGRA, DELHI, ETC. 1894.

I had often wished to visit Kashmir, and now, as I had three months' leave due—and was in need of change—I decided to do it. I hoped to have made up a party of four, but our friends could not arrange their leave to suit our time. So our party consisted of only my daughter and myself. We left Rajkote on August 15th, 1894, and Ahmedabad on the 16th by the Rajputana State Railway. Our journey from Ahmedabad was new to us, and as we would have some days of travelling, I secured a second-class compartment by paying extra fares, a proceeding in which I was by no means seconded, and which I concealed as long as I could, but L—— discovered it—fortunately after the deed was irrevocable—and I am sure she subsequently enjoyed the certainty of not being invaded by other passengers as much as I did.

Nearing Abu the flat, uninteresting plains ended, and we entered wild and picturesque scenery. Large masses of mica slate rose abruptly from the undulating forest and assumed fantastic shapes. Sometimes low, and sometimes towering 100 to 200 feet overhead. The hills were intermixed with red clay and trap and coated with jungle of various hues, amongst which the kakra (flame of the forest) abounded.

The railway stations on this line, I think, as far as Abu, are domed with stone, like Hindu temples. Every building here is domed, and all domes are alike. Even the posts which carry the wire fencing along the railway are of split stone, and make no doubt very excellent as well as economical ones.

Passing Ajmere and Jeypore, we arrived at Ferozapore and changed into the N.W. broad gauge for Lahore and were fortunate in securing the only first-class compartment. Near here we crossed the Sutlej in flood, running thick and yellow, about 1½ miles in width. The bridge is an iron girder one—carried on brick piers, and is a fine structure. We reached Lahore at 7,30, where we changed into the Peshawur train, and left for Rawal Pindi at 8 a.m.

After leaving Lahore we crossed the Rawee, a fine tributary of the Indus spanned by an iron girder bridge on brick piers. The scenery from this point is interesting and changeable. At 10.40 we stopped at a station called Wazirabad, a name I will always remember with gratitude, as also the guard who wired for our breakfast. Not even off the famous silver gridiron did I eat finer mutton chops than were brought in smoking hot for our breakfast here; never in India have I seen the like. Everything on this line reminds one more of arrangements on the Continent than in any other part of India I have travelled in. The punctuality and smartness of all is noticeable.

The scenery all the way to Pindi is fine. Every mile brings forth some new panorama, or some picturesque formation of the ever-changing mountain views, with their rivers, cascades, landslips, deep ravines, precipices, and curious formations.

We crossed the Jhelum, also in flood, a wide but rather shallow river, like a huge sinuous yellow serpent winding up the rich valley till lost in the depths of the mountains.

After a delightful evening's journey we arrived at Rawal Pindi, and drove to Powell's Hotel, which at first sight in the gloaming did not look inviting, and was at this season nearly entirely closed. However, lit up it turned out to be neat and well-appointed. It is sometimes very cold here, and each room is provided with a fireplace, but now it was exceedingly hot, and we had to sleep and eat under punkahs.

Now, the railway journey ended, we had to arrange with the transit agent for a kit cart, on which we dispatched Bica (the butler) and Nuthoo (putty walla) with our kit, and a special tonga for ourselves the following morning to take us to Murree.

For the first twelve miles to the foot of the hills there is a good made road running direct and planted with trees along each side. From the entrance of the hills to Murree the drive is simply charming. The road winds along the face of the cliffs, over bawling rivers, and sometimes it is hewn out of rock.

Presently the pine trees begin to appear, and as the summit is approached they clothe the hillsides in dense patches, giving the scenery a very Alpine look. We emerged from our comfortable tonga several times to ramble awhile and admire the views. On arrival at the tonga depot, beyond which the vehicle cannot be driven, we were met by a number of coolies, a dandy and a pony, to convey ourselves and luggage to Powell's Hotel, which is situated a good deal higher up, on a spur overlooking a deep valley, with a magnificent panorama of mountains on every side.

Everything here is English as well as the climate, and we were glad to get into warmer clothes at once. There is a fine church, and some good shops and stores. The hills are entwined in all directions by well-made roads and walks, amidst verdant and rich foliage and charming views, but I would not care to live here for any time; there is a feeling of imprisonment. When you walk or ride out you must keep to the road—a steep hill one side and a precipice the other; you are always going up or down, rarely on the level. There were a number of visitors at the hotel, including several grass widows, very gay and lively.

We stayed two days to enable our kit to go ahead, and on the third day we followed by tonga, which I had secured for the entire journey to Baramulla, at the Kashmir end of the Jhelum gorge, about 128 miles from Murree. The kit and servants went by ekha. Ponies for tonga and ekha were changed every five miles, this being the tonga mail route to Srinagar.

The first resting place beyond Murree is Kohala, on the Jhelum gorge, twenty-eight miles distant. After two miles or so through forest scenery the descent begins—about 1 in 30 all the way. One pony only is put on the tonga, and the going is delightful; but one can't help feeling a bit nervous when one shoots in and out or round a sharp corner, with a precipice on the outer side and no protection, and going at such a pace it would be impossible to pull up under one hundred yards. Our nervousness was realised at one place by the pony suddenly coming on his knees after rounding a sharp corner. We were shot up into the air, and with difficulty were able to scramble out. The pony lay under the tonga and the wheel was within six inches of the edge of a twenty feet drop into a rocky nallah. The animal was a good bit bruised, and had both knees cut, but we had no resource but to reyoke him, and he took the next stage, three miles, as fast as ever. I suppose they get used to these accidents.

At Kohala, on the Jhelum, we had some delay, as we had to put ourselves and our belongings piecemeal over the crazy suspension bridge; this was on its last legs, and since has been replaced by a fine girder bridge.

View of the Jhelum, 4 Miles from Baramulla, August, 1894.
(*See page*, 221.)

At last we got a new pair of ponies and started for Dulai dak bungalow at 2 p.m. The road was a gentle ascent cut out of the face of the hill 50 to 100 ft. above the river, and sometimes under small tunnels, very dangerous looking contrivances. The ponies had evidently just come off a stage, for we could barely get them out of a walk, and frequently they stopped altogether. We reached Dulai dak bungalow before nightfall, and found food, bed, and bath ready for us in this well-appointed rest-house.

The following day we went on to Domel by a magnificent route, with mountains, snow-capped, appearing through the gorge, hills rich with every description of vegetation, and the Jhelum dashing between rocks 100 ft. below us. L—— would persist in climbing breakneck places in pursuit of wild strawberries and cornflowers, etc. After breakfasting here, we proceeded another stage to Ghari, at the end of a considerable flat from which the hills rise abruptly, and the Jhelum is spanned by a rope bridge—a very dangerous-looking contrivance made of buffalo-hide ropes twisted, one below, on which the passenger walks, and two above, which he holds on to by each hand. At Chagoti, the next stage, there is a curious suspension bridge over the Jhelum, which is made of twisted branches, instead of ropes, *vide* illustration.

We eventually arrived at Baramulla after five days' journey from Murree. The scenery all along the Jhelum gorge is truly magnificent. Here we were at last in the famous "Valley of Kashmir," and our flotilla of boats were ready for us to carry us up to Srinagar. I had, before leaving Rajkote, undertaken to share a houseboat with some friends who were going to Kashmir a month earlier, and this boat was now awaiting our turn. With it were another two boats; one for the servants, with a kitchen on board, and a third a shikar boat to carry my shikari and attendants, for shooting.

Baramulla is a fairly good-sized town, built both sides of the river, connected by a quaint-looking timber bridge. The river from this point through the valley, some 70 miles in length, flows very quietly, and all traffic is conducted by boat. Our boat was most comfortable. We had a sitting-room and two bedrooms, with a bathroom and pantry, and on the roof we had our easy-chairs.

I may here remark, for a country where water is plentiful, the natives are without exception the dirtiest it is possible to imagine. They were dirty enough all up the Jhelum, but here they were much worse. They wear only a loose sack with sleeves at one end, and whatever the original colour of these garments may have been, they are never seen of any but a dingy drab.

We were under weigh early the following morning, and enjoyed, for the first time, the sensation of gliding silently along the glassy surface of the river.

The morning was cloudless, the temperature that of an English summer. The valley, with its orchards, fields of maize and vegetables, the patches of woodland, bounded by mountains on every side, was charming. As we advanced we passed villages and homesteads and timber depots, and groups of fantastic buildings, splendid poplar and chenar trees, also many boats to and from Srinagar, some houseboats like our own, with attendant doongas and native craft, and once a doonga paddled alongside and offered us baskets of delicious pears, for backsheesh. For one anna (a penny) we got 22 pears as good as any in our English market. At 10 o'clock we drew up beside a sloping bank for breakfast and a ramble, to give the men a rest; then on to Sopoor, a rather big village with a wooden bridge. This is the point of departure for many Kashmir trips, and a favourite rendezvous for anglers, as there is good mahseer fishing.

I at once secured a fisherman and the necessary tackle, and that evening we tried for trout and mahseer at the bridge, but were not successful (too high wind), and I hooked only one, which I lost with bad gut.

The following morning, L—— and I started with the old fisherman in his boat at 4 a.m. for the Ningle, famous for mahseer, a mile higher up the river. As the mosquitoes abound here, L—— manufactured muslin coverings for our heads and hands.

We reached the fishing-ground an hour before daybreak, and for a time trolled with frog bait, but without any success.

At daybreak we stopped to change bait and put on spoon, and very soon after we recommenced fishing a strange thing happened—I had taken up my spoon, which had got fast to mussels in the bottom, and as it swung back in the air, the triple hook struck the old fisherman, and sent one of the hooks into his nose, from which none of us could extract it. The poor old chap was in a bad way indeed;

so were we, for our morning's fishing was done; we drew up beside another boat, on which an Englishman was fishing, but he could not help, and the old man would not allow anybody to touch him, beyond removing the heavy spoon and lead weights. We set off for Sopoor as fast as the paddles could take us, and there I discovered a native doctor, but the old boy would not at first have anything to do with him, and persisted in calling the fishinghook-makers, who came on with files and pincers. I saw that unless I took the law into my own hands, nothing satisfactory would be done, so I told the doctor to go to work, and in a few seconds he had the hook out. After a hurried breakfast, we went to the bridge for fly-fishing, and almost immediately I caught two half-pound trout at the same time, but for an hour afterwards did not get a rise. It was very hot then, and we returned to the boat. At 3 p.m. the old man arrived quite fit, and said he wanted to show the Missy Sahib how to catch mahseers, so off we went to the bridge again, where we fished with live bait and fly for two hours, without any result. Considerably disgusted, we returned, and tried to find some place for a walk, but in vain. We were tired after the long day's outing, and went to rest early, after arranging for a start at five next morning.

We often heard of the beauty of Kashmir women, but up to then we saw scarcely any pleasanter to look upon than their costume. At Sopoor there was a decided improvement, and we saw several very fine-featured members of the gentler sex; they are very strong, and do lots of hard work, quite as much as, if not more than, the men, but those terrible dresses are so unsightly, in make and colour. If the Kashmir women excel, as they certainly do, in beauty of face and power of body, the Hindu women far excel them in dress and grace of figure. The Kashmir women and children, whose husbands own boats, live on board, and all take their share of paddling and punting, grinding corn, or rather pounding it, a curious process, which may be seen in operation everywhere. The maize is put in a wooden mortar made of a junk of pine tree scooped out, and pounded by two women with heavy sticks; the energy they put into the business is an earnest of what they are able to do in other ways, and of how they could treat an intractable husband. I imagine the Kashmir woman can generally hold her own all round, and in this respect scores heavily in comparison with her Indian sister.

At Sopoor I had to engage three extra boatmen, making eight in all, for the passage up the swamps, which run south of the Woolar Lake, forming indeed a part of the lake, our heavy houseboat having to be poled along all the way. We reached the swamps, and got over most of the mosquito ground before daybreak. The Woolar Lake opens out here, and looks like an inland sea, as it stretches away to the mountains some fifteen miles off, which close round it, in a magnificent amphitheatre, with their tops clothed in clouds, and the purple and blue mists below; through which, as the light increases, large masses are lit up by the morning sun. The passage for the boats is from 20 to 100 yards wide, and looks like a canal, as it twines about, through the vast extent of green, red, yellow, and brown singhara weed, varied here and there by splendid patches of water-lilies, with their red and white flowers. There is nothing to be seen looking towards the hills at the head of the lake but this extent of coloured weeds, and the effect is very fine. The weed produces a succulent berry which is greatly esteemed by the natives; indeed, whole villages live upon it. Had we been able to go by the Nuru Canal, we would have saved a day, avoiding all the swamps, and a very tedious couple of miles of another very narrow canal, through which we crawled to reach the river some three miles below Sombal, but the water was too low for the Nuru Canal. We reached Sombal, a small village, with groups of fine chenar trees, and a wooden bridge; here we moored for the night, and we tried fishing, without any result. There were three other boats here, one with some ladies, but we knew none of them. At four next morning, we started for Srinagar, passing Shadipore about 8 o'clock. This is where the Sind River flows into the Jhelum, and where the Nuru Canal flows out the name Shadipore is given to it, to denote the marriage of the Sind and the Jhelum. The scenery on to Srinagar was all alike—the broad calm river, covered with boats of all kinds, pursuing their lazy, silent way, the broad fertile country on either side, and hills rising from the plain. At 2 p.m. we entered Srinagar town, which is about two and a half miles long, built on each side of the river, and connected by seven bridges, most of which were washed away during the late high floods. They are all built of pine, in the usual pattern.

A great part of the town looks very dilapidated. The houses are not generally remarkable for their uprightness, and many are in a state of ruin. This is no doubt to be attributed to some extent to fires, earthquakes, and floods, which have been somewhat common in this locality of late years.

We halted at the house of our agent Bahar Shah, and went up to his shawl department, where we had a cup of very peculiar tea, and after arranging a few matters of business, looked over some of his shawls and rugs. Then we got into a small doonga, and were paddled up the river to the post office, where we found a packet of letters.

The river is bordered with splendid poplars, and here are the residences of Europeans ; also the Residency, enclosed within a fine park, hospital, gardens, library, polo ground, and tennis courts, and quarters for married and single travellers ; but most of the visitors live in their boats, which are moored along the river bank under the shade of the poplars and chenars.

We moved up here the following morning. The next evening we unexpectedly met two old friends, General Thatcher and Colonel Cunningham, who were at Rajkote twenty years ago, both now retired and living in houseboats on the river near us. We had a long chat about old friends and old times.

On Tuesday morning we started for the Dhal Lake, taking the houseboat, as we meant to stay a day or two there. The first part of the way is through Tsunt-i-kul Canal, which is very shady and bordered with poplars, chenars, and orchards, to the Dhal gate, which is the entrance or rather the outlet, of the lake water into the Jhelum. This gate, which is of pine, and very strong, is so arranged that when the river suddenly rises, it closes the gate and prevents the water running in and flooding the gardens. The gateway is of masonry, very roughly built. Just here is the C.M.S. Hospital, which is famous for the good it does among the natives, in charge of Dr. Neve.

After passing through the Dhal gate, we entered at once into a perfect wilderness of reeds, orchards, gardens, lotuses, huge beds of marigolds, petunias, and dahlias, lofty rows of poplars with, in many parts, vines climbing up them which were covered with bunches of ripe grapes. Through all this rich vegetation a series of canals wend their way, leading to different parts of the environs. We kept the main canal, which, after a mile, brought us to the village of Kraliyar, with two bridges, one a curious stone erection, called

Naiwidyar, built by the Emperor Akbar. Then two miles further, through gardens and openings, we passed vast patches of lotus lilies, about the most magnificent flowers in existence. They are white and rose coloured, and some of them measured ten inches in diameter, and the leaves from one to three feet.

We reached the open water after some three hours, and soon after arrived at the famous camping ground, Nasim Bagh, a large plantation of splendid chenars on a smooth velvety bank, sloping in terraces to the shore of the lake. Here we found a good many Europeans camped under the trees in small tents, while the boats were moored along the water's edge. The lake here is open, and about two miles wide by three long, that is, up to the vegetation, and all around the mountains rise like an amphitheatre. The hills themselves are without forest, all rocky spurs and precipices. Beyond the Nasim Bagh, are some State buildings and a gun factory, while on the opposite side are the Shalimar Bagh and the Nishat Bagh, both garden residences of the Maharajah.

The Shalibagh, as it is shortly called, is approached by a long narrow canal through a forest of willows ; here the banks are artificial, further on they are lined with chenar trees, and are very shady. The water in the little canal was low, so our houseboat could not go all the way, but the walk along the bank was very pleasant. There are four archways with rooms on each side spanning the canal, which runs down the entire length. Between these separate archways there are terraces about a hundred yards in length, laid out in flower beds and ornamental shrubs, and having extensive orchards of pears, apples, and peaches on either side. The last or principal building is a hall with large rooms on each side, and wide verandahs supported on black marble pillars ; this portion of the garden is called the "Abode of Love," and is said to have been the favourite resort of Jehangir's Queen, Nur Mahal. Around this there is a garden of flowers, and when the water is full it must be a very delightful place, but now the canal and tanks were dry. It was very hot by two o'clock, and we returned to the houseboat for a rest, after which we started for the Isle of Chenars, from whence we sent the houseboat back to Nasim Bagh, and took the doonga to visit the Nish Bagh, the other garden palace. This is a lovely place, built on somewhat the same fashion

Our Houseboat on the Dhal Lake, September, 1894.

(See page 226)

THE DHAL LAKE, SRINAGAR, SEPTEMBER, 1894.

(*See page* 226.)

THACKET I. SULLIMAN.

(*See page* 226.)

CHENAR BAGH SRINAGAR.

(*See page* 226.)

as the Shalibagh, but the gardens rise in a series of steep terraces, each one with a waterfall artificially formed, and the gardens are finer and more extensive. The water was not running, but one could imagine what a grand effect it would have been, with the splendid trees and mountains rising precipitously behind all. There is, however, an air of neglect about both these places. The Maharajah seldom visits them, and only now and again a European goes to see them, or stay for a day. The buildings are very poor, architecturally speaking. The beauty lies in the surroundings, and these are capable of being made earthly paradises. We had a nearly dark voyage across the lake, and arrived at the houseboat somewhat tired and hungry. I omitted to say that we brought away a quantity of peaches from both the gardens, where boats lay at the entrance steps laden with fruit.

At about nine o'clock a violent thunderstorm with lightning came on, and later it rained for some hours. The following morning was fair, but the sky was overcast, which was a pity, as we intended to photograph the beds of lotus on our way to Srinagar. Owing to the cloudy day the flowers were nearly all closed, and it was impossible to get any place to stand the camera upon, so we plucked a quantity, and carried them till we came to a solid bank, and then we arranged some on the dining-table, where we got a photo of them.

We had some business to see to, in connection with our trip to Islamabad, for which place we started the following afternoon, with our three tents and a dandy. We proceeded five miles up the river that afternoon, which would have equalled about three by the direct road. We walked most of the way along the bank, and a delightful walk it was—so cool and bracing with the soft smooth sward under our feet and glorious trees all about.

The last two days' journey up the river to Islamabad was somewhat monotonous, varied only by a walk along the bank, and on Saturday evening by a hunt for chikor. After a pretty hard walk of five miles we only saw one covey, at which I had two shots, both missfires, most unfortunately. I found that it was the fault of the gun, not the cartridges, as I at first supposed.

On the 11th we walked to Islamabad, a little more than a mile from Kambal, where everyone leaves his boat.

The road is very good, and shaded with poplars most of the way. The town is built at the foot of a conical hill, a queer old place, very tumble-down; it consists of one long straggling main street with a few others branching off it, the centre one paved with rough stones and the entire width being about eight or nine feet. At the upper end below the hill slope are a series of tanks with running water and small waterfalls. The tanks are sacred, and swarming with fish, which are worshipped, and it is believed that any person killing one of them will die within a year.

It was our intention to go direct from here up the Liddar valley, but my shikari told me that I would get no shikar there, and induced us to change our minds and go to another locality in search of bears, working round afterwards to the Liddar valley. This delayed us altogether a week at Kambal, as I found my shot gun was out of order, So I sent it to Srinagar to be repaired, at the same time hiring a Winchester repeating rifle to supplement my single barrel one. While the shikari was absent on this duty, we amused ourselves walking, sketching, photographing, etc. One evening we went in the shikar boat up the river to Wazir Bagh, a fine orchard of pears and apples, and a famous camping ground. Large boats cannot go up, and small doongas only with difficulty, as the stream is very shallow and rapid in parts. It took us an hour to reach the Bagh, where we roamed about and ate fruit. On returning, all that was needed was to guide the little boat, which flew down the rapids and round the corners, taking us to our camp in fifteen minutes.

On the 15th all preparations were made for our journey to the hills, and we started the next morning. The kotwal at Islamabad—by name Lussoo—a fine old fellow, had been to see us every day, and this morning brought us a carpet bag full of books, containing hundreds of testimonials from sahibs who had employed him, and old newspapers with mention of his name and the good services he had done. At Delhi, during the Mutiny, he saved his master's life, thereby getting a bad bayonet wound in his forehead. He is only an honorary kotwal, drawing no official pay, and lives by backsheesh from the sahibs, for whom he obtains coolies and ponies, and otherwise assists them in their expeditions. I was amused at one certificate in his collection, which he let me copy—namely:

"This is a very worthy man, as every one agrees:
It is not given to all of us to hold such chits as these.
Three cooley loads he has at least, his virtues by the score
Are numbered, merely kotwal ne'er had such a lot before;
And when good Lussoo stands at last before the golden gate,
And passes in his checks, I'm sure they'll open for him straight.
And well I know, when once inside, with all life's labour done,
He'll make St. Peter read these chits—yes, every blessed one!

(Signed) F. INCH."

L—— called him to our camp, and photographed him, to his great delight—bag, books, and all. He is sixty-seven, and looks as if he would live to a hundred.

16th.—We were up early, and by half-past seven our coolies were all loaded, eighteen for carriage of the tents and kit, and five for the dandy. We sent them all round by the bridge, and we, with the shikari and the boatman Sobano, went down the river, about two miles, in the small boat, where we met them, and from thence commenced our first day's march. I had a diminutive tat, so small that I felt it would be almost a cruelty to inflict my fifteen stone upon him; but after we had walked some two or three miles and the sun began to get hot, we decided to see how our respective modes of conveyance would answer. L—— got into the dandy, where she was very comfortable, and I mounted the small pony, which did not appear to be the least troubled with my weight, and he ambled along the narrow path between the rice fields, and negotiated small brooks and nullahs with consummate tact and intelligence, never making a false step. For ten miles the track lay across a level plain, covered with rice and other crops watered with numerous canals, and more than one large stream had to be crossed. At one place we crossed the river Vishoo in a boat. This stream is as large as the Jhelum. Every two or three miles we passed villages surrounded with groves and orchards; and at one of these we stayed for breakfast, under the shade of walnut trees. At two o'clock we arrived at the foot of the hills, and camped in an orchard.

The following morning we were up at daybreak, and got under weigh by 7 o'clock. The previous day's coolies had to be paid up, and we had new men supplied from the village. For the first mile and a half the track lay mostly across the river-beds, and as they were covered with loose round boulders the walking was bad. The rapid streams were crossed by a tree trunk or two, laid side by side, supported on a pile of boulders at either end. After getting over the last of the river-beds, a short walk through level fields brought us to the foot of the first range of low hills, and we immediately entered a narrow path in the dense forest growth. The path led upwards almost vertically, and although it was a very lovely one it was a breather! This range rises I suppose about 500 feet above the plain; it is nearly covered with underwood, shrubs, wild roses, pine and fir trees, and it presents a very home-like appearance, with its rich green sward and European flowers wherever an opening occurs.

On reaching the top of the ridge, the next great range met our view. This is covered with pine forest, and in the valley between are one or two villages and small patches of cultivation. It was at one of these villages about two miles off that we were to have camped and hunted for bears, but we were met by a messenger to say that the nullah (which really included almost the whole valley) was occupied by two sahibs who had been there for a month; and so, according to shikar law, we could not interfere with their hunting ground. We therefore decided to go four or five miles further on to another bear ground, which we reached by a most delightful path through a rich narrow valley abounding in pears, apples, peaches, and wild cherries. The fruit literally covered some of the trees, so that we could pluck large bunches of them as we passed; the cherries are white, or a pale yellow. We had some stiff climbs, some abrupt descents into small river beds, deeply shaded with forest trees, where bubbling streams swept rapidly onwards till they were lost in the dense jungle; then by a narrow path along the face of the hill, partly shaded by every kind of forest growth, amidst which our old friend the hawthorn was most abundant, while forget-me-nots and other well-known flowers covered the ground. As we both walked up all the hills and rough parts of the road, we were rather tired when we reached our halting place, under a grove of large walnut trees, on a high knob overhanging the village of Gangadhar, and with a splendid view of the mountain ranges beyond. The village people said that bears had been seen within a few days, coming out to the fields from the dense jungle on the low hills adjacent; so we arranged to halt for at least one day to try a honk. No coolies were available here, so the shikari sent to another village for them.

By 8 o'clock next morning our beaters, thirty-two in all, were ready, and we started for our first honk, a large ravine about two miles distant. It was a long and somewhat stiff walk, and a heavy climb to the opposite side, where we located ourselves at the top of a small open glade, sloping for about one hundred yards below us. It was the object of the honk to drive the bears across this open. The beaters commenced from about half a mile up the ravine, and then ensued unearthly yelling which lasted for half an hour. The beat was finished without result, beyond a report that one bear had been seen to pass down the nullah under cover. The beaters then went below and beat up, and this time the bear was driven pretty close to us, and we distinctly heard him as he grunted past, but did not break into the open. We then re-crossed to another open glade, considerably higher up, where a fresh honk was arranged, and we took our position under cover of a pine tree from which I could command the open. There we had a light breakfast, as it would be half an hour before the honk commenced. We had barely finished our repast, when suddenly we were startled by the grunt and growl of at least one bear, quite close to us, in the jungle, and we momentarily expected him to break into the open; but again we were disappointed, the yelling was now tremendous for a few moments, and when it ceased, we were told that three bears, two large and one small, had been met by the beaters. One large beast had come down the ravine while the other with the cub went through the line of beaters upwards. It was very riling, but only a bit of the usual luck of bear honking. We had three more beats during the afternoon without moving a bear. About four o'clock Bica arrived with bearers carrying tea, and we rested for an hour under the shade of a hazel grove on a smooth plot of turf. A prettier resting place it would be difficult to find, and the men brought quantities of apples for us and themselves. One of the beaters reported that the previous evening he saw a bear feasting on walnuts about a quarter of a mile down the ravine, so we decided to visit the locality and wait there till dark on the chance of his returning, so at 6 o'clock we, with the shikari and Sobano, took our way cautiously to the place. The jungle here was dense, and we descended by a narrow path into the nullah, where in the mud we saw fresh tracks of a very large bear and the smaller ones of a cub; these tracks appeared to be quite fresh, not more than a few hours old, and it might have been that they were made by bears driven down by our beaters higher up that morning. We reached the walnut trees overhanging the nullah on both sides, some of which were much broken and knocked about by the bear the previous evening. We hid ourselves in a small patch of maize about 50 yards from the trees, and silently waited till it was too dark to see 20 yards from us; it was getting very chilly, and the moon would not rise for some hours, so we decided to return to our camp, which we reached soon after 8 o'clock. It was a weird walk, partly through dense darkness, wending our way by the light of pine torches along narrow broken paths through the forest jungle. Bica, Nuthoo, and some others met us with lights near the camp, thinking we had lost our way. Wishing to give the bear honking a fair chance, we determined to stay over another day, and beat a large track of jungle not yet interfered with. We were off early the following morning while the dew was heavy on the grass, and shook upon us from the leaves of the forest trees as we passed down the narrow ravine to the place of our first honk. L—— again accompanied us, but after the first unsuccessful beat was over returned to the tents. I then went ahead, and till the sun dropped behind the mountains took literally no rest. Beat after beat was still unsuccessful, and the shikari was evidently depressed. He and his men did all in his power to find sport, but in vain! On only one occasion was a bear disturbed; but he did not break covert. It was the hardest day's exercise I had had for many years, and although so far as sport went it was a disappointment, still it was worth doing to spend such a day from early morning to nightfall wandering amidst the richest and grandest mountain and forest scenery that God has created. Here we have it almost in its natural state, for the few patches of cultivation are mere specks on the vast expanse of mountain, forest, woodland dells, glades, and ravines, pure and undefiled by the hand of man.

As our time was limited and we were anxious to explore the Liddar valley, probably ascending to the glaciers, we abandoned further bear-hunting and left the following morning for Atchibal, which we reached in the evening. We broke the journey for a few hours at a village half way, where we camped under some splendid walnut trees.

About four miles from Gangadhar, we met a sahib, with whom I had a few words on the matter of sport. He had been camped for a week at Ruzool village, hunting for bears, but had no sport whatever, and he was now moving his camp further west. It is the universal complaint. For years past no restriction has been put on shikar, and now the sportsman who wants any must take months seeking for what, a few years ago, he could have got in so many days.

Atchibal is a favourite camping ground at the foot of a spur clothed with pine forest. There is a good fruit garden and a summer residence of the Maharajah, for whom the shooting in this locality is strictly preserved. From the base of the mountain numerous streams of water issue, the source of which (it is supposed) is from the Bhingh river, which appears to escape in part through the porous limestone which forms the base of the mountain range. The streams or springs form altogether a very formidable river, and a considerable portion of the water is led through the gardens in a series of cascades in the usual Kashmiri fashion.

We put up in a quaint old bungalow, consisting of four rooms, with sloping mud floors, dirty mud walls, and a big mud verandah open to the afternoon sun, and not a scrap of furniture; however, we were independent so far, and we stayed here for a day to rest, get some clothes washed, and obtain some necessaries from Islamabad.

On the 22nd we started for Bawan, calling *en route* at Martand to inspect the ruins of the famous temple of that name, one of the most ancient and remarkable in the world. The ruins stand on the slope of the hill above the village of Martand, and are easy of approach. The buildings are constructed of huge masses of stone, carried from many miles distant and put together without cement. Some of the blocks are several tons in weight. There is (or rather was, for it is half in ruins) a central building surrounded by cloisters, forming an extensive court. The principal entrance is massive and richly carved, but only a portion of the walls are now standing; and most of the cloisters have disappeared or are lying in a mass of ruins around.

The following is a description of Martand Temple, which we copied out of books given us by one of the Bawan kotwals.

The nave is 18 ft. square, and the total length of the building 63 feet. The height is calculated to have been 75 feet. The pillared quadrangle measures 220 ft. by 142 ft. and had 84 columns, a sacred number with Hindus.

The foundations are supposed to have been laid by Hurree Rajah about 1000 B.C. The walls were built by Lattaditya Rajah, the roof by Wemdut Rajah 1337 years ago, the cloisters by Showdat Rajah same period, and the main entrance by Gabjian Master.

The walls of the main hall were ornamented with a fine entablature above, now nearly worn away, beneath which are Gothic niches containing sculptures of the Hindu gods, Brahma, Luxmee, and Vishnoo. Brahma wears the sacred thread and snake twisted round his legs, and has four hands, with a book in each. Vishnoo wears the sacred thread, and has four hands. Luxmee is depicted with a snake round her neck and feet. The friezes are ornamented with various wild animals. The east hall contained the lingam, and is quite bare of ornament.

The architecture is distinctly classical. The niches and the cloister openings are pure Gothic, and the pillars of the colonnade might be of Grecian origin. Some authorities state that the temple itself was built by Ramaditya and the side chapels, both now in ruins, by his Queen Amrita Prabha. The date of Ramaditya's reign is involved in some obscurity, but he is supposed to have died about 450 A.D.

After taking some photos and sketches of the ruins, we walked on to Bawan, where our camp equipage had preceded us. It is only one and a quarter miles from Martand, a very shady encampment under a grove of huge chenar trees, with numerous rivulets running through it. Here we decided to stay the day. In the afternoon we met Captain C—— who had just returned from a visit to Amarnath, the famous Hindu shrine at the head of the Liddar. As is usual in these chance encounters, it turned out that we had many mutual friends and acquaintances—truly the world is a little place! Captain C—— left for Martand and Kambal in the evening, and we went to visit some curious caves in the mountain side a mile further on. One of these is a natural cleft or hole in the limestone extending about 200 yards inwards, and there is another cave near it containing one

RUINS OF MARTAND.

MAHOMEDAN FORT AT URI.
(*See page* 234.)

of the most ancient temples in Kashmir, but I will refer to this on our return journey.

After this we went to try fly fishing in the Liddar, but without success. We had an early dinner, and afterwards set to to develop photographs, of which a goodly number had accumulated. While L—— worked, I had the washing to attend to, and this I did by holding the negative in the running stream. It was somewhat tiresome after a while, and I made it rather memorable once by tumbling into the stream ; after this I rebelled, and I don't think any further development was done during the trip up the Liddar.

The following morning, September 23rd, we started for Eishmakam, 12 miles up the valley, which we reached at noon. The journey was a pretty one, chiefly across the flat valley through rice fields and orchards, till near the village, when the ground rapidly ascended. The village lies well up on the hill side, and near it stands an ancient Mahomedan monastery. We camped in a fine park of chenars and walnut trees just below. The valley is narrow here, and the mountains are very grand, closing in and towering overhead with a fine view of the snow peaks above Shisnag.

The next day we reached Pailgam, stopping for breakfast at Butkot half way. This was a delightful trip, the path winding along the mountain side, now in dense shade, then through an open glade, with the river, here almost a cataract, dashing along just below. The autumn tints on the birch foliage contrasting with the sombre pine, the brilliant green of the chenars and walnuts, and the luxuriant growth of vari-coloured shrubs, interspersed with rock and verdant sward, the splendid hills towering overhead, with their crags and precipices and ice topped peaks reaching away in the far distance, formed the most glorious and ever-changing views. As we neared Pailgam we took a few photos, but marked many for our return trip. The camping ground at Pailgam is about a mile from the village (which latter consists of only a few scattered huts) on a sloping spur overhanging the river bed, flat, and thickly studded with pine. From this point upwards only pine is to be met with; the elevation is 8,500 feet ; and even at midday the air was cold and bracing, something like the Scotch Highlands, but drier. This is the great pilgrimage route to Amarnath, three days journey ahead; and although late in the season for the ascent, we hoped to go there if possible, but the path was said to be very difficult and the cold intense.

The Liddar here is joined by another river of nearly the same size, up which there is a magnificent view of the valley towards Soonamerg. As we expected a very cold night we got all hands to collect firewood, pine cones and logs, and, after an early dinner and a roast by a huge fire, we turned in.

A word here about the arrangement at each stage for our onward march. The coolies are changed at every stage, receiving four annas each for the day or stage. The stages are not less than 10 miles. On arriving at a resting place we were almost immediately met by the principal man of the locality; sometimes a kotwal, sometimes a mallee, and invariably they carried an offering of fruit, which was presented with many salaams. Orders were then given for the coolies for next day's march, and they were supposed to be ready at daybreak; occasionally there was a hitch, but generally all was plain sailing. These headmen, however, are frequently a nuisance, they bother one with the everlasting book of chits in which one has to write one's name and date of arrival and departure, and is implored to add something complimentary; then they always expect backsheesh; and if it is not given spontaneously they ask, and follow begging for it. They are not content with a small backsheesh, and for anything less than a rupee, will return almost impertinence. It is always wise to refuse to see the book or give a present till the moment of starting, and then only if all has been done satisfactorily. In visiting Martand, we were beset by no less than three of these gentlemen, who gave much annoyance, forcing upon us their books of descriptions of the ruins, which were, I found, mostly copied out of my own guide book; and when at last I lost my temper and used a little strong language they calmly retired to a safe distance, and hung about demanding backsheesh to the last moment.

Very early the following morning I was awakened by the sound of the crackling of a huge pine wood fire close to the tents; and on getting into my kit found Bica had laid the breakfast-table close to it, a very welcome sight were both, for the morning was bitterly cold, and the water almost freezing. We decided to postpone our march to Shisnag for a day, a decision all were glad of, for we had had three heavy marches without a day's rest. After chota hazri and a roast, we started for a walk to the river and to explore the valley. We returned at ten o'clock to our camp in the pine wood, where, as if to suit the surroundings, we sat down to a thoroughly

Our Camp at Pailgam, 25th September, 1894.

(*See page 237.*)

VIEW OF OUR CAMP AT PAILGAM, FROM THE LIDDAR.

(*See page* 237.)

English breakfast of rashers, boiled eggs, coffee, and excellent bread and butter, with a tumbler of familiar wild-flowers to grace the repast. After breakfast L—— went again to the river bed flat to take photos of the gorges up and down. As evening approached, we did not feel up to a heavy climbing march on the morrow, and after fully considering the matter we decided not to go up further. There was little or nothing to gain by doing so, and it was getting bitterly cold, and would be worse on a higher level.

The climate of Kashmir is in point of temperature exceedingly trying; even then, at the very end of September, the heat of the sun during the middle of the day being almost as great as on the plains, whereas in the shade of the trees or protected from the sun by a hill it was as cool as an English summer, while the mornings, evenings, and nights were so cold that fires and the warmest English clothing were indispensable. It is unsafe to travel during the day without a sun topie. We had a splendid pinewood fire lit in the evening, and another for the coolies, and a similar fire awaited us in the morning on tumbling out of the blankets. L—— took a photo of the camp, fire and all, at seven a.m., and very reluctantly we bid goodbye to our pinewood home of two days. An hour later we reached Batkot, having taken some photos on the way. We breakfasted under walnut trees which were covered with mistletoe, and gathered bunches of queen of the meadow, southernwood, woodruff, wild geranium, buttercups, and ferns, besides numerous other home flowers, but neither daisies nor heather were found; these are never seen in Kashmir in their wild state. We rode on to Eishmakam in the cool of the evening, a most delightful journey.

Before leaving Eishmakam the following morning we took two photos of the hills with the town and monastery, but the sun was not favourable. We stayed an hour for breakfast at a half-way village, and went on to Bawan, where we spent two hours sketching and photographing the cave temple of Bhavmajo. This temple is built in an enlarged natural fissure or cave in the limestone, about 60 feet above the river. The entrance to the cave is closed with an architectural doorway of classical pattern, much broken and defaced, and by it is a large lingam. The passage from this door to the temple is about 50 feet, raised in rough stone steps. The doorway of the temple is rectangular, 3 feet by 4½ feet, surmounted by a Gothic pediment, with trefoil sculptured ornaments, and it is flanked by small niches, which formerly must have held images. This is supposed to be the earliest specimen of a Kashmir temple, and dates from the first or second century of the Christian era. (*Vide* "Neve's Guide to Kashmir.")

The following morning we were early astir, and walked into Islamabad, six miles by a delightfully cool and shaded pathway under the Karrymah all the way, and by eleven o'clock we were in our boat, and on our way down the river towards Srinagar. The following morning we visited the ruins of Avantipur temple, the gateways of which alone are standing, with a few fragments of the cloisters. The temple was built by King Awantiwama, and is of the same design as Martand, but much smaller. Avantipur was once a large city, now it numbers only a few huts. The following day we arrived within five miles of Srinagar, where we moored for the night.

We arrived at Srinagar on September 30th, on Sunday morning, in time for early service. We were pretty busy all day, and went again to church in the evening, meeting General T—— and Colonel C——, who invited us to dine with them the following evening. A very funny little building is this church—wooden walls, seven feet high, very shaky and sloping, and a wooden roof covered with mud. The service was conducted by two clergymen, a lady played a small American organ, and the singing was very good. Afterwards we repaired to the library for a while. This institution has been got together by General T——, who takes a great deal of interest in it; it is a considerable boon to travellers, who are allowed for a subscription of Rs. 6 a month to take away a number of books and change them as often as they wish.

The following morning we went early to the city, and did a good deal of sight-seeing and making purchases. In the evening we dined with our friends in the General's houseboat, a very fine one, and beautifully furnished, and we had a most pleasant evening and much talk over old times and old friends, many since gone.

We remained three days at Srinagar, as we had purchases to make for friends in India. It is amusing work bargaining with the boras who come alongside in their boats. They usually ask from half to twice or three times what they will eventually accept; and I fancy no visitor escapes being done by them sometimes. However, with care and ex-

City of Srinagar.

(*See pages 238-39.*)

CITY OF SRINAGAR.
(*See pages* 238–39.)

perience this may be avoided, and there are ruling prices for many classes of wares. The pasmino and puttoo clothes are excellent, and remarkably cheap. The latter can be purchased for from four to twelve annas a yard, and I got capital suits made complete for seven rupees. There are embroidered purdahs and carpets, and rugs made of catskins, silver fox, Astrakhan sheep, etc., at prices one-sixth of what one would pay for them in Europe. Very fine silverwork in chased patterns can be got for considerably less than Kutch work, and it is much finer. Some of the handsomest work is the gold and enamel on copper, and copper chased vessels and ornaments. The prevailing colours for enamel are blue and purple, and a very beautiful blue it is. There are also quantities of brass-work, and beautiful tables of carved walnut wood, with tops of copper chased in the patterns of the country, chenar and lotus leaves, flowers, etc. These are made to fold up, and so can be conveniently carried. Srinagar is also famous for papier mâché.

As Ladak is famed for the precious stones found there, quantities of these can be purchased at Srinagar remarkably cheap. Topazes, turquoises, sapphires, and amethysts are plentiful, also onyx and catseyes. Diamonds and emeralds are not found. We bought some well-cut topazes and sapphires for a mere song.

Among the places of interest we visited was the Mission Hospital, which we were shown over by Dr. Arthur Neve, who founded it and carries it on entirely by voluntary subscription. It is an instance of success and usefulness due solely to one man's energy and zeal.

On our last day we were busy packing up our purchases in cases, most of which I had to make myself out of old boxes I got from the Parsee shops, and with tools I borrowed, for no carpenter could be found. We met again with Captain C——, *en route* for India. In the evening we said good-bye to our few friends, and early on the morning of October 3rd left Srinagar, arriving the same evening at Sombal, where we arranged to visit the Manesbal Lake on the following day.

We were unable to go up the Sind Valley *via* Sanderbal as we intended, the river being then too low to take the houseboat.

From Sombal there is a small canal connecting the river with Manesbal Lake, and as this also was too low for the houseboat we took the cook boat, a fine large doonga, and the shikar boat, with tents and provisions for the day, and started early. The doonga stuck fast at the mouth of the canal, and it took nearly an hour to clear her; the rest of the way was easy. L—— and I went ahead in the shikar boat, to look for snipe in the swamps at the foot of the lake, but we had little success, and succeeded only in getting a brace; the boat could not be poled or paddled through the thick weeds, and walking was impossible.

In the meantime the doonga had preceded us to the upper end of the lake, where on arrival we found the tents pitched on a terrace about a hundred feet over the water, under a grove of chenars. The view from this terrace was lovely; the calm lake with the forests and hills reflected therein and the distant view of the Kashmir plains with the Himalayas beyond. Certainly a grander breakfast room could not well be found, or two people better able to enjoy and appreciate it all.

Another sahib was encamped just below us, and we made his acquaintance later on in a curious way.

After breakfast L—— went for a rest in the tent, and I for a stroll till 2 p.m., when, as I had just settled myself for a sleep in an easy chair, a villager came to me imploring me to go and shoot chikor, which he assured me were in plenty less than a mile off. For a time (remembering former experiences of these men's veracity) I was proof to his entreaties, but he at length prevailed, and I started with him and two other coolies whom he called.

For one hour I walked over the roughest country I ever shot over, up and down the hill sides, in and out of ravines, through thick thorny shrubs, over boulders and river-beds, and at last had the satisfaction of seeing three chikors rise a hundred and fifty yards off! We were returning, when my friend, who had induced me to go, and was close to me, suddenly gave a jump, threw himself on the ground and shouted to me for a knife, calling out that a snake had bitten him, and roared that he was going to die; then he took the knife and nicked or pretended to cut his toe, called on me to bring the other men (who were beating on the hill side) to carry him to the village, and appeared to be in a very excited condition and in great pain. I examined his toe and found two small cuts, but they appeared to be nothing more than what a thorn would have made, and certainly did not look like the punctures a snake bite would leave, and I told him so; but he swore he saw the snake bite him. The other men came running up and made much fuss, tearing their clothes to tie up the foot, and presently the bitten man was got on to the back of one of his friends, who trotted off with him. At every halt he threw himself on his back and roared, apparently with fright and pain. In half an hour we arrived at camp, when he again threw himself down, and a crowd from the village collected round him, the ladies of his family beating their breasts and howling, and altogether the din was awful. I examined his foot again, and felt almost certain that he was not bitten by a snake, and my boatman, Subano, pronounced it to be either a cut made by himself, or a thorn, and that the man was either frightened for nothing or cleverly shamming. Not knowing how to act I tried what effect whisky would have, and poured a glass and a half neat down his throat. This brought the tears into his eyes with a vengeance, and he doubled up like an eel, spluttering and howling. The din brought the Captain out of his tent, and his opinion was the same as mine, that the fellow was either acting an old trick exceedingly well, or that he was in a terrible fright, and to compose him he prescribed and administered a large dose of neat brandy. This pretty nearly finished the wretch; the tears rolled down his face, and with a few howls and contortions he lay quiet.

I then packed him off to the village, cured, and we saw or heard no more of him. On leaving I gave his mate a rupee, with which he seemed mightily pleased. I was told that it is a trick sometimes adopted by these people to feign sudden illness or snake bite, when they have failed to show the sahib any sport, so as to excite the latter's sympathy and open his purse, instead of the stick and no pay.

Captain H—— joined us at tea. He had been eight months, including a whole winter, in Ladakh, and had made a good bag. He showed us some fine heads, and having only three days before shot a barasing, he supplied us with a haunch of venison. He was to stay four months more in Kashmir, and his accounts of his travels in Ladakh, and living for several months in the snow in an 80-lb. tent without vegetables and on the poorest native fare, was most interesting. Evidently he was a very keen sportsman!

We had a moonlight return trip over the lake, which was as smooth as glass, and arrived at our houseboat at nine, after a very pleasant and exciting day.

Next morning we voyaged on to Banyar at the mouth of the Jhelum, where it discharges itself into the Wular Lake, stopping now and then to look for snipe.

The following day we arrived at Alsoo; the lake was low, and a stretch of half a mile between the shore and the town was now dry ground. We made all arrangements for the ascent to Nagmerg on the morrow. The views from our mooring ground were very fine; especially that looking towards Hoary Haramouk, cloud-capped and glaciered, which was seen to perfection here.

In some guide books the approach to Nagmerg is said to be fairly easy, but that idea must have been taken second-hand. For the first three miles it is easy enough, but the remaining six or seven are just the stiffest piece of climbing I ever met with. The rise is about 3,500 ft. above the lake, or a full elevation of about 9,000 ft. About half-way up the pine forest is entered, and the path is not only excessively steep and slippery but very rough. At about one-third up the path to the Lolab turns off to the left, crossing a pass considerably lower than Nagmerg by a beautiful ravine clothed with pine to the summit. We stayed for breakfast in a lovely glade in the pine forest near some woodcutters' huts, and reached the open summit in the evening. This is a large meadow, so-called, sloping steeply towards the south, while from the north it descends precipitously into the Lolab valley, some 2,000 ft. below; densely clothed with pine and chestnut. The meadow may be a little over a mile long by half a mile wide, interspersed with clumps of trees and surrounded on all sides by pine forest, and at one end the mountain range rises to another smaller meadow and pass. The view from Nagberg is said to be the finest in Kashmir, certainly by far the most extensive. To the right the mountain ranges are forest clad, extending away to Hoary Haramouk, with its shining glaciers and abrupt precipices frowning 18,000 ft. over all. To the left lovely glades with clumps of pine and chestnut in the near foreground, and the Lolab pass with the snow-capped range beyond; while in front the pine slopes stretch away to the shores of the Woolar Lake, and the valley of Kashmir all lies mapped out at one's feet, with Srinagar and its Hari Parbat, Tukht-i-Sulliman, and Manesbal, and on a clear day Gulmerg, Sopor, Sombal, and all the windings of the Jhelum and the various canals, bounded beyond by the mighty range of snow-capped mountains towards the Pir Panjal.

THE "HOARY HARAMOUK," 17,000 FT. FROM NAGMERG, OCTOBER, 1894.

(*See page* 242.)

On the highest part of the meadow we found a small log hut, with two rooms each about ten feet square, and a fireplace in one of them, the floor of pine bark, and the walls and roof of split pine logs. The habitation was rough, but when we got our kit into it and lit a big fire, it was cosy enough; outside a huge pine-wood fire was kept constantly going, and there was the usual shed for the men and for cooking. This is simply a floor projecting from the hill side, and the ground underneath excavated to form a room.

We stayed one clear day exploring and sketching and photographing, and a very enjoyable day it was, and on the next morning we started for the descent. We took a more direct path straight down the grassy slope, through the pine. It was very cold and raw, and when about a mile on our way a heavy snowstorm overtook us, and for nearly an hour it snowed incessantly. It was a very wintry blast that accompanied this mountain snowstorm, and twice we took shelter under huge pines. Soon, however, we were out of it, and lower down it was presently a bright warm day, and we were glad, at twelve o'clock, to get under the shade of some birch and apple trees for a light breakfast. Here L—— consumed a large amount of blackberries—the bushes were laden with them—and we also got some honey from one of the villages; which was very acceptable. This can be got at most villages; the inhabitants keep bees in the thatch, or in the walls of their mud houses. We arrived at our boat at two, after one of the most enjoyable excursions we had had in Kashmir.

For the ascent to Nagmerg I hired a pony. A very diminutive little animal he was, but a wonderful climber. He was not more than twelve hands, and I am sure I could easily have lifted him; but he scorned my weight, and went up the steepest and roughest places with me on his back (when I allowed him) with the most apparent unconcern, but I did not let him do it much. A forbearance much wondered at by his owner, who continuously poured into my ears the names of the many great and heavy sahibs that pony had carried to the top without a rest.

During the descent, riding, of course, was impossible for the first very steep part, but lower down I did mount, and once had a ludicrous tumble. We had suddenly come on to a very steep bit of path and I got so far forward that I seemed to be sitting just at the back of the tat's ears. Certainly there was nothing visible to me but his ears, and those only for a few moments, when I lost them, and found myself sprawling on the path and the pony looking at me curiously from above.

Previous to this catastrophe L—— had at least three falls coming down the steep slope near the summit, after which she fastened herself on to me for support. The same afternoon we started to move a few miles down the lake to another mooring ground, with a view to securing an early start for Sopor in the morning. The boatmen fear to cross the Woolar Lake late in the day, as the large boats become unmanageable in squalls, which are common in the afternoon, and even on this occasion they did not move without much previous consideration. Their hopes, however, for a calm passage were partly blighted, for when we got within a mile of our halting place, a violent squall came on. The boatmen got into a terrific fright, rushed in to land, and called on us to jump out, and tried to tie up the boat, but this could not be done where we were. The wind was powerful and the shelter slight, and the big houseboat, broadside on to the squall, was being blown along shore in spite of all the efforts of the crew. Soon, however, a score of men arrived from some near village, and by means of ropes they contrived to haul the boat to the mooring place by nightfall.

The evening turned out very cold, and we kept in the boat with all doors and windows closed, and got under the blankets early.

By 4 o'clock the following morning we were under weigh, as we had eight miles to pole the big boat, and the lake here was thick with singara plant. About six o'clock the boatmen roused me with news that there were flocks of duck and geese on the lake close by, so I tumbled into my clothes and on to deck. There were large flocks of wild geese, a quarter of a mile off, and lots of teal and duck, but they all appeared very wild. I got into the shikar doonga paddled by two men, and started first for the geese, but it was no use; after half an hour's work I could not get within two hundred yards of them. The duck and teal were nearly as wild, so I was obliged to content myself by slaughtering a number of coots for the men, and returned to the boat numbed with cold.

There were two or three other boats out after the wild-fowl, but I do not think they were more successful than I was. Soon after chota hazri we reached Ningle, where we got on to the bank and walked to Sopor; it was then a bright and beautiful summer's morning. Here we took

VILLAGE OF SOPOR, ON THE JHELUM.

(*See page* 244.)

PASSING THROUGH THE SINGHARA SOUTH OF THE WOOLAR LAKE, AUGUST, 1894.

(*See page* 244.)

in some supplies, and started in the afternoon for Baramoola, where we arrived at nightfall. About ten o'clock another bad storm came on; it rained and blew, and the boat leaked from the roof, and the following morning it was again cold, and cloudy, and raw, and we kept a fire up in the dining-room all day. At daybreak we got a present of some teal and snipe from Captain C—— who had just arrived from Sombal, and he spent the afternoon and dined with us, a pleasant evening round the fire. He left by mail tonga next morning, and we started at eight o'clock, not without misgivings on account of the weather. We had one bullock cart for our heavy kit, which was always to go ahead to the place we intended to stay the night, while with us we took an ekka to carry the camera, a table, two easy chairs, and a tiffin basket for our breakfast camp. L—— had her dandy, I had nothing, but we both intended to walk all the way to Murree, about 123 miles. We stopped for our first breakfast, about eight miles from Baramulla, at a little wooden shanty on the roadside, and walked on to Ranpore in the evening, visiting on the way the ancient ruins of the Kalyar Temple, which we photographed. At Ranpore we found the entire bungalow unoccupied, and we put up in it, in preference to pitching tents, the weather was so cold. The rooms were good, and with big fires we made ourselves very comfortable for the night.

The following morning we made an early start and reached Uri at 4 p.m., carrying out the programme of the previous day. The walk of fourteen miles was very lovely, and the sharp cold bracing wind made it still more enjoyable. We stopped for breakfast at a very picturesque place near a bridge over a cataract from the mountains, and under the shade of some splendid forest trees. Near Uri the road takes a detour of some three miles to get round a deep ravine, but there is a short cut across the ravine by which some two miles can be saved; this we took to our subsequent regret, for the pull in and out was a terrible one, especially after our long walk. The new bungalow not being ready, we put up in the old shanty which, however, was very cosy with fires.

It was a bright moonlight night, and the dogs were a nuisance. I got up and went forth with a gun and vengeance n my heart to slay them, but they were evidently accustomed to such sorties, and only howled the harder while they kept a safe distance.

The following morning we started at eight and walked seven miles, taking some photos of the Jhelum gorges as we journeyed on. This and the previous day's march were about the grandest of all.

The Chagoti bungalow is picturesquely situated on the hill-side, about a hundred feet above the road, from which it is approached by a bridle-path, and some three hundred feet above the river, which is here crossed by a rope-bridge made of twisted branches. L—— took photos of both, and had a very hard climb to reach the latter the following morning, and it was consequently unusually late when we started on our march to Hatti. We breakfasted in a cool and shady nook under a precipice, which rose some hundreds of feet sheer above us, while the Jhelum rushed foaming two hundred feet below, and all around were towering ranges of mountains, on most of which the snow had already whitened the summits. It was truly a magnificent resting-place. I always thought these picnic breakfasts on the march, amidst such charming scenery and in such a bracing and delightful climate, the most enjoyable part of our wanderings, especially when we had such excellent appetites to do justice to the good things unloaded from the ekka, and it always appeared unaccountable to us, how any person who cared for scenery such as this could prefer to rush through this glorious gorge in a covered tonga, reeking with unsavory drivers and gorawalas and crushed up with kit, unable to do more than peer out at the risk of straining one's neck, and thoroughly uncomfortable. We did this going, and we did not know what we missed till we performed the same journey on our return on foot. The more we saw of the Jhelum gorge the more fascinated we were with it.

At Hatti the old bungalow was a ruin, and so we pitched tents and lit a big fire. On the next day we arrived at Ghari, where we found a heavy post awaiting us, and as we had letters to write, we were glad to find ourselves in a comfortable and well-appointed house once more.

The following day, October 20th, we reached Domel. This used to be a favourite halting-place till the dak bungalow was washed away by the floods of 1893. Another large river, the Kishenganga here joins the Jhelum, and there was a fine suspension bridge crossing the latter on the route to Abbot-tabad, which was also carried away by the floods of 1893. As a temporary measure a light foot suspension bridge has been erected. This is a lovely place, and all around is grand

Suspension Bridge over the Jhelum, made of Twisted Branches.

(*See page* 246.)

View from Domel. The Landslip which blocked the Jhelum in 1883.

(*See page 247.*)

and imposing. We visited some of the small shops in the little bazaar, where cut stones for jewellery are sold, and we purchased some and got them set in silver rings for the servants.

We put up in a temporary structure, a low range of godowns fitted up *pro tem.* as a rest-house. The views from here are magnificent, and looking down the river one of the largest landslips is seen. The falling of this blocked up the Jhelum and caused a temporary inundation. The next day's march to Dulai was only nine and a half miles, which we accomplished without any halt, and we had a quiet day in this comfortable dak bungalow. Here we met a Dr. S—— who informed us that there was a quarantine of twelve days at Kohala on all cattle coming from Kashmir, owing to rinderpest, and that our bullocks would be detained, but he promised to do his best to arrange for us. The following day we had our last march in the Jhelum gorge, breakfasting in a rocky ravine half-way to Kohala, which we reached at sundown. Many hundreds of cattle were camped for two miles along the road, which was blocked with carts laden with fruit and grain. Much of the former evidently would never reach the plains, to judge from the heavy odour therefrom. Dr. S—— met us, and said he had arranged fresh animals for our kit, and comfortable rooms in the dak bungalow were secured for us.

The following morning we commenced our ascent to Murree, twenty-seven and a half miles, which we completed the following afternoon at three. About ten miles from Kohala we met a pedestrian who had left Murree that morning, taking the old road, and did not discover his mistake till he had gone a long way, when he was directed by some villagers to the new road, which he had just joined by a hard walk over the hills. He had lost his ekka, and had had no food all day, having walked seventeen and a half miles. Fortunately our ekka just then overtook us, and we were able to provide him with food and drink which we left him engaged upon, on the roadside. A few miles further on we met his ekkas and servants, who doubtless reached him ere long.

We were delayed at Murree till the 27th, owing to all the tongas being previously engaged in a general stamp de for the plains. The hotels were almost empty, and are annually closed soon after this date, as Murree is snowed up for three months. We had nice rooms and big fires all day, and enjoyed our three days' rest exceedingly. Here we purchased a quantity of fine Kashmir honey, disposed of what kit we did not want, and returned our tents to Srinagar, and on Saturday drove into Pindi. The road was very dusty and the country considerably dried up and uninteresting after Kashmir.

At Pindi the hotels were crowded. We sent off our heavy packages by goods train, and left on Sunday night with light travelling kit for Lahore, where we arrived at ten on Monday morning and put up at Nedows hotel. Being a native holiday the banks were closed—rather unfortunate, as I was in want of money. We went to see the Chiefs' College, Museum, and Bazaars. The former is a very handsome group of buildings in red sandstone, with some fine and well-executed carving and pierced work. We were unfortunate in being too late to see the Principal, and so could only view the outside.

The following day we visited the city, which is well worth seeing, and purchased some pashmino cloth, which is made here, and is very fine. In the bazaars we got some good daggers and straw baskets. At four p.m. we left for Amritzar, arriving at seven, but only to find no accommodation available. The only hotel was occupied entirely by the Viceroy's staff, and even at the railway station the rooms were filled; we were therefore obliged to do the best we could on the platform till midnight, when we left for Saharanpur. As there was no proper resting-place at the station, it was rather tiring work; I got L—— a cane couch to lie down upon for a while, and found an easy chair for myself.

The train was late, but we got a first-class compartment to ourselves, and slept sound till morning. About eight o'clock we reached Umballa cantonment, where we were delayed for some time for no apparent reason. We arrived at Saharanpur about 12 o'clock, and had breakfast at the station, sending Bica out to the hotel to find out if we could have rooms. He returned with an answer in the affirmative, and we went at once, taking what was needed in the way of luggage, and putting the remainder in the luggage office. We got two very comfortable airy rooms in the hotel, and found it very neat and well-managed. In the afternoon we went in a gharry to see the bazaar, and visited the leather workers and wood-carvers, for which Saharanpur is famous.

Here we purchased pucca solid leather trunks for about one-fourth the price of similar trunks in Bombay. Indeed, they are superior in many ways to others I have seen three or four times their price, so light and strong, and well made. I also got leggings and rug straps, and a pair of skikar shoes, and a new case made for my binoculars, for a few rupees.

The wood-carving also was well worth a visit; they make screens, brackets, and easels, picture frames, boxes, and many other things. The carving is chiefly pierced work, but they do all kinds in floral and geometrical patterns.

It is not generally so fine as the teak and blackwood carving of Surat, and Ahmedabad, but it is excellent of its kind, and remarkably cheap. Some of these screens and tables are among the finest pieces of workmanship, taken all in all, that I have seen. The woods used are a dark brown, and light cream colour; the name of the latter is Dudia, the other I forget, but it has a pleasant perfume, something like sandalwood. The houses these people work in are so small that we had to have the articles for sale brought out into the narrow street for us to see.

The next day we visited the large Government gardens, which supply seeds and plants to many parts of India. The grounds cover one hundred and twenty acres, but they appear to be kept up more as a matter of business than for pleasure. There is a large horse-breeding establishment also, but we had no time to visit it.

We left for Delhi on the morning of the 2nd, arriving about midday, and put up at the Metropolitan Hotel, one of the nicest and best-kept hotels I have seen in India. The same evening we drove to a few of the sights near at hand,—namely the Durbar Hall, Private Hall of Audience, and Queen's apartments, and the Pearl Mosque.

The Durbar Hall is built of red sandstone, a noble arcaded building, containing the King's throne, a magnificent piece of inlaid marble work, profusely carved and ornamented. It is raised some six or seven feet from the ground.

The private audience chamber, where the peacock throne used to be, is a gorgeous building of white marble, inlaid, and carved throughout, with much gilding; the ceiling is also most beautifully worked. Beyond it on one side are the Queen's apartments, also made entirely of solid marble, every available space of which is rich in exquisite carving, mosaics, and inlaid work, and the doors and windows are marble fretwork in many beautiful

Government keeps a strict eye to the care and maintenance of these buildings, and the least injury is at once repaired. On the other side of the audience chamber is the Pearl Mosque, the private worshipping place of the Royal Family, this being also of white marble inlaid and carved exquisitely. As it was getting dark after visiting the palace, we drove through the Chandi Chowk Bazaar before returning to the hotel.

The following morning we started in a carriage for the Kotab Minar, eleven miles off. Two miles from the Delhi gate is the tomb of Humayan, the old King of Delhi, where the rebel king and his two sons took refuge after the capture of the city, and from whence they were taken by Major Hudson, and conveyed to the Delhi gate, where he shot the sons. The refugees had been concealed in a large vault beneath the building, which is a magnificent structure kept to the present day in excellent repair.

The Kotab Minar is said to be one of the highest pillars in the world, being 238 feet. It is a tapering shaft, richly carved. An inside staircase of 379 steps takes one to the top, from whence is obtained a fine view of old Dehli, and the surrounding country. Near the Kotab, and opposite the beautiful Mohammedan arch, is an iron pillar, supposed to have been placed there in A.D. 319 by the Hindus. Its height is 23 feet, all in one piece, and its weight 17 tons. There are some fine Hindu cloisters here also, which we duly inspected, and then went to a small traveller's bungalow close by, to partake of a previously ordered light breakfast. After waiting a quarter of an hour the messman in charge brought us a huge pot of very bad tea, twelve chowpatties made of country flour, and nine eggs ! apologising that these were all he was able to produce on so short a notice. What he could have done on a longer notice may be imagined ! We had an egg and chowpatti, and tasted the mixture called tea, and left again for Dehli, where we arrived about 12.30 o'clock, and at once drove to the Bazaar, in search of curiosities till tiffin time. At four o'clock we went to the ivory shop, and watched the workmen carving the wonderful ivory toys, and we were unable to resist buying one beautiful specimen in the shape of an elephant with a howdah and men in it, ladder, chains, housings, hookah and all complete, carved out of a single block of ivory.

We then went to visit the Ridge, on which we saw the monument to commemorate General Nicholson and those who fell with him during the Siege of Delhi, in 1857, then to the cemetery, where we saw General Nicholson's grave, and to other places of interest while the light lasted.

We left Delhi the following morning for Agra, which we reached at four p.m. The previous night it had rained, and all day till well on in the afternoon it continued wet and raw, like a November day in Scotland; but on reaching Agra it was a lovely bright evening; it was too late, however, to go sight-seeing. We put up at Laurie's Hotel, which was comfortable, and the following morning before breakfast we went to visit the jail, where they make very fine carpets.

After breakfast we visited the Taj Mahal, which we, like all travellers, were very anxious to see. It certainly is, of its kind, the most magnificent structure in the world, but it is one which I fancy few people would care to see a second time. It is just a splendid tomb, of magnificent dimensions and workmanship, entirely built of white marble richly carved in parts, especially in the interior.

It is, like most Mahomedan tombs, octagonal, with a gallery running round the interior, where are placed the tombs of the King Shah Jahan, and his consort Nurmahal. Immediately around the tombs is a perforated marble screen, about eight feet high, very beautifully carved in a foliated design, and the sides of the dome around are elaborately ornamented in marble mosaics.

The acoustic effects of this dome are very peculiar. The least sound—even a whisper made within the screen—is repeated louder and louder as it ascends the huge dome; it seems to circulate round it in a most musical and melodious way till it dies away at the top. A number of people talking in a low voice below has a most strange effect; the sound appears to be changed to distant music, composed of the blending of all the voices. The place, whether from those strange musical sounds that strike the ear immediately on entering, like distant chanting in some large cathedral, or from the majesty of the building, has altogether a sacred feeling about it, which induces one to remove one's hat and talk in a low voice, as one would do in a place of worship or in the presence of the dead.

The entrance to the Taj is through a handsome Mahomedan gateway of red sandstone and marble, with much stucco painting and inlaid work. From this gate to the Taj itself the approach is through a fine garden laid out on each side of an artificial masonry watercourse with small falls and pipes, through which the water plays on State occasions.

The great square on which the tomb stands is, like the Taj itself, of white marble, and the glare of it all in full sunshine was almost blinding. The Taj is best visited in the early morning or evening, or by bright moonlight. We subsequently visited the Pearl Mosque (Moti Musjid), the palace Audience Chamber, and King and Queen's apartments, all of which are of marble, inlaid and carved, and are altogether most magnificent in design and workmanship. They are all maintained by Government in perfect repair.

One cannot help wondering, when examining these splendid relics of the past splendour of the Mahomedan rule in India, if indeed it is all over; they look so new and so fresh; but a little consideration shows that all these memorials in Delhi and Agra can only for the future mark a past era, which can never be revived. The present go-ahead world would never suffer a king to spend his lifetime and the revenues of his kingdom on preparing a tomb to enclose his remains after death; and many of these old Mussulman kings appear to have had little other object in life than effeminacy and luxury while they lived and preparing magnificent resting places for their bodies afterwards.

We left Agra on the morning of the 6th, by the Rajputana State Railway, at ten a.m., and arrived at Jeypore at 10.30 p.m. We changed trains at Bandikui, where we got an excellent dinner at the railway station refreshment room.

At Jeypore we had comfortable rooms, and the following morning visited the gardens, where we met Colonel J——, to whom I had an introduction, and he went with us to the Albert Hall and Museum, which is a very beautiful white marble building, in the centre of the gardens. The Museum, which has been got together chiefly through the exertions of Dr. H—— is one of the finest general museums in India, and is kept up in splendid style. The cost of the Albert Hall was five lacs, and the garden twelve lacs. There are some fine aviaries in the gardens, which, like everything else, are well constructed and well managed.

The City of Jeypore is unlike any other in India. There are fine main streets of about forty feet wide, and from these others equally wide branch off. The houses are richly painted in red and stucco. It struck me, however, that I would have preferred more verandahs and trees, of which there are practically none for, after all, in a country like India, shade is a *sine qua non*, and one seems to look for it and to feel that nothing is perfect without it.

There is a school of art there, in which boys are taught drawing and designing for brass and woodwork and pottery. There are many workers in these arts, and very beautiful work is turned out. Jeypore is also famous for its armouries, and quantities of ancient arms of all parts of India can be purchased or made to order from original designs.

The old palace of Amber, about seven miles from Jeypore, we visited the following morning. A drive of four miles takes one to the pass of the gorge, from whence the Maharajah provides elephants to carry visitors to the palace. The scenery is very picturesque.

On Friday, the 8th, we left Jeypore by the nine o'clock train and arrived at Ajmere at half-past two, putting up at the station rooms, a very nice suite of which are set apart for the use of travellers.

After lunch we drove to see the Mayo College, and Colonel L—— the Principal, to whom he had an introduction; but we found the whole place deserted, all having gone to some tamasha. However, we had a look round as best we could.

The college was designed by the late Major Mant, and is of white marble, and very handsome. The boy's residences are separate bungalows, scattered over a considerable area. Beyond the college there is nothing of much interest. The city is large, and extends along the foot of the hill. The buildings are generally good, but the streets very narrow.

We left by the mail train at three a.m. and arrived that evening at Ahmedabad, where we stayed the night. On the following day we proceeded to Limri, and on the twelfth arrived at Rajkote, after a most enjoyable and interesting three months' holiday.

CHAPTER XXI.

SOME NOTES ON ARCHÆOLOGICAL REMAINS.

The province of Kathiawar is rich in remains of ancient temples, palaces, gateways, wells, etc., very many of which have been of remarkable magnificence in their beauty of design and ornamentation. The architecture may now be said to be extinct, for it is never reproduced in its lavish extravagance of carving, and as the temple, since their despoilment and mutilation during the Mahomedan conquest some 900 years ago, now possess no religious value, they are permitted to fall into decay unprotected and uncared for.

The material employed in their construction was principally limestone, in many instances put together without mortar. The carvings comprise figures of gods, animals, mythological and sacred emblems, geometrical designs, and beautiful elaborated cornices, capitals and frescoes. With the exceptions of the doors no timber was employed; the domed coverings are supported on pillars, carrying arches either pointed or cantilever, with architraves, all more or less highly decorated.

One of, if not the most famous and beautiful of those temples, was that of Somnath, near the famous city of Somnath Patan on the south coast of Kathiawar. The temple is said to have been first built of gold by Somraj, then of silver by Rāvāna, then of wood by Krishna, and finally of stone by Bhimadeva, of Auhilvada. There is a legend connected with the original construction of the temple as follows " Dashka was a demigod, created by Brahma for the purpose of creating animal and vegetable life; he had 50 daughters, of whom he married 27, who now shine in Heaven as the 27 lunar mansions (Nakshastras) to the Moon, but the Moon loved Rohini (the Asterism in Taurus consisting of five stars, and including the bright star Aldebaran) alone, and remained solely with her. On this the other 26 damsels complained to their father, and Dashka scolded the Moon, and desired him to treat his wives equally. But the Moon remained obdurate, on which Dashka cursed him and dmooed him to suffer from perpetual consumption.

SOUTH FACADE OF SOMNATH TEMPLE.

(*See page* 254)

Interior Somnath Temple.

(*See page* 254.)

The Moon, now stricken with grief, sought all the holy places for alleviation of his pain, and after visiting many in vain, came to Prabhas, where he worshipped Shiv with great devotion.

Shiv taking pity on him, directed that he should wane in brilliancy for 15 days, but in the following 15 days he should recover his lost splendour. In gratitude for this the Moon erected a golden temple to Shiv over the previously existing " ling " and named it Somnath, or Lord of the Moon.

The temple, though three times destroyed by the Mahomedans, was nevertheless three times rebuilt, and so late as A.D. 700, was still a place of great sanctity. It was finally destroyed by Arungzeb in A.D. 1706.

It is near Somnath that the three sacred rivers, Sararvali, Hyranya, and Kapila unite and form the sacred Triveni. Here also the Jadeos slew each other, and Krishna was shot by the Bhil.

From any accounts which can be gleaned from history or tradition, the city of Somnath Patan was originally ruled by the Chavadas, and was infested with pirates. Mahomed of Gazni conquered the city A.D. 1026, and left there a Mahomedan Governor. Subsequently, the Vajas (a branch of the Rathōd tribe) acquired Somnath and the kingdom of Nagher, and revived the glories of the ancient fane; but it was again cast down by Alagh Khan Circa in A.D. 1300, and the kingdom conquered; from this date Mahomedan supremacy prevailed, and from the reign of Mahomed Tuglak regular Governors were appointed.

The inscriptions from the time of Tuglak show a settled dominion, and this continued throughout the time of the Guzerat Sultans. After various vicissitudes the latter became paramount, and finally Pathan fell under the Moguls after the conquest of Sorath in Akbar's reign. The temple had by this time been levelled twice, first by Mazafer and again by his grandson, Akand Shâh of Guzerat, and the local chieftains were effaced. Subsequently, when the Mogul power was dissolved, Pathan was usurped by the Kharbatis, and was conquered at different times by the Sheik of Mangrole, and the Rana of Porebunder, but finally owing to the gallantry and statesmanship of Divan Amarji, it was conquered by the Nawab of Junaghud, in whose hands it now remains.—" Kathiawar Gazetteer."

At the present day there is little to remind one of the ancient glory of this splendid temple; the intricate and beautiful carvings on all but a portion of the sea face have fallen down or been removed. Of the grand dome only the hearting remains, and the huge monolithic columns and architraves supporting the domed roof are in ruins or fallen down.

Junaghud, the premier city of the province, under a Mahomedan ruler, H.H. the Nawab Sahib, is very rich in all kinds of antiquity.

It is built at the foot of the famous and sacred Girnar Mountain referred to in Chapter XI. In the Uparkot, a fortified plateau above the city, are many remarkable remains. One of these is a subterranean hall carved out of the solid rock, supposed to be 2,000 years old, and still in fair preservation. Magnificent wells over 100 ft. in depth, with stairs leading into them, all cut from the solid limestone, while below the fortifications are extensive Buddhist caves.

On the approach to the Girnar is the famous Asoka stone, B.C. 72, covered with edicts of King Asoka. These are in Sanscrit, and have all been deciphered, although 2,000 years have elapsed since they were cut in the sienite boulder, till lately unprotected from the weather.

Another very famous locality is that of the ancient city of Ghumli, the remains of which lie in a gorge of the Barda hills. This city was the most ancient capital of the Jethva Rajputs. It abounds in interesting remains, amongst the most famous of which are the Naolacka and Ghanesh Dehra temples, and the old forts on the summit of the Abapura Hills immediately overhanging the city. These last are probably the remains of palaces of the Ranas. The city is supposed to have been destroyed in the eleventh century, when the temples were cast down and mutilated by the Mahomedan conquerors.

The Naolacka temple was evidently only second to Somnath in grandeur of construction as well as size. A considerable portion of the original structure still remains, but in a ruinous condition. The hand of the destroyer is apparent here as elsewhere. The plinth of the temple represents the elephant square or phalanx. The design throughout is bold, and the carving, which covered every inch of the structure within and without, was rich and elaborate. A peculiar feature of the design is a pair of fighting elephants, placed on each of the three sides of the sanctuary immediately beneath a gigantic figure of a god. One of these groups of statues, together with many other fragments we

TEMPLE OF MATHA HARSĀD.

(*See page* 257.)

FRAGMENT OF IDOLS FOUND IN THE RUINS AT GHUMLI, 2,000 YEARS OLD.

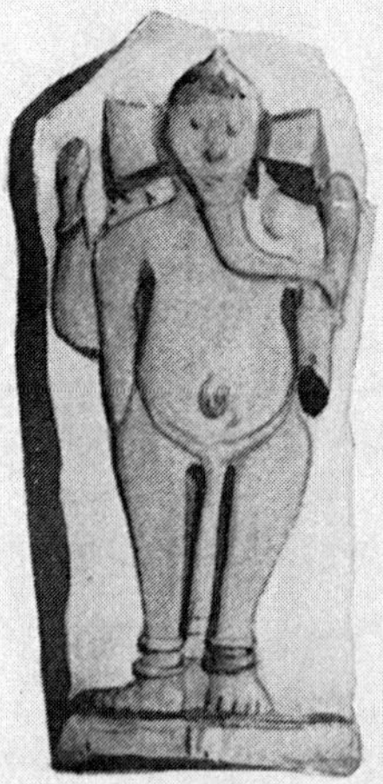

GUNESH.

NARSING.

GAROORDJEE.

VISHNU.

FRAGMENTS FROM KOILA HILL. OLD TEMPLE OF THE GODDESS MATHA HARSĀD.

SIDE OF DOORWAY TO SANCTUM SANCTORUM.

PORTION OF ONE OF THE TWO PRINCIPAL COLUMNS WHICH SPRING FROM THE FLOOR, INTERIOR OF TEMPLE.

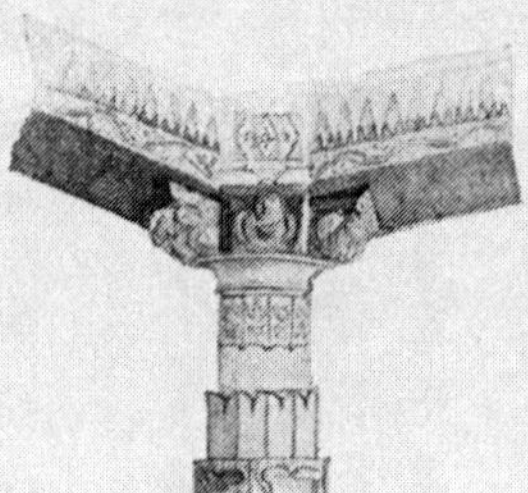

COLUMN SUPPORTING DOME, SPRINGING FROM PARAPET.

(*See page* 257.)

had removed to the Rajkote Museum by permission of H.H. the Jam Sahib. The name of the god which originally occupied this temple was Somnath. It was removed to Porebunder, and is now called Khadonath.

The next locality worthy of remark is that of Meanee, a town on the creek of that name, about 22 miles west of Porebunder. This town was at one time a remarkable centre of trade, and coasting vessels of large tonnage were able to approach it. Now the town has deteriorated. Its formerly magnificent temples are ruined or have disappeared, and the creek has silted up; and all this, according to the legends and superstitions of the locality, was due to the anger and evil will of the Goddess, Mātha Harsād, the ruin of whose original temple stands on the hill on the opposite side of the creek. The temple of Mātha Harsād is small. In design it is somewhat similar to Somnath, but varies greatly in the style of carving and ornamentation. The central figures are representations of Hindu gods, but all the remaining figures are female in the nude or nearly so, internal and external. The doorways, especially that leading to the Holy of Holies, are very richly carved, and much of the ornamentation where it is protected from the S.W. monsoon is still in fair preservation.

The temple is said to be 2,000 years in existence. I attach drawings of three fragments, which I made nearly 40 years ago.

The following legend was told to me by the ferrymen who rowed us over to the ruined temple :—

"It was formerly the custom to appease the goddess Matha Harsād (goddess of destruction) and secure her good services by the sacrifice of one animal to her daily, failing which she would vent her displeasure on those who neglected her wants by causing them heavy loss. In the sanctum of the old temple, in front of where the goddess sat, may still be seen a circular caldron-like hole, in which it was said that she daily boiled the King of Meani in oil, and devoured him, subsequently recreating him for a similar operation next day.

"The goddess was removed from her temple on the hill about 750 years ago, and placed in another building of unpretentious design at the foot of the hill facing the creek and Meani. The reason for the removal (so saith the legend) was that when the Matha occupied the hill temple her face was set towards the sea, to which fact was attributed the loss of many boats, and the property of fishermen and merchants whom it was supposed had failed to appease her by performance of the due sacrifices. To remedy this fact and reduce her power over the sea, a rich merchant of Meani, by name Jagdoosha, undertook to remove the goddess to the foot of the hill, where he constructed for her her present habitation.

"She was taken out through the dome of the temple (the orthodox manner of removing gods and goddesses, as it would contaminate them to pass where human beings had trod), and at each step down the hill, a male buffalo was sacrificed. For the last four steps there were no more male buffaloes to be found in the country, and thereupon the merchant slew, first his own wife, then his son, then his son's wife, and finally himself.

"Unfortunately, however, the goddess was placed in the new temple with her face towards Meani, then a large and prosperous city, with a fine sea trade and harbour, and from that day the estuary became unnavigable owing to a sand-bank forming across its mouth, and the city dwindled away till in course of time it became little more than a heap of ruins. Its 300 temples are now represented by two in ruins, and its population of 20,000 is reduced to 500. How far the goddess is responsible for all this may be open to doubt, but it is a fact that instead of one animal each day, only one now is sacrificed for her yearly, 12 days before the Dewali."

The goddess is said to reside at Meani from 8 a.m. to 6 p.m. daily; at the latter hour she departs to Ujan, on the other side of India, returning at 8 o'clock the following morning. Adjoining her temple is a small room in which is suspended a diminutive couch with mattress and pillows of silk, on which she is supposed to recline during the heat of the day, and a fan is placed for her use. Over her head in the temple are hundreds of little brass and copper umbrellas, being offerings from devotees and pilgrims.

Another famous remains is that of the Ranek Dēvi temple, near the city of Wudhwan.

The following is from the Ras Mala :—

The Ranek Dēvi Temple was built on the spot on which Ranek Dēvi performed suttee. She was the betrothed bride of Sidh Raj, but was carried off by Rao Khengar, King of Sorath, who married her. Subsequently Sidh Raj slew Rao Khengar and his two sons, and carried off Ranek Dēvi to Wudhwan.

TEMPLE OF RANEK DEVI, WUDHWAN.
(*See page* 258.)

On arrival at Wudhwan Sidh Raj told Ranek Dēvi he had killed her husband, and sought to induce her to marry him, but she refused, and threatened to curse him if he did not deliver up to her her husband's body. This he did, and asked what reparation he could make. She replied, build me a temple on this place and your throne shall stand firm, but as you have slain my children I lay this curse on you—that you shall die without a son to succeed you.

The funeral pile was prepared on the banks of the Bhogava, and Ranek Dēvi took her seat thereupon. Sidh Raj said to her that if she was a true suttee the pile would ignite without fire. She knelt down and prayed to the sun, then she rose and said :—

" Farewell Wudhwan, city good,
Beneath whose walls Bhogava flows,
Me Rao Khengar only enjoyed,
Enjoy me now husband Bhogava."

The wind blew so hot at this time that the pile was thereby ignited.

Sidh Raj threw his scarf over Ranek Dēvi. She cast it back to him out of the flames, and said. : " If you would become my husband in another life, you must now burn with me." Sidh Raj declined.

On the spot where Ranek Dēvi burnt, Sidh Raj erected a temple, and all Sorath submitted to him.

The funeral temple must formerly have stood on the bed of the Bhogava, but now is enclosed within the walls. It is much ruined, the dome which was richly ornamented only remaining. The anti-chamber has perished, but there is a mutilated figure of Rao Khengar's unhappy queen still in the adytum, which, on festival days, is arrayed in marriage attire with the crown, bridal veil, and royal jewels, and shares in the worship paid to other shrines in the vicinity to commemorate the virtuous devotion of the wives of the house of Wudhwan, who, with the Princes of the Jhala race, have passed through the flames to paradise.

The Madav Wao (well) at Wudhwan is a remarkable work of its kind, and must have cost a fortune to construct. It is 60 ft. in depth, with six flights of steps, and six landings, over each of which are massive carved pillars with brackets and architraves supporting cupolas ; on either side of the landings and within the cupolas are richly carved tablets with sculptured reclining figures, all now in a considerable state of decay.

Jhinjhuwada, a town in the north of Kathiawar, is of considerable antiquity and famous as being the reputed birthplace of Sidhraj Jayasing. The city was enclosed within a square, half a mile each way, and in the centre of each side were the famous Jhinjhuwada gateways, among the finest examples of old Hindu architecture to be found, but now owing to neglect very little of the elaborate carvings remain, and they are rapidly falling into decay, or being removed piecemeal by the inhabitants for the building of huts.

The gateways, which are 30 ft. in clear height, were composed of six bracket arches, grouped in threes, about 2 ft. apart on each side, with a wider space in the centre to allow of the gate leaves being folded back. The pilasters are carried vertical for about 20 ft., when they begin to project stone by stone, till the two sides meet within 4 ft. at top. A huge single stone architrave 23 ft. by 2½ ft. by 2 ft., connects the brackets. The pilasters and brackets are covered with elaborate carvings of gods, men, women, animals, dancers, musicians, etc., and there are niches at either side containing gigantic figures of Hindu gods. On many of the stones is inscribed Mahan Sri Udal, supposed to have been the minister of Sidhraj, who directed the works.

The remains of a cut stone reservoir, or tank, some 400 yards in length and width, are still to be seen, with some fine carvings on the sides of the approaches. Also a well with pillars, on which has apparently been cupolas heavily carved. But all the cupolas have disappeared except one.

At Sijakpur is one of the finest archæological remains in the province. The huge blocks of carved limestone were laid without cement, and the temple in its glory must have been a magnificent work of art. It stands alone and neglected now, half a mile from the nearest village. Pepul trees have forced their way through its rich carvings, and the shepherds use the building as a shelter for their flocks. All this is due to the desecrating hand of the conqueror, because any sacred building once so mutilated can never again possess any religious value.

In the east, towards Choteela and Thān, are some archæological remains of different, though no less beautiful, designs and ornamentation; these are built of the sandstone of the locality.

Scattered promiscuously in every part of the province are still to be seen other mementoes of bygone days, happily never to return. These are the groups of pallias (headstones) erected to commemorate suttees, when it was believed

TEMPLE AT THAN.
(*See page* 260.)

THE NAOLACKA TEMPLE, GHUMLI.
(*See page* 256.)

Ruined Temple of Sijakpur.

(*See page* 260.)

BUDDHIST CAVE, SHANA HILL. 75 feet by 65 feet by 18 feet solid rock excavation; no supports; roof flat no carving.

(*See page* 261.)

SUTTEE PALLIAS.

PILLARS FROM GHUMLI, REMOVED TO THE MEMORIAL INSTITUTE.
(See page 261.)

to be the sacred duty of every wife to immolate herself on the funeral pyre of her husband. When the pile was erected the dead body was laid on it, the living wife then mounted, sat down, and took the dead head in her lap. Ghee, oil, or other inflammable substance was thrown over her, and it was usual beforehand for her to cook rice and distribute it among the relations of the deceased. The pyre was then ignited. Instances are on record that when the unfortunate woman, on the first touch of the flames, lost courage and jumped from the pile, she was thrown back by her male relations. Happily, through the exertions of the British Raj and the progress of enlightenment and education amongst the ruling Chiefs, such terrible tragedies are at an end.

The stones which commemorate the suttees are depicted with a raised arm, while that for deceased men have a male figure. The sun and the moon are sometimes shown in the upper portion of the stone, and at the lower corners a jar of water and a loaf of bread, so that the departed may not want for food and drink. When a chief or other notable personage possessed a superfluity of wives, it was the custom that all of them should be burnt with him on his decease.

Pallia stones were also erected to commemorate all cases of sudden death, when their relations possessed the necessary means—persons who died suddenly of snake bite, or were slain in battle, and such like.

Some centuries ago Buddhism was powerful in the province, although now extinct or almost so. Temples and caves constructed and excavated for the worship of Buddha are found in many parts—the most famous remains of which are at Junaghud, Talaja, and Dedan. At Junaghud the temples were for the most part hewn out of the limestone rock, also at Talaja, but a certain proportion are built. At Shana Hill, Dedan, two ranges of low hills are literally honeycombed with caves cut out of the soft red rock, which lies near the surface and extends to a great depth. The largest is 65 ft. by 75 ft. and 18 ft. high. In excavating this a row of six square pillars were left along the entrance, possibly for ornament, but only one of these remains, and there is practically no support to the huge flat roof. These caves are without carving or ornament of any kind.

I made many drawings of these with measurements long years ago. Every part of the province has its share of interesting relics, but I have no space in this short sketch to do more than refer to a few of them.

CHAPTER XXII.

LALPURI WATERWORKS, 1895-99—IRRIGATION AND CITY SUPPLY.

The largest water project with which I was connected was that of the Lalpuri irrigation and city supply, and this had a history attached to it still more interesting than that of the Randerda.

Like the Randerda, it was another project in the Rajkote State in which the late Thakor Sahib had taken an interest, but failed for similar reasons to carry out.

This proposal for the formation of a lake for irrigation purposes only, by damming the Lalpuri valley, was put forward in 1884, and an approximate survey and estimates were prepared by me. As the scheme was then intended only for irrigation, the dam was proposed to be 40 ft. high. In 1884, Mr. C. Doig, M.I.C.E., Executive Engineer, P.W.D. Bombay, was deputed by Government, at the request of the State, to examine the project, but although his report, written in February 1885, was favourable, nothing further was done for three years, when the question of a supply of drinking water for the civil station and cantonments became an urgent necessity, and the Lalpuri project among others was re-surveyed. It was again shelved, owing to funds not being available for a dam high enough to provide a head for gravitation for the whole civil station, and the Randerda project was adopted as being more suitable for the civil station requirements. The Randerda lake and service were completed in 1891, and it was then that the city began urgently to ask for a similar boon to that provided for the civil station. During the previous year I had elaborated the surveys and plans for the Lalpuri, and had been endeavouring to get it taken up as an irrigation project, and now the Political Agent called on me to re-submit the scheme in a complete form, which I did in December, 1891, and Mr. W. Clerke, M.Inst.C.E., was invited to come to Rajkote to inspect the proposal in consultation with me. Mr.

SIR CHARLES OLLIVANT, K.C.I.E., I.C.S.

(*See page* 263)

Clerke arrived in February following, and submitted his report on April 14th. This report being in every way favourable, the entire project was submitted to Government by Sir Charles Ollivant, but as an irrigation scheme only. After some delay it was thrown out, Government being averse to undertaking irrigation projects for administered States, such projects under Government control not having hitherto proved remunerative. This decision was exceedingly disappointing, the more so because since the submission of the scheme the necessity for providing a supply of drinking water for the city had become really urgent, owing to failure of wells and the impurity of the river-bed water. His Excellency Lord Harris, Governor of Bombay, arriving in Rajkote in November 1893, he was interviewed on the subject, and urgent appeals were submitted by the State Karbarrie and Major Fenton, A.P.A., Halar, representing the great need that had lately arisen for a water supply to the city, and calling for a reconsideration of the proposal as a combined irrigation and city supply scheme. On these representations His Excellency signified his willingness to have the matter reconsidered, and as a first step the superintending engineer, Colonel Osborne, was requested to meet me at Rajkote as soon as possible for this purpose.

On Sir Charles Ollivant's arrival from furlough in November, 1894, he again took the matter up, and in February, 1895, after ten years' delay the project was at last sanctioned by the Bombay Government, and orders were issued to me to put the works in hand.

When the welcome news of the sanction of the Lalpuri was received, my eldest daughter and I were on a visit to the Political Agent's camp at Dhola, and for one reason or another, ostensibly connected with work, our visit was extended much longer than at first intended. It subsequently occurred to me that Sir Charles was just then daily expecting the Government sanction, and desired with his usual kindness to be able to acquaint me personally with the news as soon as he received it.

It was one morning when we had returned to camp after a shoot that the Lalpuri sanction arrived. I don't think I ever felt so elated. I had so often been disappointed and depressed at the rejection of the project which I believed in, and felt convinced was deserving of all support, that I was getting into the habit of thinking there was an end to it so far as I was concerned, and now it was evident that Sir Charles, while not wishing to buoy me up with hopes that might not be realised, was at the same time doing all he could to get the scheme sanctioned, and must have been pretty sure of success. We left Dhōla the following day, and within a week had all in readiness for the ceremonial laying of the foundation-stone of the Lalpuri dam. The function took place on March 18th, 1895, in a large shamiana erected on the site. The news of the sanction for a work so long and eagerly looked forward to caused much rejoicing in the city, and thousands of people flocked to the ceremony, which was attended by several of the chiefs, military and civil officers, ladies, etc.

On the arrival of Sir Charles he was conducted to his chair by the minor Thakor of Rajkote, and Mr. Motichand Tulsi, State Karbarrie, proceeded to read a lengthy address, explanatory, of the history and nature of the project. On the conclusion of which he requested the Political Agent to lay the first stone of the proposed dam. The address having been read in Guzerattee, Sir Charles proceeded to the stone, which bore the date and names of those principally concerned, and spoke as follows :—

> "Mr. Manager and Thakor Sahib, Chiefs, Ladies and Gentlemen,—I thank you very much for the compliment you have paid me in asking me to preside on this occasion, though permit me to add that I most sincerely share, for more reasons than one, your unexpressed regret that His Excellency the Governor is not here on this occasion. I wish, indeed, that the day's ceremony had been celebrated by him when he was here some fifteen months ago. I feel that it is entirely owing to the accident that at this moment I fill the office of Political Agent that I am here to-day. You have rightly said, Mr. Manager, that this will be a memorable occasion in the annals of Rajkote, and I think it is a most happy accident that this is the first appearance in public of Thakor Sahib Lakhajiraj. We congratulate him on his return to his home, and on having entered on his educational career in the Rajkumar College. It is a happy thing for him that his own educational career is co-existent with the beginning of a work which, we all hope, will contribute to the benefit of the state and the happiness of his subjects. I think you have been well advised, Mr. Manager, not to take a very sanguine view of the pecuniary profits which will be realised from

this important work. You may be quite satisfied even if it gives you no more than an ordinary return for your outlay, though if, as some people predict, a windfall of 12 per cent. should accrue, you will be fortunate indeed. I am not going to weary you, ladies and gentlemen, with the details in connection with the project, that have taken up much correspondence. I must dissociate myself from any special credit for the work, as I know that there are many here present and many absent who had a hand in writing about it. Mr. Manager, as you have mentioned, this work is to fulfil two objects. It is an irrigation project and also a project for supplying drinking water to the town of Rajkote. As regards the irrigation project, I congratulate the Rajkote State on being the first State in Kathiawar to take in hand an important enterprise of this kind. There are some present here, and notably the Chief of Jusdan, who have ventured in this direction with some success; and we know he wishes hearty success to this project; and I hope it will be so successful that other States, especially in the Jhalawad prant, will follow the example. As regards the water-supply project, I must say that water is like money, that it may be used, and that it may be abused, and the more you have the more you want. In large towns in America and England the more it is given the more it is wanted, and it is incumbent upon the people of this country to remember that when water is obtained in an artificial way it becomes a valuable commodity and is to be paid for like any other valuable commodity, and that, therefore, it must not be abused. Now, Mr. Manager, it is just about five years since you undertook the management of the State. You became Manager just about the time that I became Political Agent, and I can congratulate you on your careful and successful management. I have carefully watched your career for five years and have always found your work satisfactory, though I have received anonymous petitions against you. It seems to me that anonymous petitions are as necessary an appendage to anybody in authority as the tail is to a kite, and one of the first things that the Political Agent has to learn is to be watchful and not to be credulous. Of all people who are subjected to these vile anonymous petitions are members of the two great castes, Nagars and Vanias, who have among them respectable as well as unworthy members. One of the first things to which I have given some consideration is, how to apply the funds of the States under British management. There are those in Kathiawar who would be the first to recognise the benefits that have been derived from British management of their States during their minority. One of those first to recognise these is the Thakor Sahib of Gondal, whom we regret not to see here, although this important work concerns his own nephew. It is also, I think, generally recognised that there should not be a great accumulation of funds when a young Chief attains majority. If the funds could be applied to productive works which should yield good return, I can imagine that no manager can do better than undertake such works. Here in Rajkote you, Mr. Manager, have had the opportunity of putting funds in the railway, which promises to give a good return, and now you have undertaken this large work. I am not at all advocating that managers should fritter away funds as other States have been doing. Works that should result in benefit to the people might well be undertaken, even if they did not prove quite productive.

"Now, Mr. Motichand, after mentioning you, I pass naturally to Mr. Booth. (Cheers and applause.) Mr. Booth's name naturally evokes your applause. It is idle for me to expatiate upon the good work Mr. Booth has done for many years. I know that while my own name will be forgotten, Mr. Booth's will be associated with the progress of Kathiawar for his ability, zeal, and unselfish devotion to duty. And now, leaving the subject of the particular ceremony which has brought me here this day, I may say a word or two about myself. You have very kindly referred to the fact that this is the last occasion on which I can have an opportunity of addressing you. I really do not know that I can say much more than to thank you all, the officers of the Agency, the Chiefs, the inhabitants of the civil station of Rajkote of all classes, and of Rajkote and Kathiawar in general, for the great kindness and good feeling which has been extended to me during my five years of official connection with you. I have learnt a lesson, I have continued to learn a lesson of which I had some experience, that the two principal qualities for dealing with people are patience and accessibility; and I can believe many of you have gone away lamenting when I have not been able to see you. But the number of States in Kathiawar are so many—I forget their exact number, which is generally filed up in my office—and the Political Agent's time is so much occupied in dealing with them, that I can only plead infirmity of human nature in not being able to do many things I have wished to do. Ladies and gentlemen, I only have to bid you farewell, and to assure you that although my official relations, begun in Kathiawar five years ago, will now, in all probability end, the private relations of friendship that I have been enabled to form here will, as far as I am concerned, never end." (Loud and continued applause.) Pan supari and rose water were then distributed, and the proceedings came to an end.

That evening an entertainment was held at the Memorial Institute, to which a very large number of Chiefs, visitors, and residents were invited, and all the grounds were illuminated. The company first met at the Connaught Hall, where each guest was received by the minor Thakor Sahib and the State Manager, Mr. Motichand Tulsi. The hall was well lit up, showing off the rows of Chiefs' portraits with which the walls are hung, and a fountain played in the centre. After a little conversation the company proceeded to the grounds to witness a display of fireworks, after which all adjourned to a supper in the Lang Library.

After supper Colonel Handcock, in proposing the health of Sir Charles Ollivant, said:

"Ladies, Chiefs, and Gentlemen,—I rise to propose the health of our departing guest, Sir Charles Ollivant, and to wish him all success in his new appointment as Commissioner of Sind. For more reasons than one I ought not to have been selected for this honour. Firstly, I may be supposed to be glad that he is going (which for many reasons I am not), and secondly, because I do not possess that gift of public speaking which is necessary to enable me to do justice to the occasion. Sir Charles Ollivant himself says that he may come back to us, and thus tries to moderate our praises, but we know better, and therefore do not hesitate to tell him to his face that we do not expect to look upon his like again. For my part I have always found it much pleasanter to work under him than to act for him, and nobody sees more clearly than I do or more thoroughly appreciates all the good that he has done for the province. His efforts have really stamped out dacoity, and have given us our network of railways, as well as our grand waterworks, and the fine institute in which we are now assembled. He has also worked indefatigably to forward other public works. He has reorganised all our offices, and has done his very best to remove all abuses and to put everything upon a right and fair footing. In short, we would say of him as regards Kathiawar, all that has recently been said in praise of our late retiring Governor with regard to the Presidency; and as this is still fresh in the memory of us all, it is fortunately unnecessary for me to say any more. Fearless and fair in all his dealings, we all like him, Chiefs, and Sahib lok alike, and foresee all sorts of honours in store for him in Sind and elsewhere, wherever he may go, wishing him long life and health to enjoy them, we now bid him heartily farewell."

Sir Charles, in replying to the toast, observed to the effect that he could hardly express the feelings to which he was moved by Colonel Handcock's speech. Such kind words coming from Colonel Handcock could not but be especially gratifying, for Colonel Handcock, if any one, would gain by his leaving Kathiawar. He need hardly repeat that he, on his part, was very sorry to leave Kathiawar, and his many Kathiawar friends; he could truly say that after his English home there was no place he loved more than Kathiawar. He would propose, as a final toast, the health of the young Thakor Sahib of Rajkote and success to the Lalpuri scheme.

It would not interest the ordinary reader to describe in much detail the construction during the following three years. The works were annually closed between June and September for the monsoon season, and pushed on with vigour during the fair seasons, upwards of a thousand labourers and artisans being employed, with some miles of railway from the stone and clay quarries, fortunately found near the works.

The weir dam over the river bed portion was intended to be 600 feet in length, but during the second season's operations a formidable dyke or pocket in the trap formation at one end discovered itself. This was 60 feet wide and 73 feet below the surface of high ground, or 40 feet below the river-bed level, and one side of the dyke went down in a perpendicular face. It was an alarming discovery, and after two months' strenuous labour to negotiate the pocket fit for building in, I was obliged to shorten the weir by 200 feet

Position of Works, March, 1896, when commencing to fill Dyke.

(*See page* 268.)

EXCAVATION FOR PUDDLE TRENCH UNDER MAIN EARTH EMBANKMENT.

(*See page* 269.)

and fill in the excavation over the section and the two wings with puddled and rammed clay, and all this it was imperative to complete before the coming monsoon, otherwise heavy delay and loss of money would ensue by reason of floods entering the excavations.

The trench below the main earthen dam proved also more formidable and expensive than was anticipated from the borings, and it was found necessary to clear and blast away masses of fissured and water-bearing rock to from 30 to 40 feet in depth by 1,300 feet in length, before the true impervious bed was reached and puddling could be commenced.

The entire length of the dam was three-quarters of a mile, of which 2,180 feet was masonry and 2,100 feet earthwork.

The rains of 1896 were unusually heavy, and several floods passed over the weir at 14 feet, while the settlement over the dyke portion was quite satisfactory. By the 1st June, 1897, the main weir dam was raised to 34 feet. The under sluices were then closed and by the first rainfall on the 14th July 13 feet of water—the hot season flow—was impounded. The first rainfall was 4 inches on the evening and night of the 14th, and it filled the lake to the then level of 34 feet and overflowed 18 inches on crest.

Constant overflows took place during the rainy season. Frequently 1½ to 5 feet in depth over crest of weir at 34 feet. At the close of October, some time after the rainfall ceased, there was a considerable overflow along the entire length of the main weir.

Observations taken throughout the season discovered no signs of percolation or leakage in any part of the masonry, dam or embankments, and to enable work to be resumed, I was obliged to open two under-sluices, and these were kept open all the fair season.

For the raising of the main embankment to the full height work was kept on during the rains whenever the weather permitted, and by the close of October the entire earthwork was completed, and the moorum slope well advanced.

The works were fully resumed on the 1st December, 1897, and by the 15th May following the entire dam was completed. It was satisfactory to note that the lake during nearly the whole of the previous fair season retained its level of 34 feet, notwithstanding that the inflow by river-bed channel was very small, and that the under-sluices were kept open. This proved that there could not have been much if any loss by percolation, and that due to evaporation must have been to a great extent recouped by springs from the catchment area. The circumstance was highly satisfactory, as it promised a large supply of water for irrigation beyond what was originally estimated for.

By this time the city service had been completed and several free fountain reservoirs had been opened in the city and suburbs. These were automatic, in two compartments holding 3,000 gallons each, and furnished with twenty to forty taps, so that a large number of persons could draw water at the same time.

The rains arrived unusually early, the first falling on the 11th June, followed by another on the 12th, which rose the lake level 3½ feet. On the 18th another fall of 3.50 inches sent the level up to 48 feet. The fall on the 10th September, followed by another on the 12th, rose the lake 5 inches, and the final fall of 3 inches on the 14th September filled the lake to 50 feet with an overflow on main weir of 6 inches.

In the main weir over river bed are constructed two circular wells, one at each end, the floors of which are raised two feet above the highest arranged overflow; the wells are 9 feet diameter. That on the east, which is for irrigation purposes only, has two inlet pipes 12 in. diameter, and one outlet 15 in. diameter, fitted with valves worked from the well floor. The well on the west end has three inlet pipes of 12 in. diameter, one outlet 11 in. diameter being the city main, and one of 15 in. diameter for irrigation, the latter fixed at 26 feet and the former at 24 feet, being the lowest safe head for city supply.

The outlets lead from a recess 6 feet by 4 feet at the back of the wells, and separated therefrom by a removable sliding screen of copper cloth, supplied by the Glenfield Company, set in frames. The suspended matter thus screened is deposited at the bottom of the well, which is two feet lower than the recess, from whence it can be occasionally removed by a 12 in. diameter scouring pipe. The valve rods are worked from the iron floor of the well. Over the wells are erected small masonry towers, and steps lead up there from to the top of the embankment and hill.

For irrigation service, the 15 in. main is carried for about 2,000 feet from the dam, till the rough ground and hill are cleared, and the open flat country reached. Here it opens by means of an automatic valve, into a tank 16 feet square and 6 feet deep. From this tank a masonry aqueduct runs for 3,000 feet to the ridge or watershed com-

RAMMING PUDDLE, LALPUR DAM.

(*See page* 269.)

CITY FOUNTAIN.

(*See page* 270.)

OVERFLOW OF 6 INS. ON MAIN WEIR, ON 14TH SEPTEMBER, 1898.

(*See page 271.*)

manding the land to be irrigated. Three reservoirs are constructed on the line of duct, the last being 25 feet square and 12 feet deep, and the top of aqueduct and reservoirs are on the same level and always remain full. The duct is 15 in. wide and 18 in. deep, the floor having a small gradient. In each reservoir a number of valves 6 in. diameter are placed at 2 feet above the ground surface, where they deliver into small kundas, from whence the water overflows at any desired velocity into main earthen dhorias or ducts which radiate for long distances from the reservoirs, and from which branches will be made by the cultivators as needed for conveyance of the water over their fields.

"TIMES OF INDIA,"

DECEMBER 1ST, 1898.

LORD SANDHURST IN KATHIAWAR.

The visit of His Excellency has brought nearly all the Chiefs to the provincial capital, and has also induced a big foregathering of the officials on duty in various parts of Kathiawar. The official programme is to be supplemented by numerous unofficial entertainments, and the week promises to be a particularly lively one. The first official function was performed this morning, when his Excellency opened the Lalpuri irrigation and waterworks, and the Sir Mansingjee settling basin—the latter a generous gift to the Civil Station from the Thakor Sahib of Palitana. The character of these extensive works was fully described by the Agency Engineer, Mr. Booth, whose long and honourable connection with Kathiawar will shortly terminate. The first portion of the ceremony was in a shamiana at the dam of the new Lalpuri Lake. After Mr. Booth had described the nature of the scheme he has just completed. He went on to say :—

" The capacity of the lake above irrigation outlets is 335,000,000 cubic feet, from which it was originally proposed to deduct 7 feet, or about 89,000,000 cubic feet, for evaporation and possible percolation, but from our experience of last year, during which the lake maintained an uniform level of 34 feet with a small overflow and passage from under sluices, we may safely assume that in ordinary years the evaporation and any other loss will be nearly if not quite recouped from inflow by river-channel and side-springs, and this will allow of a much larger amount of water for irrigation than was originally estimated, or roughly 300,000,000 cubic feet. Now the quantity of water drawn from wells for wheat irrigation in these districts is roughly 20,000 cubic feet per acre, and the cost of lifting this water by bullock-power is about Rs.18 per acre. But for safety we have estimated that 40,000 cubic feet of water may be required for an acre of wheat, and that the price we may receive for it will be Rs.5. On this basis, and assuming that a varied crop would bring in about the same average return, we would have sufficient water to irrigate 7,000 acres, and would receive for it Rs.35,000, which, assuming the cost of the irrigation work to be half the total cost, or, say, two lacs, would mean 17 per cent. on outlay, or, making a liberal reduction for maintenance establishment, etc., at least 15 per cent. This is, of course, a forecast only of what the scheme may be worked to in the course of a few years, when the irrigation is fully developed. These good returns will, in the first place, be due to the unusual cheapness of the construction, and in the future will depend on good management and careful expenditure of water. The cultivator who can take as much water as he pleases without stint or measurement from an open aqueduct running through his fields is likely to become more indifferent to waste than when he had to lift the water from wells at his own expense. For the present year I believe some 2,000 acres will be placed under irrigation, which, at an average rate of Rs.5, will yield an immediate 5 per cent. on outlay. Several reservoirs for free drinking purposes are constructed in the city and puras—and private house connections will be taken in hand as soon as a committee of management is formed. For irrigation the 15 in. main delivers water under pressure into a system of masonry tanks and aqueducts, at 2,000 feet from the lake. These aqueducts continue for a further 3,000 feet to the ridge, from whence the whole of the irrigable land is commanded. The supply is automatic, and the water is drawn off in any required quantity from these tanks into main earthen dhorias (aqueducts) which radiate from them. From these main aqueducts the cultivators will construct branch channels to convey the water to their fields. I wish to take the opportunity of expressing my appreciation of the good and faithful service rendered by the head mistri, Jiwa Ramji, and the sub-mistris employed under him from time to time, and the good service of these men is all the more worthy of notice when it is remembered that I had no assistant on this work. I was necessarily often absent from Rajkote, and during such times the head mistri was solely responsible to me. It is scarcely necessary for me to explain how much the success or failure of a large lake dam depends upon the honest and careful supervision exercised over the builders, who are frequently task or piece-workers under the contractor, and how much exposed to temptation is the supervisor over these men who have it in their power, in collusion with the overseer, to scamp the work in a way it would be impossible to detect until too late to rectify it and some irreparable disaster occurred. That no leakages have occurred in the masonry under fullest pressure during two years is proof that the work is sound, and that the supervisors have done their duty, and the contractor also. The Political Agent has permitted me to ask your Excellency to present, on the part of the Rajkote State, a purse of Rs.500 and a dress-of honour to the head mistri, Jiwa Ramji, as a reward for faithful service on the Lalpuri Waterworks."

The next function which your Excellency will be asked to execute this morning is the opening of the "Mansingji Settling Basin." Soon after the formation of the Randerda Lake six years ago, it was found that the water at certain periods of the year became discoloured by suspended matter, due to the action of high winds on the shallows at the exposed head of the lake, and the latter being of small area the disturbance affected the whole of the water. To remedy this it was proposed to construct filter beds, but for want of funds nothing could be accomplished until two years ago, when Sir Mansingj, Thakor Sahib of Palitana, generously came forward with an offer of Rs. 20,000 towards meeting this want. By that time, however, the draw-off from the lake was so greatly increased it was found that a much larger sum of money would be needed than was originally estimated, especially as it was impossible to separate the drinking water from that required for public and private gardens, roads, etc. At this juncture it was discovered that the conformation of the ground at the lake would enable us to form a considerable reservoir by bunding the valley behind the main dam, by which means we could secure, at a comparatively small cost, a well-protected settling basin 26,000 square yards in superficial area, with a greatest depth of 35 feet and capable of holding 1½ million gallons of water above the assumed draw-off. This basin would be bounded on three sides by masonry dams, and on the fourth by a rocky hill, and it was considered the water filled into it from the lake would soon settle and become clear; but to assist this operation, it was decided to construct what we may term filter channels in the saddle dividing he lake from the basin. These were to be made by cutting a channel between the lake and basin and therein to construct three compartments protected by masonry bunds on the extreme ends The central compartment was to contain sand, and the other two to be receiving tanks, one for lake water direct and the other for receiving it after passing through the central sand compartment. We have been able to construct only one filter channel at present, on trial, and owing to the high level the lake maintained during the past fair season, this is only 10 feet below full lake level; and again, owing to the last unprecedented scanty rainfall, we received only 3½ feet of water in the lake this year, so the level is unusually low. The trial filter channel has, however, worked satisfactorily, and the Waterworks Committee have decided to construct another one with a double filtering compartment, at a depth of 22 feet below full lake level. When this is finished I do not anticipate that there will be further trouble about discoloured water. The maintenance of the filter channels will be only a trivial cost. I may state that a sample of this water was lately sent by the Agency Surgeon to Bombay, and has been favourably reported on by the chemical analyser to Government. The total cost of the settling basin has been Rs. 33,000, and Sir Mansingji generously increased his original gift to that amount. The cost of the filter channels will be borne by the Waterworks.

The young Thakor Sahib of Rajkote then, in a bold, clear voice and excellent English, bade His Excellency welcome to Rajkote, and requested him to open the lake and settling basin.

His Excellency having walked over the weir, opened the valve with a handsomely chased silver key, then driving across to Randerda, he performed a like office at the settling basin, and briefly addressed a large assembly of the chiefs, and officials, etc., as follows:—

"Your Highnesses and Chiefs, Ladies and Gentlemen,— I sincerely wish Sir Charles Ollivant was here to see the completion of a scheme of which he was one of the first to see the importance, and also induce Government to

Opening Ceremony of the Waterworks.

(See page 271.)

take the same view. He commenced the work by laying the foundation stone in 1895. However, we must content ourselves with that regret, for the exigencies of office work are overwhelming. The young Chief of Rajkote made his first public appearance on the occasion of the laying of the foundation-stone. I congratulate him on the completion of a scheme which ensures such great benefits, and which will add to the value of the State which he, in the natural course of things, should one day rule over. I doubt whether, reviewing in my mind the number of projects to which I have put the finishing touch or formally commenced since I came to the Presidency, I have been connected with any individual project which has greater possibilities in it for the health of a populous town or for the benefit of the agricultural area surrounding it. As regards the health of the town, we all know the dangers of a tainted water supply; also we know that in Kathiawar there is ever present the fear and possibility of a water famine. I believe that this very year the record is the worst for nearly half a century, and that your wells are almost dry. I need not dwell on the horrors that must ensue from such a scarcity. But while the horrors of a water famine must have been ever present to many minds, I can imagine no position more anxious, hardly any tension of the mind greater, than that which must be the condition of the ryot who keeps on continually waiting and watching for the rain which does not come, and when the time is reached when no more rain is available (the former supply having been insufficient) that feeling of anxious longing must give way to one bordering on despair. It is not too much to say that now that this scheme is completed, from the moment that I have set the water in motion, those anxieties should never recur in Rajkote town and the area to be covered by the irrigation. In regard to the irrigation works, I may add that all the cultivators concerned have agreed in writing to pay the water-rate, which will yield, it is calculated, six per cent. on the capital outlay. You have heard the very interesting paper read by Mr. Booth, in which it is set out that 300,000,000 cubic feet of water will be available for use, and that special care is taken that the town supply should not suffer owing to too extensive demands for irrigation. In regard to the supply to the Rajkote Civil Station, purification of the water of the Randerda Lake has been rendered simple by the provisions of the settling basin—a generous gift of Sir Mansingji, the Thakor Sahib of Palitana—a public-spirited gift for which the inhabitants of Rajkote Civil Station cannot be too grateful to him. You have heard the details of the cost of construction, and some allusion to the difficulties too lightly glossed over by Mr. Booth, and the possibilities of the lake and its contents. I need not repeat them. They speak for themselves. But I am constrained to say a word about the engineer who devised and worked ceaselessly to overcome by his knowledge, patience, and courage succeeding difficulties as they arose. This is a stupendous work. Much has to be done before the ceremonial of opening is performed by the Governor. The land for the catchment has to be selected and surveyed, and then the work commenced, and in this case three years' patience and incessant supervision and extreme resourcefulness were required. As Mr. Booth has pointed out, a dishonest or careless subordinate can easily do harm that will take a fortune to repair, and perhaps delay the works and their benefits for a lengthy period. Again, Mr. Booth remarked that he has had no assistant, the responsibility and anxiety has been entirely his own, as much as is the brain which worked out the project brought to-day to its successful issue. Mr. Booth has been well served as he generously recognises, by his head mistri, Jiwa Ramji, and the sub-mistris; but the anxiety must have been very great, and we therefore congratulate him all the more upon the completion of a work which cannot fail to be of the most enduring benefit.

"But, ladies and gentlemen, Mr. Booth has been your friend far longer than he has been mine, and I am telling you what you all know. I lately referred to the enduring and useful work of an engineer, and its fascination as a profession. Kathiawar has had much to be grateful for to that profession in the last 32 years, during which Mr. Booth has been in charge, especially the Rajkote State. In whatever direction we may turn our eyes, we see your works, Mr. Booth—these lakes, the roads, the Rajkumar College, the Jubilee Hall and Museum, and a host of others too numerous to mention. It is a fact to say that every public work in this State owes its existence to your abilities. This work may be said to be the crowning work of your career, now drawing to a close, and I can assure you that your loyal and thorough work throughout that long and honourable career is fully appreciated by all, and their good wishes follow you on your retirement, and they are grateful to you for the health and strength you have expended in their service. I beg to congratulate you on the completion of the works I now declare open."

The following monsoon of 1899 was a failure, and caused the severest famine on record in Kathiawar. The Lalpuri Lake proved then to be the saviour of Rajkote and its surroundings.

CHAPTER XXIII.

THE DEATH OF CHESTER MACNAGHTEN, AND THAT OF THE MAHARAJAH OF BHAVNAGAR—FURLOUGH.

In the early part of 1896 two most sad occurrences took place. First, the sudden and very unexpected death of the Maharajah of Bhavnagar, one of the first pupils of the Rajkumar College, and a ruler beloved by all who had the privilege of knowing him; and secondly, the sad and very sudden death, on February 6th, of our dear old friend Chester Macnaghten. He had always been delicate and much subject to asthma, and of late years had been obliged to visit England on two or three occasions. His last absence was for nearly two years, and although his medical advisers did not recommend his return to work, he decided to try once more to take up charge of his beloved college. He had returned only eighteen months when his last illness took place. On February 1st he attended, with his wife and niece, an "At Home" at the Kothie, after which he walked home with me and my eldest daughter, and was apparently in good form and spirits.

The next evening I called at his bungalow, and found him lying on a couch, complaining of much pain in the side. He told me he had asked the civil surgeon to come and see him; that he had suffered a little from similar pains for some days, but did not think anything of them, and did not wish to alarm his wife. After sitting a while with him, and seeing he was suffering a good deal, I went for the doctor, and fortunately found him just come in. He went to Macnaghten at once, and that night stayed with him, but in the morning there was no improvement. The following day Macnaghten was seriously ill, and we learnt that an immediate operation was possibly the only thing that could save him; but there was no time to procure a surgeon from Bombay. On Sunday he became unconscious, and remained in that condition till he passed away on Monday evening.

It was strange that about a fortnight before, when he was with me in the cemetery, he pointed out a place, near where lay our old friend Colonel Scott, as the spot he would like to rest in if he died at Rajkote. In concurrence with his expressed wish, I had his tomb prepared there. And four of us, his oldest friends, carried his coffin to the grave the morning after he died.

With Chester Macnaghten seemed to have passed away the best part of our Rajkote life, and we all felt that the place could never be to us again as it had been for five and twenty years. His influence, character, and personality were so strong with everything connected with the College and Rajkote. He was a man in ten thousand, and we could never hope to see his like again. Mrs. Macnaghten had perforce to remain at Rajkote for nearly a month, while his affairs were settled up. A very sad settling indeed for her, in her great loss and loneliness.

I had been suffering a good deal in health during the last season. The heavy responsibility attached to the Water-works, in addition to all my other charges throughout the province, gave me little or no time for rest. My raids to other districts were done under pressure, and office work was exceptionally heavy.

It was a relief when, after the first season's work, by June 15th, we had everything safe, and were able to close the works, and pack up for a four months' run home. Mr. Benson, the State Engineer of Porebunder, was appointed to act for me during my absence.

My eldest daughter accompanied me, and we travelled to Trieste on the Austrian Lloyd's s.s. "Poseidon," arriving there early in July. From there we went to Venice, where we stayed for some days, and enjoyed it immensely. Travelling with us were Mr. Bennett, Editor of the "Times of India," General Briscoe, and Colonel Jackson, all excellent companions. They stayed with us till we reached Lucerne, travelling *via* Milan and the Italian lakes, and we remained nearly a week in those delightful localities, seeing all that time allowed us to see. The St. Gothard route was specially fine, and my daughter was in raptures with the scenery; it was her first visit. The corkscrew tunnels bored into the heart of the mountain are engineering triumphs; we wished we could have got out of the train and walked all the way, inspecting every wonderful bit of that most lovely and remarkable passage. We had, however, one rather nasty experience. My daughter and I were standing in the corridor at the foremost end of the carriage when we stopped at the station just before entering the great tunnel. I had forgotten that the train on starting, would immediately enter the tunnel, otherwise I would have taken her back into the carriage. In a few moments we were in intense darkness; the carriages all being closed, we were now standing on the narrow footway in front of the corridor connecting with the next carriage, a false step would have sent us off. The noise was so great we could scarcely distinguish our voices, and we held on to each other for some time, while we gradually felt our way, bit by bit, to the end of the corridor, and through the thick smoke which nearly suffocated us, till we got a glimpse of light from the closed windows of our carriage, and found Colonel Jackson inside very astonished to see us. He thought we had got into the carriage in front. It takes half an hour to pass through this tunnel of nine miles. and we were pleased indeed that we were not doomed to spend all that time on the open footboard of the train in rushing wind, thick smoke, and intense darkness.

At the exit from the tunnel on the Swiss side, Wassen, we stopped for an excellent lunch, and from thence the run to Lucerne was a succession of the most exquisite lake and mountain scenery. We reached Lucerne about 6 p.m.. and put up in the Schweitzer Hoff Hotel.

We stayed at Lucerne for some days longer than Jackson or Briscoe, hoping for a fine day to visit the mountains, but it rained much, and heavy clouds obscured the views. We, however, saw a good deal of the town and low country, and had many walks and drives, besides excursions on the lake. The hotels were very crowded with Americans and other foreigners doing the tour. From Lucerne we travelled to Paris, and stayed two days only, being anxious to reach London. But with the assistance of an excellent guide we contrived to make very good use of our limited time, seeing much of the city and its treasures. From Paris we went direct to London, and stayed for a fortnight with my son, then a doctor at Fulham. From thence we proceeded to Harrogate, having been advised to drink the waters there. Major Gott, whom we knew at Rajkote, was now on furlough, and living with his mother at Harrogate, and he secured rooms for us. I placed myself under the care of Dr. Ozanne, and for a fortnight religiously attended the pump rooms and imbibed the disgusting liquid served to me. We did not, however, on the whole, enjoy our visit to Harrogate. At the end of the fortnight Dr. Ozanne informed me that it was evident I did not need any pump waters or medicine of any description; so our visit to Harrogate was really a loss of time we might have spent more pleasantly elsewhere. We now went to Ireland on a visit to my brother at Williamstadt, near Dublin.

In London I had some business to attend to in connection with our waterworks, and I had to arrange with the sculptor for the statue of the late Chester Macnaghten, as also with an artist for his portrait for the College, and for his wife. I met Sir Charles Ollivant (also home on furlough) in London, and under his advice decided to give the statue work to Mr. R. Mullins; and under Mr. Manning's advice, the portrait painting was given to Mr. Trevor Haddon.

Before the end of my leave we spent a week with Sir Charles and his daughters at his place at Sunningdale, near Windsor, which we enjoyed greatly. We visited Windsor Castle and Park several times, and took long walks in the lovely country. We regretted much being unable, for want of time, to pay a visit to our old friends Dr. and Mrs. MacDougall, who were living at Stroud, near Wales, and who had most kindly invited us. Dr. MacDougall soon after this time inherited his brother's property at Oban, in Scotland, but he did not live long to enjoy his lairdship, and I never saw him again.

We returned to India by the same route, but did not break the journey except for one night at Venice. We arrived at Rajkote in time for the recommencement of the Lalpuri Works.

CHAPTER XXIV.

FIRST WOMEN'S HOSPITAL—RAJKOTE CIVIL HOSPITAL—BALLACHERI AND JAMNUGGER.

Up to the year 1896 there did not exist in Kathiawar any public hospital for the care of women other than those of the lowest or some of the middle classes. All ladies of the Durbar or higher classes being "purdah," were debarred from receiving medical attendance from any qualified male physician, native or European, and under the strict rules of the zenana it can well be imagined that serious, and what would now be called criminal, neglect was the cause of suffering and death which might otherwise have been prevented. Some of the enlightened Chiefs (notably H.H. The Thakor Sahib of Gondal) in their own States endeavoured to improve the existing state of things, but any departure from the old-established customs was naturally exceedingly difficult except maybe in some isolated and extreme cases, where, for state or other special reason, a medical man might be consulted, but in no case could he personally see the patient.

The first important move towards remedying this want was made by Colonel Hunter, the Political Agent, in consultation with the Chiefs' representatives in 1897, when H.H. the Nawab Sahib of Junaghud undertook to pay for the erection of a Women's Hospital at Rajkote for the benefit of the entire Province, and agreed to Col. Hunter's proposal to procure from England a duly qualified lady doctor to take sole charge of the institution.

In addition to the reception and treatment of purdah ladies at this hospital, the lady doctor would be available for attendance on any zenana lady at her own home who would not be able, owing to illness or other causes, to come to the hospital.

On my return from furlough in 1897, I found the proposal sanctioned, and I was called upon to prepare the necessary designs for the hospital, and residence for the lady doctor, so that the foundation stone could be laid within a fortnight.

Miss Wickham, M.D. of London, had been already appointed, and was on her way to Bombay.

As the case was an urgent one, and it would take several months to erect the necessary buildings, it was decided to make use of an old school building near the bazaar for hospital purposes in the meantime.

The buildings were completed and opened by H.E. Lord Sandhurst, Governor of Bombay, in November 1897, and the hospital, under the excellent control and devotion of Miss Wickham and her assistants, has continued to effectually fulfil all that was expected from it, and has proved one of great blessing to the Province.

RAJKOTE CIVIL HOSPITAL.

The old hospital in Keatinge's time was small and inconvenient, like most things in those early days, but as time went on many enlargements and needful additions were carried out, till in the course of thirty years it became as extensive and well-appointed in all branches as any. Its general design from the beginning was essentially suited to hospital requirements—large, airy and well-ventilated wards, with wide shady verandahs, so arranged that they could be closed in with movable venetians when so needed. When I first saw the hospital Dr. (now surgeon-general) Joynt was in acting charge, Dr. Butler being on furlough, and I often watched him operating, etc.

At this time and for years previous, and subsequently, the assistant medical officer was a Eurasian, Dr. Edroos, a name so inseparably connected with the hospital, it can never be forgotten. Dr. Edroos was an enthusiast, the hospital work was his life. He was the invaluable and trusted assistant of each successive civil surgeon; he never took a holiday, was never ill, and for nigh half a century worked indefatigably at his beloved charge.

Another name which will live for all time in the annals of the Rajkote hospital is that of Miss Goldney, the first professional European nurse appointed in the province. From the day Miss Goldney arrived she assumed charge of the hospital and dominated it. Little could be done without her. She trained native nurses, advised on each improvement carried out, personally attended to every detail of hospital management and duties, was popular in Rajkote society, respected and valued by the medical authorities, and beloved by the natives. One of the last additions I had the pleasure of carrying out was an upper-storey residence for Miss Goldney, over the new women's ward, in front of which she had laid out a lovely garden, where her assistants and convalescents could enjoy the open air. It may well be said the present efficiency of the hospital, and the blessing it has been to thousands in late years, are in a great measure due to Miss Goldney's kind and capable management and personality for over fifteen years.

Another who was for many years civil surgeon in charge and took a keen interest in the welfare of the hospital was the late Col. F. C. Barker, I.M.D.

BALLACHERI AND JAMNUGGER.

We were peculiarly fortunate in Kathiawar in possessing many seaside resorts, to which one could, when work permitted, adjourn for a few weeks to enjoy the cool sea breezes in the hot season.

Pre-eminent among these, and beloved by us all, was Ballacheri. This locality was situated on the west coast, facing the Gulf of Kutch. Although the place had been discovered years before Col. Keatinge's time, it was he who had the first bungalow erected there on a prominent little head overhanging the sea. On the south side from this stretched a fine strand for two miles, while on the north the foreshore was broken by innumerable rocky bays and islands, with their coves of silvery sand. Near the bungalow were a number of small hills, and high flats on which camps could be pitched, and further on the north side was a large rocky knob we called Lang Island, because, during Colonel Lang's reign as Political Agent in 1846 to 1859, he annually transferred his camp to this spot for the hot weather. In this retreat, often cut off from the mainland by floods and tides, he would be secure from tapals and office worries, and was enabled to enjoy the peaceful life he loved. Inland from Ballacheri the land was mostly flat or slightly undulating, with many streams, and large stretches of sandy mounds covered with aloe plants, an excellent cover for hares, partridges, and hyenas, while sand grouse were plentiful, and near by antelope. Along the sea coast were to be found curlew and golden plover, and other sea birds. When the tide receded there was a wide stretch of even sand for fully a mile. During the outgoing tide the breeze usually lulled, but immediately it turned the refreshing south-west wind came with it, and then it was delightful, and the sea washed up to the shore beneath the camps.

BALLACHERI.
(*See page* 284.)

It was a glorious change from the stifling heat inland, and many a merry party have I joined there; quantities of oysters, crabs, pomphlets, and all kinds of fish were daily caught. The way this was done was by means of paddocks, so-called. A mile or so out on the flat sands certain areas were enclosed by means of little rough stone walls about three feet high, and the stones forming these were cemented together by mussels; here and there only were small openings where the water could pass through.

When the tide flowed in and filled these paddocks, quantities of fish came with it, but as the tide receded numbers of the fish were unable to escape with it, and when the water remained a foot deep or so, the fishermen went out and secured them. Frequently young sharks were caught—the full-grown ones were unable to come into such shallows. Sometimes fine turtles were secured, but the best of all were the pomphlets.

Crab catching was a favourite amusement with us in the early mornings, and one in which the ladies excelled. When the tide had receded, we started with iron rods, crooked at one end; presently a crab would be detected near some rocks. A stealthy approach and he might be secured, but not unfrequently he would bolt for a hole and disappear. On our return we would sit down to a crab or oyster breakfast, only a preliminary, however, to the square meal to follow.

The morning's sand grouse shooting was another "diversion." We sometimes took a light breakfast with us, and rode or tongaed a few miles. Here we would dispose ourselves in various shelters to await the arrival of the grouse, which were accustomed to come to certain localities at a regular hour each morning, and settle along the sandy river beds. Their advent would be heralded by their calling, and presently a flock of 10 to 50 maybe would appear, and after flying around would settle. Then they had to be stalked and shot.

The early mornings and evenings were given up to riding, bathing, shooting, crabbing, and general fun, while during the day we worked in our office tents; but, as well as I recollect, we did as little work as possible during our Ballacheri holiday, letting the office hands have a fling as well.

Jamnugger was only twenty miles from Ballacheri, and a visit there was not uncommon. The late Jam Sahib was a splendid old chief, and his like will never be seen again.

He was the essence of generosity and hospitality, and was never more delighted than when entertaining his European friends to nautch and dinner. The former was held for an hour before dinner in a hall adjoining the banqueting room. The chief sat in the centre, with his native and European guests on either side. In front were twelve or fourteen nautch girls, for the most part young and good-looking, dressed in the usual dancing and singing costumes, with numerous gold and silver bangles and bracelets adorning feet and arms. In singles or pairs they danced or sang or acted, and after each performance a cup of some liquid refreshment was handed to them, or the cup which each girl had in front of her was filled by an attendant. The musicians (two always) stood immediately behind the performers. At the Jam Sahib's feet throughout the hour's performance stood a stand on which was a small clock, while his cupbearer, squatting on the floor, held a bottle of rose wine in one hand, and in the other a small silver cup filled. I think the bottle of rose wine held twelve of these cups, and so many times did his Highness partake of the refreshment. To us guests were brought silver trays with glasses of champagne.

On the conclusion of the nautch, his Highness would sign certain orders, which were handed to the performers, and then he would offer his arm to the principal lady, if one was there, and lead the way to the dining hall.

Here dinner in European style was provided for the European guests at one table, while H.H. dined alone at another. When he had finished, and that indeed was not infrequently before we had well begun, he would ask us if we had had a good dinner, and on being assured in the affirmative, he would rise and propose the health of her Majesty the Queen. This was followed by the principal European guest's proposing His Highness's health, which was the signal for an immediate break-up.

H.H. then escorted the lady, or maybe two ladies, one on each arm to the door, and was at once conducted to his sleeping apartments by his attendants in waiting.

H.H. SIR VIKHAJI, K.C.S.I., LATE JAM SAHIB OF NOWANAGAR.

(*See page* 286.)

CHAPTER XXV.

RAJKOTE STATE PADDOCK.

In 1896-97 I was engaged on the construction of a home for the above institution, which was started under the auspices of the Political Agent, Col. J. M. Hunter, and the late State Karbarrie, Mr. Motichand Tulsi. At one time Kathiawar enjoyed a high reputation for its special breed of horses, which were famous throughout the Presidency. Every chief in those warlike days bred his own horses, and was independent of outside aid, which indeed was not then available. During recent years this condition became changed, and all kinds of animals were imported, so that the pure Kathie breed bid fair to die out, and few of the modern chiefs took so keen an interest in the matter as their forefathers had done. One old chief, who was pre-eminent as a sportsman and horsebreeder, was the late Thakor Sahib of Palitana, who died, I think, in the 'seventies. He not only maintained the old blood, but improved it with the best from England and Australia.

It was intended to start the Rajkote institution on a commercial basis for the supply of provincial needs, as well as for Government remounts and Imperial service cavalry, etc.

Three hundred and fifty acres of waste grass land in the vicinity of the Lalpuri Lake, and bounded by a running stream, were taken over. Extensive stables, hospital, and all needful buildings were erected, and as a quantity of milk would be required for the young stock, a dairy farm was projected near by, with all the necessary machinery on the most up-to-date principle for the separation of cream and butter, as it was a part of the project to supply these necessaries to the Rajkote civil state, cantonments, etc.

As H.H. Lord Sandhurst was to come to Rajkote in November 1897, and had expressed his willingness formally to open the Institution, by that date all was in readiness. A veterinary establishment had been put in charge, a large number of mares selected, land for Lucern grass put into cultivation, arrangements made for a sufficient supply of milk for cows and buffaloes, the dairy in full swing and milk carts daily running into Rajkote.

At the opening ceremony, which was attended by a great concourse of people, Mr. Motichand Tulsi read an exhaustive address, describing in detail the project from the date of its conception to its realisation. To which H.H. Lord Sandhurst replied as follows :—

"When I am asked to declare open any building or institution it always seems to me that the lightest task of the undertaking has fallen to my share. I am glad to see that the management of this State have undertaken the promotion of these paddocks, and I have every hope that when the youthful Chief succeeds to the Gadi, he may find the paddocks what we may call a going concern. Paddocks and their occupants form a subject in which a chief, however youthful, may at once begin to take an interest, and with the fostering care that will be bestowed upon him, I hope that his attention will be turned carefully in the direction of the horses which will occupy this paddock. It was very satisfactory to hear in the address of the prosperous condition of the Rajkote State, for while I am assured that these paddocks are so arranged as to be model paddocks, they may be at first somewhat expensive. It is also satisfactory to all concerned to learn that the paddocks are to be conducted upon a commercial basis, and this is a matter which I hope will not be lost sight of. I have not yet seen the buildings which form a portion of the paddocks mentioned in the address. . . . The subject of horse-breeding is, to my mind, one of the most interesting, and did I propose to go into it at all fully, those of us who partake of breakfast might have that meal delayed for some time. It is a subject of peculiar interest to you, the chiefs of Kathiawar, from the historical associations which horse-breeding has with this district, and the excellence which that breed is acknowledged to have attained, but I regretted to hear in the address that there had been some falling off in the latter respect. I know that in two cases, Palitana and Wankanir, the breed of horses is noted, and I should like to see one and all of the Chiefs taking the same interest in horses and horse-breeding and doing all they can to foster and improve them. I was struck by one or two passages in the address which seemed to me to be of an eminently practical character, and those were the proposals with regard to keeping in touch with the mares and the young stock. Every encouragement should be given to the subordinate cultivators to improve their stock, and I should like to lay stress upon what is noted in the address as to the necessity of paying every attention to young stock. There are one or two points to which I may allude in regard to the breeding of horses. They are simple, and ought to be known to everyone, but matters which are the simplest, and appeal most to common sense are often amongst those left out of calculation. The points I would wish to emphasise in connection with the breeding of young stock are the necessity of giving them as much space as you can, and side by side with that as much good food as you find they will eat. It was also interesting to note the reference made in the address of the desire on the part of the management to assist the Government, as well as to provide horses for the State. The question of remounting our cavalry is a very important one, and also the provision of animals for transport, and in that respect the allusion made to the breeding of mules is of especial interest. A noteworthy feature of this establishment is the dairy farm, and I have little doubt that it will be found of very great value in conjunction with the breeding of horses. In regard to this particular paddock which I am to declare open, the circumstances are peculiarly auspicious in view of the brilliant assemblage I see before me. I have observed in regard to the Imperial Service Cavalry which I shall shortly have a chance of inspecting, as well as in the youth of the Rajkumar College, how soldier-like was their bearing on horseback, which showed signs of careful instruction. It seems to me that these two institutions, the College on the one hand, and the Imperial Service Cavalry on the other, are institutions of which you should be most proud, as well as of this establishment, which shows your desire to improve the breed of the horses of the Province. Now I will without further delay declare this paddock open, and I hope that on a future occasion I shall have the opportunity of congratulating the minor Chief of the Rajkote State upon the success of the operations undertaken for him." (Applause.)

CHAPTER XXVI.

RAILWAYS—RAJKOTE DRAINAGE.

I referred in Chapter VI. to the advent of railways into Kathiawar—namely, the extension of the broad gauge from Ahmedabad to Wudhwan, 78 miles, carried out in 1872-73.

This was followed in 1877-78 by the construction of a metre gauge line from Wudhwan to Bhavnagar, 104 miles, *via* Dhola, under Mr. Izat, M.Inst.C.E. The next was an extension from Dhola to Dhoraji, 84 miles, under Mr. Dangerfield in 1880-82, followed by another from Jetalsar Junction to Verawul, about 60 miles, in 1888-90 by Mr. Knox, M.I.C.E., under Col. Gardiner, R.E.

Then in 1892, a line was run from Dhoraji to Porebunder, 80 miles, followed in 1894 by an extension from Jetalsar to Rajkote, 48 miles, under Mr. W. H. White, M.I.C.E., in direct charge of Mr. Davies, M.I.C.E., and from Rajkote to Jamnugger, 54 miles, in 1896-97, followed by a final metre gauge connecting Drangadra, with Wudhwan Junction, 24 miles, under the same engineers.

The narrow-gauge railway between Wudhwan, Morvi, and Rajkote, 76 miles, was constructed in 1884-86, and was altered to metre gauge 1903, all under Mr. White.

So between 1876 and 1897 the province was intersected by about 530 miles of railway, independent of the broad gauge extension from Ahmedabad.

The States who built and owned this railway system, were Junaghud, Bhavnagar, Gondal, Jamnugger, Morvi, Porebunder, and Drangadra, and they were conducted until 1910 (with the exception of Morvi) under a general manager and a railway committee consisting of the Political Agent and State representatives. Subsequently this was changed to separate management by each State.

I had no connection with the railway works, beyond that some of my road bridges were utilised for railway purposes as well as road. The large road bridge over the Bhadur at Jetpur has carried the metre-gauge railway for 30 years, and the narrow gauge ran over the iron road bridge at

MR. W. H. WHITE, M. INST. C.E.

(*See pages* 58 *and* 290.)

Wudhwan, together with 20 miles of bridged road, for many years. I should have considered this a compliment, and maybe I did, but I think at the time I would have preferred seeing the railway men build their own bridges.

In the very early days of railways some amusing incidents occurred. Once in passing near a herd of antelope a sporting driver of the metre gauge deliberately pulled up and shot a black buck—doubtless he was a European, and maybe the only one on the train. On the arrival of the narrow gauge the pace was so slow that it was said a jovial kumbi on a smart tat raced it successfully for the first stage.

I recollect that on one of the occasions when T.R.H's. the Duke and Duchess of Connaught were coming to Rajkote on an official visit, it was decided that they should be the first to pass over the new line. All went well till within three miles of Rajkote, when the fresh embankment gave way and the Royal party were delayed some hours before the train was got into motion again. It was a cold dark night, and we had a long wait at the terminus, and a very late dinner at the Residency.

DRAINAGE AND SANITATION OF RAJKOTE CIVIL STATION AND CITY STATION IMPROVEMENTS, ETC.

During the last three or four years of my service I was also engaged on the drainage and sanitation of the city and civil stations of Rajkote, and this became especially necessary after the opening of the water supply.

Previous to this the native population, having to procure water for domestic purposes from wells or streams, often at a considerable distance from their dwellings, naturally took care not to waste it; but when an unlimited supply was laid on practically at their doors by means of public free fountains, or at a small primary cost direct to their houses, many wasted it so reprehensibly that measures for protecting the supply as much from economical motives as for the saving of public health, became urgent.

The uneducated resident then at least saw no need for conservancy innovations. His forefathers did without, why not he? He was content to live as they lived, and if he sickened and died it was God's will. There was no reason to search for causes. It is hard to deal with this class.

When the civil station had been supplied with free water for a few years, it was found that waste and saturation of the ground was becoming deplorable. There was no drainage under or above the surface beyond the ordinary gutters formed by the monsoon floods, which, happily, during the rainy season scoured away the accumulated filth of months.

In April 1895, I represented to the Political Agent the condition of the cantonment bazaars and adjacent quarters, and proposed and obtained sanction for a system of surface drainage for them.

The scheme was carried into effect for the civil station bazaars during the following year, and proved successful.

In February 1899, I had again to obtain sanction for the application of a similar scheme of drainage and conservancy for the city, which became urgently needed since the supply of Lalpuri water was laid on. This work was put into hand, and had progressed considerably when I left the Province.

Another improvement in connection with the bazaars made at this time was the removal of butchers' shops from the neighbourhood of the dwellings to an open site where they were surrounded with pure air, and protected from flies by enclosures covered with fine wire netting.

By 1899 the civil station of Rajkote had vastly improved from the conditions I described in 1866. The old tumble-down residences for civil officers had been replaced by new up-to-date buildings, fenced and gardened. Public buildings to meet all necessities had been erected. New roads had been opened up and old ones put into proper condition, all bridged, footpathed, and planted with road-side trees. Unsightly fences of cactus and prickly pear were replaced by neat masonry walls ; a fire brigade established ; new markets, drainage sanitation, and waterworks established—all due to the interest of successive Political Officers and the chiefs who generously provided funds for making the head-quarters of the Province what it should be.

VICTORIA CLOCK TOWER OVER RHAIA GATE, RAJKOTE.
(*See page* 292.)

CHAPTER XXVII.

1898-99.

The opening of the Lalpuri, the new College Hall, and unveiling of the statues of Chester Macnaghten and his Highness the Maharajah of Bhavnagar, were the last public functions with which I was destined to be connected.

Although the States wished me to continue to hold the appointment for as long further as I desired, I was constrained, much to my sorrow, by medical advice as well as by friends, to retire while I was yet strong enough, and I felt that without at the least a considerable rest in Europe I could not hope to be effective in the future. Although returning to one's own land and relatives after a long life of work in foreign parts is an attraction and an event looked forward to by most people, in my special case there was a considerable set-off. Had I been in ordinary Government service, liable to and frequently moved to different charges, I would not have felt the leaving so much, but I had had thirty-three years' continuous service in the same appointment, for the most part independent of any other professional control. My life's work lay around me on all sides—work which was all my own, and I felt it very hard to part with it, and all my life's interest therein; hard to part from my many good friends among the Chiefs, gentlemen, and people of the Province, and employees who had been so long associated with me.

During the Christmas holidays we all went to the Nal Bauli with Major and Mrs. Abud and some Bombay friends for a last shoot, and spent a remarkably pleasant fortnight. Our old friend the late Chief of Limri came and camped with us, and brought with him a fine boat. We slew some thousands of duck, teal and snipe, the ladies joining us at lunch, and after dinner we sat round camp fires in the open.

Immediately on the conclusion of the shoot I heard from Sir C. Ollivant that he with his two daughters were coming to Rajkote, and we had to return to make arrangements for their stay with us. Soon afterwards my daughter and I went to Bombay, and stayed with them on Malabar Hill, meeting many old friends. The following three months passed quickly, being much employed on matters relating to city drainage, and leaving all my charge in readiness for handing over.

One of my last duties was the placing of the splendid statue of Her Imperial Majesty Queen Victoria on the daïs of the Durbar Hall. This statue had just arrived from England, and had cost £4,000. As it weighed nearly ten tons, it was not a particularly easy matter to move it from Bombay, tranship it from the broad gauge at Wudhwan to a metre railway truck, and from thence to move it on extemporised rails to its place; but it was all safely accomplished by the beginning of May, my mechanical engineer, Sheik Ali, taking charge of the work.

To accommodate the statue on the daïs, the entire end of the hall was removed and thrown out in a semicircle, which provided an extra width of 25 feet. This was lit by four windows each 7 feet by 14 feet; the fanlights of which were executed in stained glass subjects, representing the four continents the Queen reigned over. The fanlight designs were by Horace Van Ruith.

I have mentioned a few of the many friends we knew in Kathiawar, and chiefly those only who happened to be associated with me in official work. Others who were not so associated, but who were amongst our valued friends, were first Mr. and Mrs. Beaman, I.C.S. He was for a long time Judicial A.P.A. at Rajkote, now judge of the High Court, Bombay. Also Col. Seely, a most popular officer, who held various official charges from time to time, and from whom, also in his retirement, we sometimes hear. Other old and valued friends were the Rev. Mr. and Mrs. Bailey (he was at one time chaplain at Ahmedabad), who occasionally visited Rajkote. They were both shikaries, she eminently so, and her record of big game shooting could not be beaten by many men. I have pleasant recollections of morning small game shoots with her when they stayed with us. Nobody meeting this charming and delicate-looking lady in a drawing-room would imagine that the same morning she had slain a tiger or a panther.

Many of the Rajkote ladies were excellent rifle shots, and during the monsoon weekly rifle shooting competitions were instituted, at which the ladies as a rule topped the scores.

The Rev. Mr. and Mrs. Scott, of the Presbyterian Mission, were among our best friends. They were long resident at Rajkote, and very popular with natives as well as Europeans. They both possessed a marvellous power of attracting the natives, who held them in high esteem, and their mission schools were well attended. Mr. Scott, like other good ministers, could enjoy a day's fishing, shooting, or golf, and hold his own with any man.

I would like to mention others we have kindly recollections of, and it is to me a great pleasure to write, and think of our friends of the old working days, but my notes and reminiscences have extended far beyond what I intended.

We packed up to take home with us many movable articles which we prized as old friends, the remainder being sold by auction, with horses and traps, except my old red pony (thirty years of age), which was pensioned off at Wankanir, and our faithful little terrier, Judy, which we gave to Sargeant Pryde, of the police, and often heard of afterwards.

I handed over charge on June 1st, 1899, to Mr. Maussen, Ex-Engineer and late Secretary to the Government in the P.W.D., and on June 2nd we left for Bombay, having taken our passages by the Austrian Lloyd steamer to sail on June 7th.

Notwithstanding the proximity of the monsoon we had a most pleasant voyage. Owing to our having started from a plague port we were prohibited from landing at any place *en route*, and to enable us after we entered the Mediterranean to take in certain supplies which were run out, the Captain adopted a course *via* Zante and the Ionian Islands, passing also near Corfu. It was a delightful voyage here in the cool European waters after the Indian heat, and the sweltering passage through the Red Sea, which we were never to experience again.

On arrival at Trieste we were passed clean. It is an amusing spectacle to observe the progress of the medical examination. The passengers are placed in a line on the deck, and one by one tongues are put out for inspection. Very unclean tongues, too, some of them were; and the poor folk, and the doctors too, have to run the gauntlet of many a joke.

We spent the day at Trieste, visiting the beauties of the neighbourhood, and driving, etc. The neat dresses of the pretty women who wander about bareheaded and the wealth of flowers for sale in the open streets are remarkable.

At midnight we left in another steamer for Venice, where we arrived in the early morning. We put up at the Bauer Grünwald Hotel on the Grand Canal, and remained for a fortnight, thoroughly enjoying our visit, and the perfect climate. We purchased some lovely walnut furniture for our prospective residence in the old country.

After Venice we stayed a few days at Milan and then on to Lucerne by that enchanting journey by the Italian lakes and the St. Gothard tunnel. We fortunately secured accommodation in a pretty pension overlooking the lake, and did the usual sightseeing for a fortnight.

Our next move was to Lausanne, where, having received letters calling me to England on urgent private matters, I left my wife and the girls and proceeded to London, where a week afterwards they joined me.

There is little more to add. We remained in London for nine months, much of the time being spent in house-hunting, it being then my intention to settle in or near London, in the hope that I would be able to find something to employ myself with; but old pensioners from India don't find it easy to get into harness in England, and after a time I found that I was getting almost reconciled to an idle life.

We came over to Ireland the following year, being much urged thereto by my brother, and settled for three years at Bray. Then we moved to our present home, which I bought and renamed "Lalpuri," to commemorate the ultimately successful fight with the Bombay Government for sanction for the waterworks.

With gardening, fishing, painting, occasional shoots, visiting and receiving old Indian friends, we continue to get along very comfortably, and we have made many good friends, some of whom are old Indians and near neighbours.

On my arrival at home I received the following extract from the Government Gazette, Bombay Castle Extract, par. 3, from Government Resolution No. 4,305, dated 10th June, 1899, Political Department.

"His Excellency the Governor in Council desires to take this opportunity of placing on record his high appreciation of the services rendered by Mr. Booth to the province of Kathiawar."

Also I received from the members of my office staff an expression of goodwill in the form of a handsomely designed and engraved silver inkstand and tray, designed by themselves, and made at Rajkote at their own cost. It was a graceful tribute, after I had left the province and them, and will always be a valued possession. I sometimes hear from my friend Mr. Ratanshaw Damri, my late head accountant, and am glad to know that he and all of them are prospering.